Love You to Death

the unofficial companion to the Vampire Diaries

Love You to Death

the unofficial companion to

the Vampire Diaries

Crissy Calhoun

ECW Press

Published by ECW Press

2120 Queen Street East, Suite 200, Toronto, Ontario, Canada M4E 1E2
416-694-3348 / info@ecwpress.com

LIBRARY AND ARCHIVES CANADA CATALOGUING IN PUBLICATION

Calhoun, Crissy
Love you to death : the unofficial companion to the Vampire
diaries / Crissy Calhoun.

ISBN 978-1-55022-978-3

1. Vampire diaries (Television program). 1. Title.

PN1992.77.V34C34 2010   791.45'72   C2010-901402-2

Typesetting: Gail Nina
Text design: Melissa Kaita
Cover and color photo section design: Rachel Ironstone
Cover photo: Michael Muller/Contour by Getty Images
Printing: Lake Book Manufacturing   2   3   4   5

Interior photo credits by page: 11, 43: Sue Schneider/MGP Agency; 14: The CW/Joe Magnini/Landov; 16: Amy Graves/PictureGroup/AP Photo; 21, 45: ML Agency; 23, 94: RD/Erik Kabik/Retna Digital; 26, 174: PseudoImage/Shooting Star; 30: Kristian Dowling/Warner Bros. Television Entertainment/PictureGroup/AP Photo; 34, 105: Matt Sayles/AP Photo; 37, 163: Grady Agency; 40: MJT/AdMedia/Keystone Press; 48: Albert Michael/startraks photo.com; 51: Eugene Biscardi/Shooting Star; 53: Gaas/AP Photo; 57: Seth Browarnik/startraksphoto.com; 65: Dan Curtis Productions, Inc.; 68, 101, 120, 149, 181, 201: Jennifer Ridings; 71, 115, 134: The CW/Quantrell Colbert/Landov; 77: Johann Georg Sturm, *Deutschlands Flora in Abbildungen* (1796); 85: Byron Purvis/AdMedia/Keystone Press; 89: Michael Didyoung/Retna Ltd.; 124: The CW/Bob Mahoney/Landov; 150, 186: Ritschel/interTOPICS/Retna Ltd.; 156: Andy Fossum/startraksphoto.com; 178: Jennifer Graylock/AP Photo; 191: Ruthie Heard; 195: courtesy of Smart Pop Books; 204: courtesy of Koopman Management; 223: Lee Weston Photography.
Photo section credits by page: 1, 3 (bottom), 7: The CW/Quantrell Colbert/Landov; 2: Rob Kim/Retna Ltd.; 3 (top): The CW/Guy D'Alema/Landov; 4, 6: The CW/Bob Mahoney/Landov; 5 (top): Jeff Vespa/WireImage; 5 (bottom): Kristian Dowling/Warner Bros. Television Entertainment/PictureGroup/AP Photo; 8: John Spellman/Retna Ltd.

The publication of *Love You to Death: The Unofficial Companion to The Vampire Diaries* has been generously supported by the Government of Ontario through the Ontario Book Publishing Tax Credit, by the OMDC Book Fund, an initiative of the Ontario Media Development Corporation, and by the Government of Canada through the Canada Book Fund.

Canada

PRINTED AND BOUND IN THE UNITED STATES

You've gotten into my bloodstream

— Stateless ("Bloodstream")

Contents

Rob Pralgo as Mayor Lockwood and Susan Walters as Carol Lockwood

Introduction

I've never watched a television show the way I do *The Vampire Diaries*. Each Thursday night, I head over to my friends' house with two others for dinner and to catch up, and then we tune in to the show. There's always some Team Stefan versus Team Damon trash-talking, some shrieks, and loads of theorizing during commercial breaks and after the episode ends, inevitably, on a cliffhanger. It's always a great time, thanks to the brilliance of the show and the company of good friends. But just like the show itself, these evenings together are about more than just light-hearted fun. One of the creators of *The Vampire Diaries* television series, Julie Plec, said in an interview in the spring of 2010 that the show's two primary themes are love and loss — and that's precisely what brings my group of friends together every week.

After an unimaginable loss in the spring of 2009, my dear friend asked if we could have a regular hangout (which came to be known as "knitting club"), to be there for her and her husband, providing distraction, company, and an opportunity to talk openly. In September, we watched as Elena Gilbert tried to return to "normal" after the death of her parents, and it was clear right from *The Vampire Diaries'* pilot episode that, for us, this show wasn't just about hot vampires and teen romance. It resonated.

As I got to know *The Vampire Diaries* fans online over the course of the first season, I could see how connected we all were to the series. This show isn't popular because we're in the throes of a vampire craze. That may be why The CW wanted this show on the network, but the success of Twilight and *True Blood* didn't guarantee that *The Vampire Diaries* would be the runaway hit it is. The series has earned the loyalty of its devoted fan base by being unrelentingly captivating, exciting, and emotionally honest. Stefan, Damon, Elena, and the rest of our friends in Mystic Falls want nothing more than real connections in their lives, and the audience at home responds to how heartfelt and human this supernatural world is. I wanted to write this companion guide to *The Vampire Diaries* because of that strong reaction we have to the series. *Love You to Death* is my tribute to a show that's come to mean quite a lot to me personally in just one season, to the people who create *The Vampire Diaries* and the audience who keeps the discussion alive offscreen.

In these pages, you'll find chapters on L.J. Smith and her book series, on the creation of the show and the masterminds behind it, and background on the main cast members. After that is the episode-by-episode companion to the first season. Here's a mini guide to the guide:

Each episode's write-up begins with a bit of dialogue that stood out for me either because it captures the episode in a pithy few lines . . . or it was just too well written not to acknowledge. From there, I provide an analysis of the episode, looking at its main themes, the character development, and the questions it raises followed by these sections:

COMPELLING MOMENT: Here I choose one moment that stands out — a turning point, a character standing up for herself, or a long-awaited relationship scene (usually involving kissing).

CIRCLE OF KNOWLEDGE: In my interview with Vampire-Diaries.net's Red and Vee (see page 189), Vee talks about the "circle of knowledge": who in Mystic Falls is in on its supernatural secrets. In this section of the episode guide, you'll find all the need-to-know info for our circle of knowledge — the details you may have missed on first watch, character insights, the cultural references, and the connections between episodes. Often episode titles are plays on film titles; those are explained in this section.

THE RULES: Any work of fiction relating to the supernatural has its own particular spin on how that world operates. Here I catalog what we've learned about what goes bump in the night.

THE DIABOLICAL PLAN: One of *The Vampire Diaries*' defining qualities is its lightning-fast pacing, so "The Diabolical Plan" tracks the various forces at work in Mystic Falls and raises questions about what their next steps may be.

HISTORY LESSON: The only class at Mystic Falls High School that gets considerable screen time is history. In the characters' back stories, the town's history, and subtle references, history — both real and imaginary — is important in this series, and "History Lesson" is your study aid.

BITE MARKS: Bite marks, stake wounds, necks snapped, and good old-fashioned slaps to the face — this section is all about the violence on the show, cataloguing injuries inflicted by the immortal and mortal.

MEANWHILE IN FELL'S CHURCH: Here we travel from one TVD universe to another and I draw comparisons between L.J. Smith's original plotting and characterization and that of the TV series. Because production of the TV show was underway before The Vampire Diaries: The Return was published, this section focuses only on *The Awakening*, *The Struggle*, *The Fury*, and *Dark Reunion*. (Fans of The Return, please don your Wings of Understanding.)

OFF CAMERA: Here we leave the fictional world behind to hear what the cast and crew has to say about filming an episode, or I provide background details on a guest star or other filming details.

FOGGY MOMENTS: Elena, surprised by Stefan in the cemetery in the pilot episode, tells him the fog is making her foggy. "Foggy Moments" is a collection of confusing moments for the viewer. Containing continuity errors, arguable nitpicks, and full-on inconsistencies, this section is not meant as an attack on the show. Few of these inconsistencies make a significant impact on the characters' behavior. (And it's comforting to know that even the great Kevin Williamson and Julie Plec aren't infallible.)

MUSIC: An important part of *The Vampire Diaries* is its soundtrack, and in this section, I tell you what song is playing in each scene.

Make sure you watch an episode before reading its corresponding guide — it contains spoilers for that episode (but not for anything that follows). Within the pages of the guide, you'll also find short biographies of the actors who bring the recurring characters to life as well as sidebars about other elements of the show and its influences. After the episode guide, you'll find an interview section featuring Q&As with three leaders of the fandom, with a fan who works on the show as an extra, and with actors Benjamin Ayres (Coach Tanner) and Malese Jow (Anna). Finally, I've pieced together a timeline for the past few hundred years in the TVD universe.

If there's something you think I missed, or that I completely read your mind about, drop me at a note at crissycalhoun@gmail.com, @reply me on Twitter (@crissycalhoun), and/or stop by my blog at crissycalhoun.com for a weekly reaction to *The Vampire Diaries*.

xoxo
Crissy Calhoun
July 2010

Writing Like Magic: The World of L.J. Smith

"Since I was too young to really remember . . . I looked for magic." Lisa Jane Smith read all about magical worlds in her favorite books by C.S. Lewis, E. Nesbit, and J.R.R. Tolkien. Smith wanted "to write for kids when I was a kid. I knew the kind of books I liked to read and there just weren't enough of them. Nothing to do but write them myself. I'd been telling myself stories ever since I was four or five, and writing them down was just the next step." With encouragement from a teacher who praised a poem she wrote in grade school (a poem which Lisa Jane now calls "horrible"), the budding writer started her first novel while she was in high school. In fact, the idea for the story came to her while she was babysitting. She took her time writing it, working on it slowly through college as she got her BA in experimental psychology at the University of California, Santa Barbara. Looking back, Lisa Jane can see that she took to writing naturally: "It felt easy to write, I enjoyed doing it tremendously." But her parents warned her that making a living as a writer was a very difficult thing. So L.J. became a kindergarten and special education teacher, and she wrote in the evenings after spending her days at school.

Since she didn't own a typewriter, let alone a computer, Lisa Jane took her first finished manuscript to a professional typist. "She said it was the best manuscript she'd seen . . . and asked if I was interested in being agented." The answer, of course, was yes. Though it took a little while, the manuscript for *The Night of the Solstice* eventually sold to Macmillan, and it was published in 1987. L.J. wrote in a blog post, "I'd started writing a book at 15 and it had only taken 10 years to get it published!" Her editor at Macmillan picked up the book's sequel, *Heart of Valor*, which was published in 1990. Both books were well reviewed but failed to generate a lot of sales, which L.J. suspects was in part the result of abysmal cover designs. Lisa Jane excelled at her teaching job and was nominated best teacher in the district by her school, but the amount of energy it took to work all day *and* write novels in her nonexistent spare time was too much. She left teaching behind to become a full-time novelist. "Every fall I get very nostalgic about teaching, but writing is more fun."

With her focus completely on her writing, the 1990s would be an extraordinarily prolific decade for L.J. Smith: she would publish 22 books. The first four novels were a series, The Vampire Diaries, about a beautiful, self-centered teenage girl in a small Virginia town who meets two brothers with a dark secret that leads her and her best friends into the world of the supernatural. L.J. explains, "I was given a call by some people who wanted a trilogy of vampire books [. . .] and they said that they wanted me, within nine months, to produce three books about vampires. So the idea was that there were two brothers who were both in love with the same girl: one good brother, one bad brother. And I kind of like the bad brother better. That's Damon, and he's one of my favorite characters to work with. So it didn't come out exactly perhaps as it was intended, but it seems that people enjoy the effect, so I can't complain." In 1991, just months apart, Harper published *The Awakening*, *The Struggle*, *The Fury*, and *The Dark Reunion* known collectively as The Vampire Diaries. "The story is one of redemption," says L.J., "of how a girl who's really kind of a social butterfly and an egoist learns that she's not the [center] of the universe; she's not the thing the world turns around. And she realizes that other people mean a lot more than she does. And it's a story of redemption for the boys too, especially for Damon, who ends up finding himself with a choice to sort of stick by her side or to perhaps go with a greater villain and stay alive."

The next year L.J. had another series for Harper, The Secret Circle, which centered on a young girl named Cassie who finds herself drawn into the world of witchcraft. In 1994 and 1995, L.J. Smith created two more three-book series, The Forbidden Game and Dark Visions. In 1996, the first book in the Night World series, *Secret Vampire*, was published. L.J. would stay in this world of vampires, witches, werewolves, and all manner of supernatural creatures for nine more installments. In each book, a Night World being and a human are drawn together by the "soul mate principle," which is not dissimilar to Stefan and Elena's initial attraction to one another.

As the 1990s drew to a close, L.J. Smith's personal and professional lives entered a period of crisis. Her focus was on her family — on her brother's serious illness and on her mother's battle with terminal lung cancer. "For 10 years actually, just like a faucet, my imagination was turned off," said L.J. "And you can imagine what agony that is for a writer. I really wanted to write that whole time and was trying to, but I was not able to." After her mother passed away, L.J. began writing poetry about her mother. This helped her to continue writing, first short stories and then full-length novels; in fact, Smith felt this return to her craft was a gift from her mother.

In the meantime, vampires had clawed their way back to the top of bestseller lists with the enormous success of Stephenie Meyer's Twilight Saga (2005–2008), and L.J. Smith's publisher wisely rereleased The Vampire Diaries with updated cover designs. "I was busy nursing my mom, and I didn't know that they had republished my books until they were telling me that the second one had debuted at number five on the *New York Times* bestseller list," said L.J. in an interview. Though she hasn't read any of the Twilight books or seen the films, L.J. is well aware of the similarities between her and Meyer's stories of human girls who fall in love with a good, animal-blood-only vampires. "There's the floods of mail from people accusing me of stealing, and they list about 30 things from *Twilight*. I usually write back just one sentence: 'Look at the copyright date.' Actually, I get a tremendous amount of apologies back."

In her trademark style, once L.J. was able to write again, she worked at a frenetic pace and signed up for five more books, including The Vampire Diaries: The Return. "I had been negotiating with Harper to write an adult book for the series, but the YA department didn't want to let go of it. So there was a year and a half which ended with the negotiations going nowhere, but with me writing scenes for an adult book." That work wasn't lost; the world of YA had changed since the first Vampire Diaries books were published, and she could "essentially write my adult epic as three decent-sized YA books." (To compare length, the first TVD book is 253 pages; the first in The Return, 586.) The new group of books tell "the story of Elena falling in love with Damon to the same extent that she is in love with Stefan. So we have a real love triangle."

Though Smith's writing explores supernatural worlds, it's consistently grounded by strong female characters, whether they are of the mortal realm or not. Characters like Elena, Bonnie, and Meredith from TVD and Cassie from The Secret Circle are strong-willed, courageous, and clever. L.J. calls this network of women the "velociraptor sisterhood" — after the "smart, fast, and utterly scary" velociraptors in *Jurassic Park* — who "[stand] up for your female friends and sisters when they need you most." Her advice for aspiring writers is simple: write, write, write ("Write anything and everything you like, and don't be critical of yourself. Just let it come out and worry about whether it's good later") and read, read, read ("Read all you can and read a variety of books. You'll absorb all sorts of good things, grammar, vocabulary, plot structure — even if you don't realize it. Try the classics, and keep trying them as you get older").

Lisa Jane Smith, who lives in the Bay Area of California, always favors the novel she is currently writing, but when asked to choose her all-time favorite of her books, she reluctantly admits it was "the first omnibus of The Vampire Diaries, because I put my entire self into the Vampire Diaries books. It's like the old maxim, 'Writing's easy. Just sit down at the keyboard and then open a vein.' Singularly appropriate, yes?"

"High School Is a Horror Movie": Kevin Williamson and Julie Plec Turn The Vampire Diaries

"I've had other things optioned before," said L.J. Smith about finding out The Vampire Diaries was to be adapted for television, "so my reaction was at first, 'Okay, another one of those.' But then when they said it was by Kevin Williamson, I realized it was probably a little bit more serious."

Kevin Williamson says he "grew up sleeping in front of the TV. I always wanted to make TV and film. I always wanted to live in a fantasy world." Born on March 14, 1965, in New Bern, North Carolina (not too far from a little spot known as Dawson's Creek), Kevin, his older brother John, and parents Faye and Wade, moved to Texas when Kevin was small, returning to Oriental, North Carolina, when Kevin was in his teens. Kevin's father was a commercial fisherman. Though in early interviews Kevin would joke that he grew up "white trash," he clarifies, "We didn't have a lot of money, but weren't white trash. I had wonderful parents, and they always provided. I always got what I needed." The resourceful 10-year-old requested that his local library subscribe to *Variety* and *The Hollywood Reporter*, so he could keep up on industry news. He loved reading books and watching movies, but growing up a Southern Baptist in the Bible Belt was difficult for a boy who always knew he was gay. When his preacher spoke about sinners, homosexuals were mentioned in the same breath as murderers and rapists.

A self-described loner in high school, Kevin did his BA at East Carolina University, studied theater arts, and dated his best friend Fannie. He moved to New York City to become an actor and landed bit parts, including a turn on *Another World* in 1990. The struggle to make a living eventually drove Kevin to Los Angeles to try his luck in the film industry there. In 1993, he decided to finally shrug off the words of a discouraging high school English teacher, who, in marking a short story, had told Kevin, "Yours is a voice that shouldn't be heard." He took a writing class at UCLA and wrote his first script, *Killing Mrs. Tingle* (a revenge story inspired by that nasty teacher), and it got optioned. Kevin used that money to pay down his college loans, but the script languished with its production company. By 1995, Kevin was 30 and working odd jobs — walking dogs, taking shifts as a word-processing temp, slogging hours as an assistant; he needed a career to keep himself afloat.

One night, alone in his apartment, Kevin heard a strange noise and, as he went to investigate it, he noticed a window standing open that he could have sworn he had shut. A little spooked, he locked the window and called up a friend. The two started throwing horror-movie trivia questions at each other, and with that, the opening scene for *Scream* was born. Williamson wrote the script very quickly, reportedly in three days. As he says, "The movie just came out of my youth. I grew up with a VCR; Blockbuster was my friend. The dialogue in the film comes from conversations I had with my friends about films from that era." He hoped to at least use the script as a writing sample; he did not expect *Scream* (which was originally titled *Scary Movie*) to provoke a bidding war. Dimension Films, a division of Miramax started in 1992, picked it up, and the legendary horror film director Wes Craven signed on.

Kevin was nervous as he began his working relationship with Wes Craven, mostly thanks to "all the Hollywood stories about directors mutilating scripts." At their first meeting, however, "[Craven] handed me back the script and there were pages and pages of notes. It turned out they were all typos. He said to me, 'I'm sorry, Kevin. I used to teach English and this sort of thing bothers me.'" The two would go on to work together again on the other Scream films and on *Cursed*.

Released on December 20, 1996, *Scream* became the highest grossing slasher movie of all time, a rank it still holds over a decade later. Williamson was widely praised for revitalizing a tired genre, and he won the 1997 Saturn Award for Best Writing. It was a huge change for the formerly unemployed writer, who was now considered one of the hottest screenwriters in

Hollywood. "Suddenly Miramax was looking for any Kevin Williamson project. I wasn't writing them fast enough, which I didn't understand, because I was writing them as fast as I fucking could." A year after *Scream's* release came *I Know What You Did Last Summer*, which performed well at the box office but didn't receive the glowing reviews *Scream* had. The film's villain was modeled, in appearance only, on Kevin's fisherman father. In December 1997, the same month that *Scream 2* came out, Kevin signed a $20 million contract to write, produce, and direct movies and TV shows for Miramax. Bob Weinstein, then co-chairman of Miramax, said, "Writers that don't pander [to teens] win the game. Kevin understands this brilliantly, and he's got the talent to go with it."

As Kevin Williamson readily admits, "Everything I do is autobiographical," and nowhere was that more evident than in his first television series, *Dawson's Creek*. First pitched to Fox but picked up by The WB, the teen drama centered on Dawson Leery, an idealistic wannabe filmmaker obsessed with Steven Spielberg films and struggling with his first romances in Capeside, a fictional Massachusetts town based on Oriental, NC. "I love the teen experience," said Kevin. "There is something very potent about teen drama in the sense that everyone is dealing with their first love." The show's teenagers talked about sex and feelings in an explicit and nuanced way not heard before on TV, and *Dawson's Creek* garnered a lot of attention for its language, content, and for that season 1 affair between Pacey Witter and Ms. Jacobs. The WB wisely slotted the show at 9 p.m., rather than during the 8 p.m. "family hour," airing it after *Buffy the Vampire Slayer*. *Dawson's Creek* premiered on January 20, 1998, to great ratings in its core demographic. Part of the show's magic came from filming on location in Wilmington, North Carolina. It "forces the cast to bond because we don't know anyone else," said Katie "Joey Potter" Holmes during *Dawson's* first season. In season 2, Kevin introduced the character Jack McPhee, a gay teen, whose experiences in a small-town high school were informed by Kevin's own. While discussing Jack's coming-out episode with the media, Kevin seized the opportunity to publicly confirm his sexual orientation. (He had come out to his parents back in 1992.)

Kevin Williamson didn't leave horror movies behind while working on the *Creek*. On December 25, 1998, *The Faculty* was released. Directed by Robert Rodriguez, Williamson's story of a high school whose faculty is taken over by water-starved aliens was a cross between *Invasion of the Body Snatchers* and *The Breakfast Club*. As Kevin said, "That whole theme of conformity versus individuality fits perfectly into the high school metaphor. I got into that and tried to create the characters that interweave in a *Breakfast Club* way and then left all the cool alien shit to Robert." (In fact, a viewer familiar with the films of John Hughes can spot the alien-in-disguise among the main cast right away: there's the brain, the athlete, the basket case, the princess, the criminal, and the sweet-as-pie new girl. Hmmm.)

After season 2 of *Dawson's Creek*, Kevin decided to move on to other projects. "I feel in my heart of hearts that it could have been better. If it was my full-time job — and I had nothing else tugging at me — it would have been better." His attention had been split between his directorial debut, *Teaching Mrs. Tingle*, and *Wasteland*, a new series for ABC about 20-somethings in New York City. The TV show centered on Dawnie, a late-blooming grad student writing her thesis on her friends' lives, one of whom is a gay but closeted soap opera actor. It premiered in October 1999, was ravaged by critics, and was canceled three episodes in. *Teaching Mrs. Tingle* didn't fare much better. The film, which was Kevin's very first screenplay, had been modified in the wake of the 1999 Columbine Massacre, and resulted in, as the *New York Times* said, "the incongruously toothless version of a sadistic fantasy." *Entertainment Weekly* had named Kevin an Entertainer of the Year in 1997, and yet their reviewer wrote, "Williamson, whose best work has melded humanity with a kind of media-savvy meta-playfulness, [made] a movie that dances so clumsily on the grave of empathy, pandering to the worst instincts in young audiences."

The reason his work was lackluster was obvious to Kevin and everyone around him: he was badly overextended. Katie Holmes became close with Kevin and used to stay with him while in L.A. In 1999, she commented, "He works nonstop. All of us are always telling him to take a break. He is hard on himself because he's a perfectionist." Looking back on the late '90s, Kevin said, "It's what I call my insane period. . . . I did not know how to say no." In three years, he had written five screenplays, directed his first feature film, and created two television series. "I worked so much, I didn't have any personal life . . . I had a great home that I didn't see. I was sleeping on the floor with no pillow so I wouldn't sleep, so I would wake up every few hours and go back to the computer. That's insane! But I had deadlines. I was self-destructing. There's no way anybody could have met the timelines that I had, but I kept trying. I fell apart."

He wrote an outline for *Scream 3* but handed over the screenwriting duties to Ehren Kruger, and after *Wasteland*'s cancelation he took a year off. "One of the things I learned while I was doing *Wasteland* is that writing about people in their 20s — who cares? . . . Nothing's life or death then. When you're 25, who cares if a love doesn't work out? You will find another one. But when you're 16, it's life and death. . . . There's your first love and your last love. Those are the epic moments."

But his return to teen-focused television was still a few projects away. In January 2002, Williamson's *Glory Days* premiered on The WB as a midseason replacement; described by *Entertainment Weekly* as "a *Northern Exposure*–cum-*X-Files* murder mystery for the MTV set," it was aimed at young men. Williamson didn't originally envision the show as a thriller, but the network asked for more scares. The story focuses on writer Mike Dolan, who returns to his small Washington hometown where strange things are happening (*Twin Peaks*, anyone?) and discovers he's unwelcome because his novel was too revealingly autobiographical for the town folks' comfort, a predicament Kevin was familiar with. "*Dawson's* was autobiographical," he said in 2002, "and I exposed things in the storylines that I got flak for — things about my family that people saw. I'd change the names and sometimes the outcomes, but you still hear about it. If I were dating someone and we got into a big fight, Dawson and Joey would get into a fight in the same manner." *Glory Days* didn't fare much better than *Wasteland*, and after only nine episodes had aired, the show was canceled.

Though he hadn't written for *Dawson's Creek* since its second season, Kevin was asked to write the series finale in 2003. Opting for a flashforward so fans could see where the Capesiders ended up, Kevin said, "I put my heart into it, and I cried the whole time I was writing it." Fans still ask him about his resolution to the series' long question: who does Joey truly belong with — Pacey or Dawson? At the 2009 Paley Fest where *Dawson's Creek* was being honored, Kevin said, "Dawson and Joey are soul mates. And they always will be. . . . My whole goal for that was to show that, you know, your soul mate might not necessarily be the person [who's] your romantic love."

After their writer-director partnership on *Scream* and *Scream 2*, Kevin was back working with Wes Craven on a Dimension Films werewolf horror movie starring Christina Ricci, Jesse Eisenberg, and Joshua Jackson. It was aptly titled *Cursed*, as the *New York Times* said, as it had to be "recast, reshot, and recut" before finally being released in February 2005. It was a box-office flop, and the *Toronto Star* opined that the "only thing worse than a bad horror movie is a bad horror movie made by good people." Kevin couldn't seem to catch a break; his next project, *Hidden Palms*, suffered the same fate as his last two TV projects. The CW series about the dark secrets of a gated community in Palm Springs premiered in May 2007 and was off the air by July. But Kevin was undeterred and was about to join forces with someone whom he'd met over a decade earlier.

Julie Plec first met Kevin on the set of *Scream* in 1996. "I was Wes's assistant on *Scream*. It was [Kevin's] first movie that ever got made. My first movie. I was 22, just out of college. We were two kids in a candy store, up in Santa Rosa, California, on location, making a movie." Plec had graduated from Northwestern University's School of Communications in 1994 where she had become friends with Greg Berlanti. Before Berlanti would work on *Dawson's Creek* or go on to run shows like *Everwood* and *Brothers & Sisters*, he was a disillusioned and stalled writer in Los Angeles, and he credits Julie with convincing him to take another stab at writing. "[She] took me out for lunch where she read me the riot act for giving up on my dream before I even had a chance to fail at it. . . . Julie reminded me that there was a time in my life when I never cared about how successful I was at writing, just how much I loved it."

After working as Wes Craven's assistant, Julie was promoted to his director of development. She worked as an associate producer on *Scream 2* and *Teaching Mrs. Tingle* and became the VP of production and development at Outerbanks Entertainment (Kevin Williamson's production company, responsible for *Dawson's Creek* and *Wasteland*). Julie co-produced Greg Berlanti's romantic comedy *The Broken Hearts Club* (2000) and was back for *Scream 3*, this time as co-producer. In 2000, she left Outerbanks and landed at Ricochet Entertainment where she worked with Ricky Strauss as head of production and development. Said Strauss, "Julie's background in film and television is outstanding. She has excellent taste, and her commercial sensibility is right on the money." By 2005, she was once again working with Wes Craven and Kevin Williamson on *Cursed* as co-producer.

On her next project, Julie began as a producer but was soon writing her first TV episodes and working her way up to co-executive producer. Premiering on June 26, 2006, *Kyle XY* was an ABC Family series about a teenage boy who wakes up in a forest outside Seattle with no memories, no idea how he got there, and no bellybutton. The Trager family, headed by psychologist Nicole (Marguerite MacIntyre), takes in the extraordinarily gifted

"We're a very romantic show but we kill people," said Kevin Williamson, seen here with Julie Plec at the Paley Center's Television Festival in March 2010.

Kyle (Matt Dallas) and helps him acclimatize. The Tragers try to figure out where he came from and why his mind is as fast as a computer. The show was a charming combination of sci-fi mystery and teen drama, following Kyle and the Trager siblings, Lori and Josh, as they navigate high school. In its first season, *Kyle XY* had huge ratings for ABC Family, but by its second, the ratings dropped and, in January 2009 as its third season was airing, the show was canceled. Without a chance to properly resolve *Kyle XY*'s storylines, Julie and the writers settled for including a featurette on the season 3 DVDs, "*Kyle XY*: Future Revealed," to let the show's loyal fans know where Kyle and the Tragers would have headed. As Julie Plec said, "We were only just getting started on all the stories left to tell about Kyle XY. On behalf of myself, all the writers, producers, and the cast, we're very grateful that we had the opportunity to do this show and to tell Kyle's story. The fans' loyalty and passion for the show was like nothing any of us had ever experienced. It was a true gift . . . so thank you." *Kyle XY*'s final episode aired on March 16, 2009.

Though that gig ended abruptly, Julie didn't have to wait long for another project she was passionate about to come her way. Kevin Williamson wanted to collaborate on a show with her. "It was a matter of wanting to do something with Julie Plec. We've worked together off and on over the last several hundred years. The timing was right." The pair had a friendly lunch with Jennifer Breslow, who once worked at Outerbanks Entertainment and was currently the VP of drama development at The CW; they ended up discussing ideas for TV shows. "We were talking to [Jennifer] about vampires and how much we love them," recalled Julie, "and one of us said, 'We'd love to do a vampire show, but *nobody*'s going to do another vampire story.'" Stephenie Meyer's Twilight Saga (where the undead sparkled) had ushered in a new vampire craze, and HBO's *True Blood* satisfied those who liked their vampire stories with more bite, blood, and fangbanging. But The CW wasn't opposed to the idea of creating a third major vamp franchise to fill that vast void between abstinence and orgies. "They said, 'Actually, we have a property that we've been dying to do. We absolutely want to do a vampire show, and we'd love for you to look at it. And so we did." The "property" was L.J. Smith's The Vampire Diaries represented by Alloy Entertainment, the company responsible for other CW shows like *Gossip Girl* and *Privileged*.

Though The CW execs were keen, Kevin Williamson didn't want to be involved in a knockoff: "I said I didn't want to do this. It's *Twilight*." But Julie had read further into the book series than Kevin had and she urged him, "'Keep reading. Keep reading.' And then I kept reading and was like, 'Oh, okay, I get it.' . . . The premise is the same but the themes are different. It goes beyond just a love story and really goes into everything that goes bump in the night. It's more sort of a *Dark Shadows*. This town has a lot going on in it, and we just start with the vampires." Asked at 2009's Comic-Con about doing a vampire show in the wake of the Twilight Saga and *True Blood*, Kevin said that despite having "a lot a lot a lot" of reservations about doing *The Vampire Diaries*, after reading the books "suddenly it all changed. The whole backstory, the mythology, everything about this story is just completely 100 percent different and I kind of got into it. And because of *Twilight* and because of *True Blood* is why I'm here." Kevin Williamson and Julie Plec made no pretence about the fact that their show was green-lit because of the other projects' successes, and they fully acknowledged their vampire predecessors, promising that their show would be original.

"We're dealing with a cross-genre [series], in a way," said Williamson. "There's a lot going on here. We have the teen element, the teen-drama aspect, which you can compare to *Dawson's Creek*. . . . But it's not just a teen show. This is not a high-school show. It's more of a small-town show . . . we're telling a story about a town. That's one of the things I loved about the books — L.J. Smith created this huge, rich mythology — and we're immersing ourselves into that. The vampire story is our way in."

The Vampire Diaries was a natural fit for The CW, which had made its mark as the go-to network for women aged 18 to 35. Taking its "C" and "W" from its two parent companies, CBS and Warner Brothers, The CW Television Network was born from a merger of UPN and The WB; its freshman season in 2006 featured existing shows like The WB's *Smallville, One Tree Hill,* and *Supernatural,* and UPN's *America's Next Top Model, Veronica Mars,* and *Everybody Hates Chris.* President of entertainment Dawn Ostroff worked to create an identity for The CW brand, focusing "intensely on finding shows that would finally define The CW as a net for young people, especially younger women."

For Dawn Ostroff, everything about *The Vampire Diaries* works: "Great writing, great casting, a topic that's in the zeitgeist, and a known franchise is always what we look for. It's the perfect example of the kind of qualities we stress in every show we pick up." Because *The Vampire Diaries* shared a few things with both *Supernatural* and *Gossip Girl,* Ostroff suggests that "[w]hat *Vampire Diaries* has done so well is that it's not just a genre show, it has romance and humor and friends that feel like family. There are so many elements that work on different levels. So although it is a genre or sci-fi show, it has a lot of other elements that make the show work for all of our audience." Her showrunners agreed. Julie Plec summed it up: "Specifically, on our network, it's the perfect amalgamation of what they've been doing, that takes all the genres they've been dabbling in and combines them into one

show." And Kevin emphasized the importance of *The Vampire Diaries'* soapiness: "It's also different from the *Buffy* and *Smallville* and *Supernatural* model in that they're sort of monster-of-the-week shows, and we're not that. This is actually closer to *Gossip Girl* . . . it's a serialized ensemble teen soap with a supernatural element. It's more about characters and romance."

On September 10, 2009, *The Vampire Diaries* would premiere during a vampire craze that was already in full swing: 2005 saw the first Twilight novel, 2008 saw the film adaptation as well as the premiere of *True Blood* (adapted from Charlaine Harris's Sookie Stackhouse novels). Add in films like *30 Days of Night* (2007), *Cirque de Freak: The Vampire's Assistant* (2009), and *Daybreakers* (2010). Pop culture was all undead all the time. The explosion of fanged heroes didn't surprise Melissa Rosenberg, screenwriter for the Twilight Saga films. "When one vampire story is successful, everyone else jumps on the bandwagon — that's just how studios and networks operate. It all comes down to money, but it's born out of very creative writers reinventing a genre and reinventing the mythology. Of course, every time it's reinvented, you have a whole new generation of people for whom it's really brand new."

Asked why he thinks vampires are the current obsession, Kevin Williamson said, "I'm sure there's some psychological ramification to the psyche of America and culture at the moment and politics and the state of the world. I'm sure we could go analyze it till the cows come home. But I think they're cool, they're fun, they're sexy, and they took off." He also pointed out that this wasn't the first time vampires had come to the front of the culture's psyche: "Everything is cyclical. Who knows? I mean . . . when I think of *The Lost Boys* [1987], I get all excited. And *Near Dark* [1987], I have great, fond memories of that." Cyclical it is: L.J. Smith's good boy "vegetarian" vampire predates *Twilight*'s Edward Cullen by more than a decade.

Julie Plec calls the vampire "the new James Dean." She counts herself as a devoted fan of the Twilight Saga, so she understands the appeal: "Edward has rejected all humanity, but he is struggling to be human. There is always the question, 'Does this person have it in him to be good, to make the right decision?' It's a theme that works like gangbusters in films and television." And for those of us wishing our next beau could be a biter, she suggests the lure is in the "epic amounts of knowledge and soul and spirituality and intelligence lurking behind those eyes. So in a vampire, by definition, you are getting the bad boy with the brain."

A self-described "sucker for an epic love story," Kevin Williamson describes vampires with the word that became a touchstone for Stefan and Elena early on in their romance: "Vampires are the bad boys. They're dangerous, but they're also just sexy and they can protect you. You can challenge them. There's so much there — epic love, epic romance, epic epic! Everyone wants their life to be epic."

The themes common to vampire stories — like immortality, lust, and fear — work beautifully in a high school setting in Kevin Williamson's opinion. "I always said that the teenage years are just one big horror movie. High school is a horror movie." As Joss Whedon did on *Buffy the Vampire Slayer*, Kevin and Julie work to balance the everyday life of small-town American teenagers with the Big Bad: "Life and death stakes, and prom night. Keeping it real and grounded is our big challenge, and telling stories with emotion so that I want to cry. I want to be emotional, at the end. . . . Doing all that is hard on a weekly basis."

If *The Vampire Diaries* was going to work, a critical factor was the three lead actors. Casting was all-important; if the audience didn't take to Elena Gilbert, it wouldn't care about the vampires falling for her. "It is always hard to find that anchor," said Kevin. In fact, casting the "mega-talented" Nina Dobrev as Elena almost didn't happen. As Kevin relates, the actress came in feeling ill and had the "worst audition ever. We didn't even look at her a second time. And she went home, went back to Canada, and she was just miserable. . . . So she put herself on videotape . . . and we were like, 'Who's that?' 'Oh, she came in and auditioned.' 'No, she didn't.' 'Oh, the sick girl?' She was a totally different girl, *totally*. . . . I had such luck with that with Katie Holmes back in the day, with videotapes, and so I said, 'Let's see if we can get lucky again.'" Nina Dobrev fits the part so well that, now, Kevin Williamson says, "I feel like I'm writing for Elena/Nina. They're all one and the same now." For Stefan, "Paul Wesley came in the very, very beginning and we thought he was a great actor but we didn't have our Elena yet so we couldn't make a decision. . . . When we had Nina we brought him in to read with her and that was it."

Getting Ian Somerhalder as Damon Salvatore was a bit trickier. "I heard Ian Somerhalder was interested in the part," says Kevin Williamson, "as far as I was concerned, he had it. . . . But to be honest, the first time he read for Damon, he didn't really bring it. Everyone said oh, he's definitely got the look, . . . but he just didn't bring it when he read. Still, I knew he had it in him. . . . it was just about getting him the role, convincing the network to roll the dice with him. . . . We took a gamble on him, and he delivered."

The pilot for *The Vampire Diaries* was shot in Vancouver, British Columbia, where, coincidentally, *The Twilight Saga: New Moon* was also filming — in fact, the two casts stayed in the same hotel. When the network ordered more episodes of the series in May 2009, production moved to Georgia because of tax credit incentives offered by that state. Filming mostly takes place in Covington, a town accustomed to film and television crews. "The word gets around when a specific locale is film friendly, is an easy place to do business, and provides all of the resources, locations, and inspiration needed for a producer to realize his or her vision," said Bill Thompson from the Georgia Department of Economic Development. Covington's proximity to Atlanta was a big part of the appeal, as was its picturesque town square. "When the writers came and visited Covington and saw the square, it was exactly what they had pictured for Mystic Falls," said Jessica Royal, who works with Bonanza Productions, the production company associated with *The Vampire Diaries*. Shooting on location meant the cast, who were apart from their families and friends, quickly became close, much like the cast of *Dawson's Creek* had while shooting in Wilmington, North Carolina. "They're a family and they're friends and they hang out," said Kevin. The camaraderie and familiarity comes across onscreen, and for the first time since *Dawson's*, Kevin Williamson felt the same kind of magic among his actors. Executive producer Bob Levy, from Alloy Entertainment, knew the show would work once he saw the onscreen chemistry between Nina and Paul in the pilot episode.

Kevin, Julie, and the rest of TVD's writers work out of Los Angeles, away from the day-to-day production of the show. Says Kevin, "We're so lucky because we have Marcos Siega, our supervising producer, and he's out in Atlanta a lot. . . . he's really responsible for the look of the show and the tone. He's out there making sure that the quality stays up to our standard. We don't have a big budget, but I think we really stand up to other shows with a much larger budget, and that's because of Marcos. Give him a light bulb, and he can make anything look good."

As The CW's "Love Sucks" promotional campaign for *The Vampire Diaries* rolled out, Kevin Williamson wondered, "Is there enough room for one more vampire show on people's DVRs? I don't know. I have room, but I don't know how America feels. It will be interesting to see if this show is one too many and tries people's patience, but I feel like the vampires are still popular." On September 10, 2009, the pilot episode aired and people tuned in. It was The CW's most-watched series premiere ever.

The early reviews were promising. Most identified the show as a mix of *Twilight*, *Dawson's Creek*, and *True Blood* or *Buffy the Vampire Slayer*. The *Calgary Herald* praised the show for being "something much smarter, sexier, and more profound than anyone could have expected"; *USA Today* described it as "a TV amalgam of *Twilight's* teen-angst broodiness, *True Blood's* humor-spiced chills, and the good boy/bad boy dynamic that is a teen soap's lifeblood"; and *Entertainment Weekly* called it "fun stuff mixing soap with blood." The *New York Times*, which had skewered Williamson's *Wasteland*, *Glory Days*, and *Hidden Palms*, wrote, "Mr. Williamson understands the modern American teenager more fully than Ms. Meyer" and called the show "slickly produced" with "engrossing moodiness." Viewers cast their votes for *The Vampire Diaries* by tuning in week after week, and brought the freshman show its first award, the 2010 People's Choice for Favorite New TV Drama. By February 2010, the show received an early pick-up for a second season. With a hit on their hands, Kevin Williamson and Julie Plec were able to make more long-term plans — what sets should they build, how many guest stars could they afford, will they have more series regulars in the future? Kevin advised, "You always save money when you plan long term." He also announced that the much-rumored *Scream 4* was going ahead, with Wes Craven directing and the original cast of Neve Campbell, Courtney Cox, and David Arquette returning. Kevin was also contracted to pen *Scream 5*, and at time of writing, is working on a remake of the 1987 thriller *The Bedroom Window*.

Though L.J. Smith was busy furiously writing The Vampire Diaries: The Return series in September 2009, she made sure to tune in to The CW when *The Vampire Diaries* premiered — which turned out to be a bit of a problem for a writer with no TV set. She bought one and had the cable guy come out, all so she could watch TVD. "They deviated in a number of places," said L.J., "but I think they did, overall, a magnificent job. I was so thrilled that it was Kevin Williamson who was doing this, you know, because it was just so exciting to get the guy who had done *Dawson's Creek* to be doing my work." Praising the music and the cinematography, L.J. also singled out a dynamic that was a fan favorite too: "It looks like they're starting off with a very strong Elena, one that's going to stand up to Damon, which I love. The scenes between them are going to be terrific."

The show was, in a word, epic.

From Fell's Church to Mystic Falls

Asked about her thoughts on readers' widely varying interpretations of her characters, L.J. Smith said, "My official opinion is that once I make up a character and then put him or her into a book, and that book is published, the character is the property of everyone, to do with as they please." Smith's open-minded perspective on her work meant that when Kevin Williamson and Julie Plec began working on their adaptation of The Vampire Diaries for The CW, they had the freedom to make that world work in the very different medium of television. Kevin Williamson said, "We want to do the books justice. We're going where the story takes us, but at the same time, we're really trying to honor the original books. A novel doesn't really lend itself to a 22-episode season, though, so there are obviously major differences. Our main concern is to honor the tone of the books and the major themes," which he identified as: romance, friendship, betrayal, deception, and redemption. What interested the show creators in the book series were those rich themes, as well as the fully realized world of Fell's Church. "We've had to make some hard choices, and we've made some changes," said Williamson. "But what I loved so much about what L.J. Smith did was she created a world and a mythology that is a writer's dream. That is the hardest thing to do, is come up with the backstory."

Expanding on her writing partner's point, Julie Plec said at the time of the show's premiere, "If you look at the gross content of the books, we're following it incredibly closely. But if you look at the timeline, it's varying quite a bit. We're telling some of the stories a lot faster, some of them a lot slower.

But the core relationships are very specific, and very much what we're playing with. We've got about five books that we're hopefully turning into many, many seasons."

One of the more controversial changes was a surprisingly simple one — and there was nothing the writers could do to change it. "There is a core fan base for the books," said Plec. "And they're mad that the lead character is not blonde. So when you start there, there's not a lot you can do." The casting of brunette Nina Dobrev in the role of Elena Gilbert was shocking to the dedicated fans of the book series. When readers first meet Elena in *The Awakening*, she is described as "cool and blond and slender, the fashion trendsetter, the high school senior, the girl every boy wanted and every girl wanted to be." While Elena's character changes dramatically over the course of that novel and the series as a whole, she begins her journey as someone quite aware of her position in the school hierarchy and of her power over others because of her appearance and confidence. She uses both her status and her beauty to her advantage. Armed with fierce determination, Elena Gilbert makes it her mission in *The Awakening* to win over Stefan Salvatore. In reimagining their heroine for television, Kevin and Julie knew she had to be more immediately relatable, the "anchor girl" the audience connects to and follows into the world of Mystic Falls. They needed the right actress, regardless of hair color. Said Kevin, "Once we saw Nina, we just couldn't get back to the blonde thing." L.J. Smith didn't understand their casting choice until seeing Nina in action. Said the author to MTV News, "I really, really like the Elena that they picked, Nina Dobrev. Even though she's brunette, and not blonde, which took some getting used to for me, she's a great actress." Though Elena is orphaned in the books as well, the tragedy was made more recent; instead of three years earlier, Elena loses her parents in the spring before the action begins, and was involved in the car accident herself.

More physically similar to their book counterparts were the actors cast as the brothers Salvatore, Stefan and Damon. Stefan Salvatore arrives in Fell's Church a mysterious stranger with a hot car and excellent personal style; though Mystic Falls' Stefan lost the Porsche, he retained the leather jacket and sunglasses for his first walk through the high school's halls. In L.J. Smith's novel, Stefan has never before been to Fell's Church, arriving there in the hopes of creating a semi-normal existence for himself — he wants to play the role of high school student, walk among the living with his lapis ring, and hide his true identity from the townsfolk. Stefan is shocked at Elena's

uncanny resemblance to Katherine. Because he feeds only on animals and his hunger is never truly satisfied, Stefan tries to stay far away from Elena, because she's a huge temptation for him. (A detail dropped perhaps due to *Twilight*'s similar trope.) Stefan's character — noble, mysterious, loyal, and secretly a vampire — remained the same in his transition to television, but Kevin and Julie altered his backstory. They gave him a purpose in coming to this small Virginia town: Stefan is returning to visit his hometown, and he chooses to stay because of Elena. As he says in the pilot episode's opening narration, "I had no choice. I have to know her."

In the novels, the Salvatore brothers are originally from Renaissance-era Italy, two sons of Giuseppe, Conti de Salvatore, in love with the same pale blonde girl, Katherine, daughter of the German Baron van Swartzchild, who is rarely seen in public before twilight. In present day, when Stefan comes to Fell's Church, he has no ties to the town, nor does his brother Damon, who follows him. L.J. Smith's Fell's Church is a fictional town with strong ties to the Civil War — the high school is named after the commander of the Confederate Army, Robert E. Lee, and the town cemetery is full of fallen soldiers. In changing the backstory for Stefan and Damon, the show's creators rooted the Salvatores' history in that of the town: Mystic Fall's Civil War past was witnessed by Stefan and Damon firsthand. The town's founders were their father's contemporaries. Though the re-imagined brothers are now roughly 350 years younger, they still possess an old-fashioned charm, not that of Renaissance men but of Old Southern gentlemen.

The dynamic between the brothers was another core element transferred faithfully from page to screen. Damon is stronger than his little brother because he feeds on human blood, and he is unashamed that he's a vampire. Where Stefan hates his monstrous side, Damon revels in it, using the Powers to torment his brother and the citizens of Fell's Church. In the book, Damon aggressively pursues Elena, trying to bring her to the dark side, to lure her away from Stefan. But for the show, Kevin and Julie opted for a slower build. Of the actors' portrayals of her beloved Salvatores, L.J. Smith was beyond satisfied: "I especially like Damon; Ian Somerhalder does very well. . . . And I love the Stefan they've picked."

As important to The Vampire Diaries' books as the love triangle is (that between Elena, Stefan, and Damon) there is another all-important trio — girlfriends Elena, Meredith, and Bonnie. Short, redheaded Bonnie McCullough is fascinated by the Druids, and believes her ancestry leads back to them. She's kind-hearted, bubbly, and tries very much to be as courageous as Meredith and Elena. Losing her distinctly Scottish last name as she was adapted for television, Bonnie became a Bennett (the writers borrowed the surname from the books' Vickie), and the Druids were dropped. Instead, her lineage traces to Salem and the witch trials of the 1690s. Tying Bonnie's history to something distinctly American had the same effect as swapping the Civil War for the Renaissance era: it grounded the show's action in something

Steven R. McQueen, Candice Accola, Nina Dobrev, Zach Roerig, Sara Canning, and Kayla Ewell pose for the photographers at a party for Nina's 21st birthday in Las Vegas.

more accessible to its primary audience. Bonnie herself became quite a grounded person as played by Katerina Graham. In her portrayal, Bonnie's insecurity about her latent abilities is secured by her core faith in herself.

But where is Meredith? Level-headed, dark-haired beauty Meredith Sulez helps keep her two best friends focused and rational when things get freaky in Fell's Church, but she's nowhere to be found on the TV show. When word reached fans that there would be no Meredith among the main cast, back in April 2009, Julie Plec wrote, "Be patient, Meredith fans." In a tweet after the premiere, Julie wrote about the no-Meredith situation: "Time, money and a lack of story at the beginning. Plenty for her to do in the long run." Kevin Williamson discussed the broader subject of the adaptation: "There are a couple of characters we have yet to introduce. We have a lot of things from the book that we have up on the board, ready to go. We've just got to figure out when [to introduce them]. It's all about a puzzle and putting all the pieces together. There's so much story, it's the puzzle of how you tell it." It's possible that Meredith is a no-show onscreen because of how much of that character made its way into Elena. Beyond the physical similarities between the natural dark beauty of Meredith and Nina Dobrev, TV Elena has the grounded, strong, and self-assured characteristics of Meredith.

Moving into the position of third bestie is Caroline Forbes. As imagined by L.J. Smith, Caroline is a beautiful green-eyed, auburn-haired social climber, interested in taking over Elena's spot as queen of Robert E. Lee High School. She's a schemer, a conniver, and susceptible to the influence of dark Powers. She and Elena were once close friends, but as *The Awakening* begins, the mild competitiveness between them has escalated into hostility, though Elena does not know why. Played by Candice Accola, Caroline vacillates between self-absorption and insecurity; she loves Elena and Bonnie but knows they value each other's friendship more than they value hers.

Perhaps the most faithful adaptation from the book is the character of Matt Honeycutt, the blond, blue-eyed, all-American athlete, a close friend of Elena, though he wishes she loved him another way, too. Coming from a poorer family than the rest of the characters, Matt's a stand-up, good guy, who befriends Stefan despite the fact they are in direct competition for Elena's heart. Matt became a Donovan in the move to Mystic Falls and got an older sister, Vicki. Based on the minor fictional character Vickie Bennett, who parties with jerk jocks Tyler Smallwood and Dick Carter in *The Awakening* before being targeted by the dark Powers, Vicki Donovan has a larger role to play as a love interest for Jeremy, a character who didn't even exist in Fell's Church.

L.J. Smith gave her heroine a little sister, Margaret. But because a cute four year old would limit the storyline possibilities, Kevin and Julie reimagined Elena's sibling as a kid brother, Jeremy, who's reeling after the death of their parents. Steven R. McQueen, who plays Jeremy, explained the choice: "When our characters are closer in age, it allows us to interact in more ways than we would be able to . . . if I was a young girl [laughs]. Our storylines wouldn't really cross. So I think they were just making sure that we all have a kind of a web, a connection. . . . But sorry, fans, that I'm not Margaret. And in preschool. Well, mentally I might be, but . . ."

With that same goal in mind, Aunt Judith Gilbert became Aunt Jenna Sommers so her character wouldn't be as removed from the lives of the high-schoolers. Though her maternal experience is just as non-existent, Jenna is younger than Judith, a grad student whose high school days are not that distant a memory.

L.J. Smith was not very involved in the adaptation of The Vampire Diaries, but the author seems content with this: "[Kevin] doesn't call me up and say, 'What do we do now?' I think they have their very definite ideas about their way that they're doing it, and I have very definite ideas that I have about my way that I'm doing it." Now existing in two vastly different media, The Vampire Diaries has separate and distinct narratives — one is laid out in the pages of Smith's seven novels, the other is being revealed episode by episode on The CW's breakout hit of the 2009 TV season. "We're plotting it out for longevity and we're plotting out all of the character arcs," said Kevin Williamson, reassuring the fans of the books. "If your character doesn't resemble the one that it did in the book, maybe we backed it up and started it somewhere else so maybe they can grow into that character, because we're a series and we have to tell a story every week."

The Cast

Nina Dobrev
(Elena Gilbert/Katherine Pierce)

Nina Constantinova Dobreva was born on January 9, 1989, in Sofia, Bulgaria. When Nina was two years old, she, her older brother Alexander, and their parents moved to Toronto, Canada, where the family settled. "I have spent most of my life in Toronto, but I also have gone back and forth to Bulgaria during summers and Christmas breaks," says Dobrev. "Most of my extended family is still there, and I definitely am bilingual and relate to both cultures." But before they could afford trips back home, Nina says, her parents "literally started out with nothing." Her father is a computer specialist; her mother an artist. Nina "just went to [J.B. Tyrrell Senior Public School], and started dancing and doing that kind of stuff just for fun." She took ballet and jazz classes, and competed in rhythmic gymnastics, even traveling to Europe for meets. Besides school, playing volleyball, and her dance and gymnastics classes, Nina had a busy schedule before the age of 16. Once she could find a job, it only got busier. "If I wanted the things everyone else had, I had to earn them myself," so the teen had a paper route, and later a job working at Hollister in the local mall.

Nina attended Wexford Collegiate School for the Arts and, as she likes to describe it, "lived a *Fame* life. It was very competitive but it was productive, too. . . . That's how I got started in the business." She began by modeling and then auditioned for commercials and acting roles for TV and film projects. In 2006, she had small parts in the TV movie *Playing House* as well as in films *Repo! The Genetic Opera* and *Away From Her*, which was adapted from a story by Alice Munro. That year Nina landed her defining role (that is, before Elena came along): she was cast in the Canadian teen drama *Degrassi: The Next Generation* as Mia Jones, who struggles to balance being a mom with being a high school student (and fashion model). Arriving on the set of *Degrassi* feeling "really new to the business," she was as "nervous as you can get. Meeting new people, making a good first impression, seeing the studio. It was strange." Mia stuck around from seasons 6 through 8 (with two episodes in season 9 to resolve her character's arc), and during that time, Nina became really close with her *Degrassi* family. Like the teen stars who came out of the 1990s *Mickey Mouse Club*, several *Degrassi* alumni have gone on to great success south of the border: Shenae Grimes plays Annie on *90210* and Aubrey Drake Graham is now better known as the Grammy-nominated rapper Drake. *Degrassi* provided a kind of training ground for young actors. "We worked with great people and were supported, and they really took the time to teach us," says Nina.

Nina gained more on-set experience with two more TV movies in 2007 (*Too Young to Marry* and *My Daughter's Secret*) and appeared in the films *The Poet* and *Fugitive Pieces*, an adaptation from Anne Michaels' novel of the same name. A project that would put her performing arts education to the test came her way in the form of *The American Mall*, an MTV-produced musical in which Nina starred as Ally, a struggling singer-songwriter. Shooting in Salt Lake City, Utah, the TV-movie musical required four weeks of boot-camp performance training followed by three weeks of intensive rehearsals before shooting even began. As she began shooting, she was as nervous as her first day on the *Degrassi* set: "It's my first American thing, it was the lead, there was a lot of pressure but good pressure. It was something I was very excited about. I couldn't sleep." Nina was confident with her dancing and lip-synching skills ("I was one of those girls who would watch TV and try to lip-synch, try to be Britney Spears"). But she worried about her vocal abilities, so she had some assistance in the studio for the notes that she couldn't quite knock out of the park. "It was my first time going in the studio, and recording and doing that whole thing. So I had help, I definitely had help." Perhaps because it was targeting an audience older than the tweens who'd made *High School Musical* such an insane success, *The American Mall* failed to make the same kind of splash. But Nina loved the experience: "I thought it was so much fun. I would do another one, if we had the opportunity."

In addition to her ongoing role on *Degrassi*, Nina appeared in *Mookie's Law*, *The Border*, *You Got That Light*, *Never Cry Werewolf*, and *Eleventh Hour* — *and* she managed to graduate high school and enroll at Toronto's Ryerson University where she was a sociology major. It sounds like too much for one person to juggle, and it was. As Nina admitted in 2008, "I love what I'm doing, and I couldn't wish for anything better, but I'm also trying to go to university, in my first year, and I'm never there. People go to university to learn how to be what they want to be in life. I'm already doing it, so I'm conflicted." The overachiever realized that she just couldn't do everything all at once: "I wasn't able to do any of them [school, *Degrassi*, and film work] perfectly. I was just kind of mediocre. I was trying to divide myself in three ways, and each was suffering. I wanted to be this perfect person . . . I had to realize there is no such thing as perfect — you do the best you can and have fun. But it took a couple of anxiety attacks to figure that out!" So Nina decided to defer her education, and focused on her acting career.

In the winter of 2009, Nina Dobrev moved to Los Angeles. Her first audition for a TV show pilot was *The Vampire Diaries*. It didn't go so well. "I was sick for that first audition, and then I had to go back to Toronto to shoot a film [*Chloe*]. So I [later] put myself on tape. The tape is what eventually got me the part." The scene Nina was given for that audition was of Elena alone in the graveyard talking to the crow. Said Nina, "It was a really awkward audition to do!" The casting agent liked the tape, and they asked her to come back. "So I flew in and auditioned in front of the studio, then the network, then the producers . . . It was very nerve-wracking, especially when you're standing in front of so many influential and powerful people." In her early auditions, Nina initially played Elena like the book's character — selfish and less relatable — but Kevin Williamson and Julie Plec steered her away from that: "'just be yourself. Do what you'd do if in this situation.' They wanted her to be more likable." Nina tried to portray Elena as "a little bit more vulnerable. . . . I'm not the most comedic person, so I tried to make it real, and sometimes the comedy is in the reality and the awkward moments. So they just liked my natural approach to it." After shooting the pilot episode in Vancouver, Nina moved with the production to Georgia, despite having just recently relocated to L.A. She initially shared an apartment with Kayla Ewell (Vicki Donovan) before bunking with her onscreen aunt, Sara Canning.

After *Degrassi*, Nina had to adjust to life as the heroine on a vampire TV show, which meant long night shoots. But she definitely feels she's grown since starting the show. "I think I've attained a comfort level on the set I didn't have before. I'm more responsible. I think I can take on a lot more now than I did [before]." It's much easier to throw yourself into your work when you love it, and Nina has a lot of admiration for her character: "Elena is definitely the moral center, I think. Or at least she tries to be. She sees her brother who is struggling and she tries to help him out. And she's always trying to be positive and move forward. . . . You have morals, but everyone makes mistakes." Nina's confidence shows in her performance: "I feel like I can pick up a script, read it, analyze it, and feel good knowing that when I get there, I'll do the best I can and it will translate and it works."

Though she is still very close with her friends from *Degrassi* (the producers sent her flowers when she got the part of Elena, and again when the show was picked up), Nina has a special bond with *The Vampire Diaries* cast and crew. Of Kevin and Julie she says, "We've become each other's people," and of her male leads, she says, "Ian and Paul are like my brothers." Though she and the rest of *The Vampire Diaries* family work incredibly hard, you'll never hear Nina Dobrev complaining. "Going to work is not like going to work. I get to do stunts, wear cool makeup, get bloodied, and be around people I love — basically my life is like the merry-go-round at a theme park. It's so fun."

But the fun doesn't stop there for Nina: playing the second, much different character of Katherine allows the actress to be conniving, narcissistic, and selfish, not to mention a lot more monstrous than Elena. Of the flashback scenes, Nina says, "It's a lot of fun for me to put on the corsets and the big dresses and do something completely different for a few days." Interestingly, her portrayal of Katherine is drawn from Ian Somerhalder's

Damon: "Damon gets a lot of who he is from Katherine. . . . So I actually adopted Ian's performance and some of Ian's quirks, so that the transition would make sense. Damon picked things up from Katherine, so in turn I drew inspiration from Ian."

At the 12th Annual Young Hollywood Awards, Nina was recognized for her performance in the show's first season and picked up the Making Their Mark award along with the Cast to Watch award with her TVD castmates. Despite now being famous enough to require her own personal publicist (a first for the actress), Nina is still humble and grateful for all the opportunities the show has brought her. In the break after season 1, Nina filmed *Deathgames* opposite Kellan Lutz (*Twilight*'s Emmett Cullen) and was cast in *American Empire*. But she'd rather spend her hiatus time not working than filming a movie or getting an endorsement deal for a product she doesn't believe in. And she believes in *The Vampire Diaries*. "It may be a vampire show, but there doesn't seem to be anything unreal about it, to me."

Paul Wesley
(Stefan Salvatore)

Paul Thomas Wasilewski, born in New Brunswick, New Jersey, on July 23, 1982, was the second child for Polish immigrants Agnieszka and Thomas. Paul has an older sister, Monika, an attorney, and two younger sisters, Julia and Leah. Growing up in Marlboro, New Jersey (rated among the safest and best places to live in the USA), Paul's passion was playing hockey until he was about 14 years old and was pushed into performing. As Paul says, "[I] had no real ambitions to act until I was forced to do a school play in elementary school, and then they're like, 'You have to sing.' The teacher put me in everything. I did this play and my mom was like, 'Oh I love what you're doing.' And I'm like, 'I love this, too,' so she threw me into modeling." Paul ended up at the prestigious Ford Modeling Agency in New York, where he stayed for two years. His first professional acting gig, on the other hand, was a little less glamorous: "I was an extra in a Great Adventure commercial and I was a kid and had to ride a roller coaster 14 times in a row. I vomited at the end."

In 1999, when he was still known as Paul Wasilewski, the 17 year old got a part on the soap opera *Another World*, followed shortly thereafter by a six-episode arc on *The Guiding Light* as Max Nickerson, acting opposite Brittany Snow. It was great news for his acting career, not such good news for his life as a student at Christian Brothers Academy. As Paul put it, he didn't "jive well with them" at the Academy, so he transferred to Marlboro High School. Sadly he didn't fare much better there. "I went to three different high schools because a lot of them weren't very accommodating [to my career]. I got kicked out of Marlboro High School because they couldn't tolerate the way I was missing school." The teen, who had always earned good grades and participated in extra-curricular activities when he could, finally found the right school for his unusual schedule. At Lakewood Prep in Howell, "I would go to school once or twice a week, but they were really awesome and let me do the work from home. They facilitated it so I was able to get a high school degree," which he did in 2000. Since he was moving around so much, Paul wasn't really part of the high school social scene: "I wasn't some weird loner in school, but I definitely wasn't invited to the cool parties."

For one semester, Paul attended Rutgers University, in New Brunswick, NJ, but he admits he "wasn't concentrating." He told his parents that though his plan had been to "get my degree and have a regular job just like everyone else," he'd changed his mind and wanted to continue working as an actor. "[My parents] constantly preached, 'You've got to get good grades. You've got to go to a good school.' When I made the decision to drop out of college to pursue acting, I had already been moderately successful doing the soap opera. Instead of being hesitant, they said, 'Do it,' which was really cool. I respect that." Says his mother, Agnieszka, "I'm the number one supporter of following your passion. I believe that if you have something that you really want to do, I'm not going to tell you that you have to stay in school first."

With his parents' blessing, Paul parlayed his experience on the soaps into getting his next set of roles, in HBO's *Shot in the Heart* (2001) and in the short-lived werewolf series *Wolf Lake* (2001–2002), in which he played a lead, Luke Cates. (Also in that series was Mia Kirshner, who plays Isobel Flemming on

The Vampire Diaries.) Paul soon had another potential series ahead of him, playing Lancelot in *Young Arthur*: "I did the pilot for a show that shot in Prague, and if it had gotten picked up, I would have had to live there for seven years. I knew that if the show was that successful to be showing on NBC for seven years, that by the time I got back, I would be a well-known actor. So I decided to do it." While his time as a knight of the Round Table was limited to the two-hour pilot (which was repackaged as a TV movie), Paul's performance in it attracted the attention of producers working on yet another new TV series, *American Dreams*. He was cast as Tommy DeFelice and appeared in 10 episodes from 2002 to 2005. He'd made his primetime debut, and it helped him land part after part on series like *Law & Order: Special Victims Unit*, *The Education of Max Bickford*, *Law & Order: Criminal Intent*, *Smallville* (as Lex Luthor's brother Lucas), *The O.C.*, *8 Simple Rules*, *CSI: Miami*, *CSI: NY*, and *Crossing Jordan*.

Those parts were all limited to one or two episodes, but on The WB's *Everwood*, Paul had nine episodes, from 2002 to 2003, as Tommy Callahan, a sensitive outcast with a drug problem. From bad boy to angel, Paul's next notable turn on TV was in ABC Family's 2007 miniseries *Fallen* about human-angel hybrids living on earth. Aaron Corbett was Paul's second supernatural role, after playing a werewolf in *Wolf Lake*, and he loved that *Fallen* was "dark and interesting and heroic." It was around this time that Paul decided Wasilewski was too hard to pronounce, and, with his family's permission, he adopted the surname Wesley.

In addition to smaller roles on *Cane*, *Shark*, and *Cold Case*, Paul Wesley played Logan Atwater in Lifetime's *Army Wives* in 2008. That year also saw Paul pick up his first lead in a film. Though he'd had smaller roles in other features like *The Last Run*, *Roll Bounce*, *Cloud 9*, and *Peaceful Warrior*, in comedy-horror *Killer Movie*, which premiered at the Tribeca Film Festival, Paul had a lead role as Jake Tanner, the director of a reality TV show whose set is plagued by a serial killer. In 2009's *Elsewhere*, Paul starred opposite Anna Kendrick (*Up in the Air*, *Twilight*) and Tania Raymonde (Alex Rousseau on *Lost*). Released in 2010, *Beneath the Blue*, which filmed in the Bahamas in 2008, saw Paul as the romantic lead, Craig Morrison, caught up in espionage relating to naval bases where sonar is affecting marine mammals. Though Paul confesses he doesn't really watch TV, he had seen *24* and was impressed with it. "I auditioned for it about seven times, for different parts," and in late 2008 he was cast as Kim Bauer's husband, Stephen, in the show's eighth season. Ever modest, he says, "I don't do much. I have a couple of lines."

Getting the part of Stefan Salvatore was an even more grueling experience: "I auditioned for the role of Damon three or four times. I went back and forth. They wouldn't see me for Stefan," he says. "They thought I wasn't right for it." But after casting Ian Somerhalder, says Paul, the showrunners thought "'Maybe this will work.' . . . I read for [Stefan] four times and then [screen] tested. They had already tested for the role of Stefan and [they] saw hundreds of guys. At the screen test, I had to go against three guys from Australia, three guys from London, four guys from New York, and five guys from L.A. It was like *American Idol.*" Paul was in love with the part: "When I read about a 160-year-old guy who was stuck in a kid's body, I thought, 'Well, this is going to be the most challenging role of my life, if I get it.' And it has been. Try encompassing 160 years of knowledge into your brain. My grandfather is 80 and my hero. He's the wisest man I've ever met in my life, and I'm playing a character that's twice his age."

Of the characters on the show, Paul's is one that most closely compares to the books, and Paul did his homework on Stefan: "The minute I was cast, I plowed through all the books." His younger sisters were already readers of the series, and Paul counts them and his mother as his first fans. In fact, at his sister Julia's 13th birthday party, Paul was the main event: "I showed up and it was literally an hour of me, having fun and hanging out with her friends. That's what they wanted. I was like, 'This is going to be really boring,' and she was like, 'No, they love *The Vampire Diaries.*'" Paul is coming to realize that it's not just 13-year-old girls who are watching but a much wider audience. "The businessman in the elevator, who's just standing there minding his own business in awkward silence, goes, 'Love your show.' That kind of thing happens all the time. It's awesome."

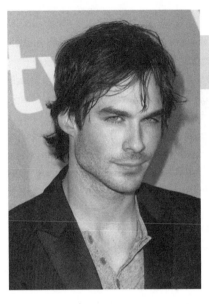

Ian Somerhalder
(Damon Salvatore)

Thanks to the impact of Anne Rice's Vampire Chronicles novels, when Ian Somerhalder was a little boy growing up on the north shore of Lake Pontchartrain, looking across the water at the skyline of New Orleans, he thought "There's vampires over there." Born December 8, 1978, in Covington, Louisiana, to mother Edna and father Robert, Ian spent his formative years in nearby Mandeville with "horses and land." After making his acting debut at age six in a school production of *The Sound of Music*, Ian became a child model at age 10 when he wanted money to buy a bicycle and fishing gear. His mother, a massage therapist, helped him find an agency, and the youngster quickly became a sought-after child model. It wasn't long before he was in campaigns for Gucci, Guess, and Versace. At age 16, he left home and headed for Europe to model. "My parents trusted me. There's a whole emancipation process [that happens when] you can live on your own. We just had this understanding that it was okay." Landing in Italy by himself, teenaged Ian grew up quickly: "You're 16 years old and by yourself, and you look around and see this other world happening you never knew about. You realize, 'I'm totally at home in the world, not just my hometown. . . . We're all part of this gigantic thing.'" Though he had no trouble getting work, it wasn't without its embarrassing moments. At a press show for Valentino, where Ian was wearing black underwear under his white suit, a stylist asked him to take them off. Ian obliged, disrobing behind a rack of clothes. "I went to grab the pants, but a guy had taken them away to steam them. And all of a sudden — cue the clothing cart moving away. And I'm just standing there. Sixteen, right out of New Orleans, and I'm in Italy and now I'm naked in this room."

Around the age of 18, his focus shifted from modeling to acting; he took classes, found a talent agent, and began auditioning. His first major part was on The WB's *Young Americans* (2000), a spin-off of *Dawson's Creek*. He played Hamilton Fleming, a prep school student with confused feelings about another boy (who, it turns out, is a girl in disguise). Ian also appeared in the films *Life As a House* and *Changing Hearts*; TV shows *Now and Again*, *Law & Order: Special Victims Unit*, *CSI*, and *CSI: Miami*; and in the TV movies *Anatomy of a Hate Crime* and *Fearless*. Opposite James van der Beek (*Dawson's Creek*) in 2002's *The Rules of Attraction*, Ian gained attention for his portrayal of the bisexual Paul. In 2004, Ian had a six-episode arc as Adam Knight in season 3 of *Smallville*. That year also saw Ian in what became a career-defining role as Boone Carlyle on *Lost* — and it came at just the right time for him. "I went through a really big breakup . . . I wasn't working that much because I couldn't figure out what I wanted. And that comes through. People can see that. . . . You're putting this out and there's only so much you can hide. I was just a wreck."

On *Lost*, which filmed in Hawaii, Ian played Boone, one of the original castaways and spends much of his time bantering with his sister Shannon (Maggie Grace). "I'm sure most of the public thinks, 'Oh God, there's that yappy blonde and the other dude,'" said Ian at the time. "The island is starting to change people, and I think I'm the first one it's changed. All the things I didn't like about Boone, I now understand." Just as his character began to get interesting and one week before Ian planned to go house hunting in Hawaii, he got the call that his character was going to die. Said showrunner Carlton Cuse, "It was a narrative imperative that we kill Boone." It didn't take long for Ian to bounce back from the blow, and he reasoned, "Everybody knew [that being killed off was a possibility]. Look, it was very hard for the audience to sympathize with a good-looking, spoiled, white, rich kid. I get that. I think it was hard for the writers to do so, as well. I don't fault them for it at all." His *Lost* castmates had become a second family, and Ian remains close with them. "One night there was a beautiful moon. Everyone was swimming. Naveen Andrews was playing guitar. Matt Fox said, 'Cherish this time because it will go.' He's right; it did."

A variety of roles came Ian's way post-*Lost*: he played a high-school aged Pigpen from Peanuts in an off-Broadway play called *Dog Eats God*; he starred opposite Kristen Bell in the tech-thriller *Pulse*; and he traveled to China as Marco Polo in a TV movie about the thirteenth-century explorer. In 2007, Ian could be seen in six episodes of the steamy HBO show *Tell Me You Love Me* as Nick. As the actor neared 30, he came across in press interviews as calmer and more confident in his work: "I couldn't be more focused now if you paid me. It's not a race. It's a steady climb. It's not how high you climb. It's not how high you fly, it's how long you fly high. You don't want to be Icarus. You don't want to burn out." Ian filmed a few more movies — *The Lost Samaritan*, *Wake*, and *The Tournament* (with *The Vampire Diaries'* Kelly Hu) — as well as TV movies *Fireball* and *Lost City Raiders* before hearing about a casting call for a vampire show. It was called . . . *True Blood*.

Somerhalder was desperate for a part in it and was honored that show creator Alan Ball met with him to audition for *True Blood*, which is set in Ian's home state of Louisiana. Ian tested for the role of Jason Stackhouse, Sookie's brother (a part that eventually went to Ryan Kwanten). "I so badly wanted that show, and I had a *really* bad meeting with Alan Ball and I blew it in the room. And I was so pissed off at myself that I couldn't bring myself to watch that show." At least not until he found himself starring in another vampire series.

Ian was in the Vegas desert with his girlfriend when his manager called to remind him about a very important meeting the next morning — to read for *The Vampire Diaries*. Studying his lines during the drive back to L.A., Ian wasn't very prepared when he met with the show's producers. "I'm personally not a very good auditioner and testing for a show is so nerve-wracking, especially when you want it. That process, man. The meetings and the network and the studio and the tests and all that stuff is very intense. It was just a week of sweaty palms. And Kevin fought for me, I knew he was fighting for me and that's . . . why I have such a connection to him. We both really wanted this." Ian calls the experience of playing Damon Salvatore "the most fun I've ever had, in the entire run of my career," and he credits that to "the fact that I haven't really gotten a chance to play those characters [who get into trouble] and really have fun. I've sorta learned that I'm so tired of taking myself so seriously. It's so great to show up at work and truly enjoy every word you say."

Ian draws inspiration from disparate sources for his take on the undead bad boy — Josh Holloway's portrayal of Sawyer on *Lost*, Cary Grant, and Dionysus. "The marriage of a crazy crass redneck with the class of an eloquent man like Cary Grant is an interesting way to play a crazy well-rounded 150-year-old guy who likes a dance and the finer things in life — like blood, wine, and Beethoven. Then you add in Dionysus — Damon is essentially Bacchus, he is that figure." Somerhalder had the opportunity to study Josh

Holloway firsthand when he returned to Hawaii to film two episodes for the final season of *Lost*. Ian kept his movie career going with *Cradlewood* and *How to Make Love to a Woman*.

But Somerhalder was really happy to be back living in the South while filming *TVD* in Atlanta ("That night air in Georgia is just like in Louisiana. It smells like when I was a kid."), closer to his family who still lives in the area he was raised. Ian uses his time off to promote charitable initiatives, like blood drives for the Red Cross or fundraisers for animal rescue organizations, and to raise awareness about the impact of the BP oil spill disaster. Though his fans won't be happy to hear it, the actor's dream is early retirement — to "spend about six years on this show and [do] a couple of movies and then cash out and spend the rest of my life on a horse," somewhere "on the bayou where I grew up — on the Tchefuncte [river] or on the lake. Those are my roots."

Katerina Graham
(Bonnie Bennett)

Unlike her small-town-girl character on *The Vampire Diaries*, Katerina Graham has had an adventurous life thus far, and it has exposed her to many cultures and countries. Born September 5, 1989, in Geneva, Switzerland, to a Russian-Jewish mother, Natasha, and Liberian father, Joseph who was working as a journalist at the UN, Katerina Alexandra Graham spent time in London, England, and in Portugal during her youth. Her international adventures led the youngster to pick up a number of languages: "I speak English, Spanish, French, a little bit of Portuguese, and Hebrew. My mom raised me. She's Jewish, so she spoke Hebrew and put me in Hebrew school, and before that she had me in French school. And my father speaks fluent French." But Katerina grew up "in the heart of Hollywood," where she would skateboard on Sunset Boulevard. For most Americans, Hollywood is an almost mythical place; for Katerina, "It was my neighborhood. I knew everyone and they knew me." She began acting at a very young age; her mother brought her to auditions, mostly for commercials, as early as three years old. Little Kat landed gigs in campaigns for Barbie, Kmart, Pop-Tarts, and Old Navy, and in 1998's *The Parent Trap* remake with Lindsay Lohan. Though she never made a conscious decision to be an actor as a child, she now can't imagine her life without acting: "I just stuck with it over the years. . . . It was like eating breakfast to me. I couldn't go a day without it." She studied acting, dance, and piano, and her training paid off in one-episode parts on *Movie Surfers* (2002), *Lizzie McGuire* (2002), *Malcolm in the Middle* (2003), *Joan of Arcadia* (2004), *Grounded for Life* (2004), *The O.C.* (2006), and *CSI* (2006).

As her acting resumé was growing longer and more impressive, Katerina was also busy at work on her singing and dancing career. She performed as a backup dancer for rapper Bow Wow's performance at the BET Awards when she was just 15 years old: "I was petrified! I could see Jay-Z in the front row!" That gig led to work with more high-profile choreographers and artists like Missy Elliott, Jamie Foxx, and Pharell, and appearances in music videos like "Mr. Lonely" (Akon), "Used to Love You" (John Legend), and "Why I Love You" (B2K). Katerina also found success as a songwriter; one of her first songs, "Derailed," found its way onto the soundtrack for the Jean-Claude Van Damme movie of the same name. She used the money she earned from that track to buy music production equipment and she taught herself how to use it, recording her own original songs.

At age 17, Katerina had an unusual opportunity to combine her acting, singing, dancing, and love of travel when she was picked by Coca-Cola to be one of four "mod" Fantanas, the high-energy pop group who sings the impossible-to-get-out-of-your-head jingle "Wanna Fanta," about the soda pop. Kat was "Capri" who loves the strawberry flavor, and she sharpened her Spanish skills doing international interviews for the campaign. Around that time, she recorded the female vocals on another infectious track, will.i.am's 2006 single "I Got it From My Mama." That connection led to Katerina going on the road with will.i.am's supergroup the Black Eyed Peas for four months, as a dancer and backup singer. "It was surreal and amazing and exhausting and it reminded me how much I love music."

As she continued producing her own songs (which stream on her website, katgraham.com), the overachiever was also picking up more credits as an actress: she played Allison on three episodes of *Hannah Montana* and worked with Disney-alum Zac Efron in *17 Again*, playing Jaime, one of the high school girls attracted to Zac's character Mike. Katerina is glad she doesn't have to choose just one profession — music or acting: "It's like being born half black and half white, it's just what I am. I can't be one without the other. I've been acting longer than I have been doing music. Acting is a huge passion of mine; I spend hours working on my craft, sometimes obsessing over one scene. But I could never stop making music." In 2010 and 2011, Kat is back on the big screen in *Bleachers*, a remake of *The Breakfast Club*; *Chicago Pulaski Jones*, directed by Cedric the Entertainer; *Boogie Town*, a heavy-on-dance-sequences, futuristic retelling of *West Side Story*; *Honey 2*; and *The Roommate* opposite *Friday Night Lights'* Minka Kelly, *Gossip Girl's* Leighton Meester, and *Hellcats'* Aly Michelka. The latter two combine singing and acting in their careers, and Kat loved working with them as they "shared similar mentalities."

Not too long before landing the part of Bonnie Bennett, Katerina said of the acting roles coming her way, "Because of my age, the roles that I'm in [don't] have as much depth as I would like, but that will change. Halle Berry, Angelina Jolie, they play heavy, meaty roles, which are the sort that I want to play." At first glance, the part of Elena Gilbert's best friend on *The Vampire Diaries* may not have seemed like an opportunity for a nuanced performance, but playing Bonnie is something Katerina considers a "blessing" and her "best role." What makes the job so important to her are the friendships she's developed with her castmates and *TVD*'s crew, as well as the opportunity to play a part that means so much to the original Vampire Diaries fans. "I have all of [the books] and I study them constantly. I realized that, in the beginning, before the pilot even came out, the fans were fans of L.J. Smith's novels."

Of her character, Katerina says, "What makes Bonnie beautiful is that she was coming into being a witch. It wasn't like she was just born a witch. It wasn't all very mystical from the beginning. I try to play her as real as possible and as normal as I could, and then have the discoveries, for the fans, about all her new abilities. . . . It's so important that people can relate to her and that she's just little Bonnie Bennett, thrown into this powerful world."

Katerina succeeds in creating a Bonnie that viewers can relate to, winning the fan-voted 2010 E! Online CW Award for Best Supporting Actress; despite her unusual and exciting career trajectory, Kat makes sure her fans can relate to her too. She is always replying to her fan mail and her fan's tweets, and she even created a web series, Road to Oz, that chronicles her journey so she can share her experiences with Team Kat Graham. Among her influences and idols, Kat names actresses Tilda Swinton, Helena Bonham Carter, and Thandie Newton, and musical performers like Lady Gaga, M.I.A., Gwen Stefani, Robyn, and Janet Jackson. With her success thus far and her fiercely independent spirit and determination, there are already those out there who consider Katerina Graham their role model.

Candice Accola
(Caroline Forbes)

That clichéd phrase "big in Japan" rings true for Candice Accola. Of course, these days, she spends her time as Mystic Falls' "misunderstood" Caroline Forbes, but in 2008 Candice was a rising star in the land of the rising sun; her album, *It's Always the Innocent Ones*, was a hit in Japan, and it brought her popular and critical acclaim.

Candice grew up in Edgewood, Florida, just south of Orlando, with her parents, Dr. Kevin Accola, a renowned surgeon, and mother Carolyn, a homemaker and active political campaigner. (Her parents and teenage brother still live in the area, on Lake Jessamine.) Born May 13, 1987, Candice was only in middle school when she first began performing, as Daisy Mae in the *Li'l Abner* musical. For young Candice, it was singing rather than acting that first appealed to her: "When I was eight or nine years old, I came home and told my mom that I was starting a girl group and that we were going to be the next Spice Girls." She took vocal lessons and sang in her school choir. But despite her noble aspirations and follow-through, her group, Girl Zone, didn't get past the retirement home circuit.

At the ripe old age of 16, having secured an agent to represent her, Candice left Lake Highland Preparatory School and headed to L.A. and a new career in music. (Don't worry: she finished her high school education over the next two years by correspondence.) In her first six months in L.A., Candice landed a deal with Maverick Records/Warner Music Group and began recording the pop-rock album *It's Always the Innocent Ones*. The singer ditched her last name, going just by "Candice" for her music career. The deal with Maverick/Warner went sour, due to the label's internal problems, and then-red-haired Candice's big debut was released on an independent label, Beverly Martel Music, in 2006 and is available on iTunes. (The Japanese label Spinning Art picked up the album, repackaged it, and released it in 2008.)

Advice Candice's father gave her as she was growing up stuck with the 19 year old as she struggled to find success; he always told her: "No doesn't mean never, no means not yet." It was around this time that Candice's attention turned to acting roles. Though she'd studied acting as a kid, Candice's interest in it blossomed while living in L.A.; she swears "something is in the water out there." She knows she found more jobs, more quickly than a lot of L.A. wannabes, and admits, "I was fortunate enough to work and then continue working and [take] more classes and continue working. . . ." Her first onscreen role was in 2007's *Pirate Camp*. After that, she landed a bit part in *Juno*; her character was "Girl Lab Partner." She picked up parts in two more films that year, *X's and O's* and *On the Doll*, and Candice realized how happy she was. "The more I started working, the more I just really loved the job."

But as had happened with her music career, just as Candice's acting career was picking up steam, the 2007–2008 Writers Guild of America strike kicked in and production in Hollywood soon came to a standstill. But plucky Candice didn't let that stop her; she got a job as a backup singer for Miley Cyrus on the bestselling tour in a decade. The Best of Both Worlds Tour felt like the best of all worlds for Candice: "It was a blast. I'd worked with the band director before; he'd produced my record. . . . And I was friends with the rest of the band, so I was basically getting to go on the road with a bunch of my friends. And Miley was a sassy little thing who's super talented!" With her stop-and-start career, Candice took some inspiration from the precocious pop star: "I was definitely taking notes in how she met people, always with gratitude and being excited. At the time she was 15 and she pretty much hit overnight and always enjoyed it. She always had fun and [was] appreciative. As you get older you forget it's supposed to be fun. That definitely gave me insight to have fun and just appreciate the hell out of it." That tour also gave Candice more big-screen time, and in 3-D no less, as part of the *Hannah Montana & Miley Cyrus: Best of Both Worlds Concert* movie (2008).

Back in L.A. and acting, Candice added some higher-profile TV shows to her resumé like *How I Met Your Mother, Supernatural,* and *Greek,* as well as the horror movie *Dead Girl.* When she heard about the audition for *The Vampire Diaries,* Candice saw the names attached to it — Kevin Williamson, Julie Plec, and Marcos Siega — and was "incredibly interested and excited . . . I love Kevin Williamson; I grew up watching *Dawson's Creek* and all the *Scream* and *I Know What You Did Last Summer*s. And what Julie Plec had done on *Kyle XY* was just incredible." The audition process was lengthy but in the end, the young actress, who was applying for waitress jobs when she found out she had the part, calls the whole experience "completely nerve-wracking and completely gratifying." *The Vampire Diaries'* Caroline Forbes was Candice's first recurring television role. "The most surprising thing going into a series is you really don't know what's going to happen . . . whereas when you're doing a film, you get that beginning, middle, and end. You know where your character arc is. . . . Not only is the audience learning about who you are as a character, but as an actor you're learning that just as much."

It seems like Candice couldn't be happier: she lives with her aunt, uncle, and cousins while she films in Georgia, and with Nina Dobrev when they're in Los Angeles. She loves the cast and crew of the show, who, even after spending long days together, socialize on their time off, and she enjoys playing Caroline, a girl she considers not to be self-absorbed or shallow but misunderstood. Says the actress, "Caroline just puts so much effort into the way she appears and getting together school activities and into the amount of flirtation she plays with the boys, and she just wants to be appreciated by the people around her. And I think that's what makes it so hard for her, that Elena doesn't even *try* and everybody just appreciates her."

An avid reader, Candice loves splurging on books and tearing through fiction like *City of Thieves* (David Benioff), *Love Me* (Garrison Keillor), or *The Road* (Cormac McCarthy), which she lent to costar Paul Wesley after reading. Music is still a big part of her life, and she's happy she doesn't have to choose one career path or the other. She continues working on projects outside of Mystic Falls, with two films, *Kingshighway* and *The Truth About Angels*, already wrapped.

Though Candice says she shares Caroline's knack for saying things she shouldn't, the two are otherwise rather different. Each day on set, getting into her character's "always very done" hair and wardrobe helps Candice "get into the Caroline essence, if you will. And I think just before they call action, just taking a beat, and standing up a little bit straighter, head a little higher, and here we go. Here's Caroline."

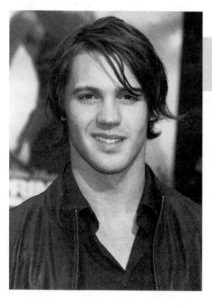

Steven R. McQueen
(Jeremy Gilbert)

While the rest of his name is rather familiar, the "R" is still a mystery. The grandson of film icon Steve McQueen, he has been variously reported as having the given names Steven Chadwick McQueen and Terrence Steven McQueen II. The young actor now known as Steven R. McQueen was born on July 13, 1988, in Los Angeles, California, to mother Stacey Toten and father Chad McQueen. Just as Chad dealt with his father's legacy as a huge Hollywood star when he began acting in his early 20s, Steven now finds himself facing the same scrutiny and expectations.

As a child, Steven didn't plan to follow in his father's or grandfather's footsteps: "I think my mom wanted me to stay out of it, to be honest. So I stayed out of it when I was younger." Around age 16, Steven began taking acting classes and auditioning for roles. His first part was in the sci-fi series *Threshold* in 2005. "Once I started [acting], I knew it was something I would love. It just kind of became my passion," said the actor. For seven episodes in the fourth season of *Everwood*, Steven played Kyle Hunter, a talented but troubled piano student. That WB show didn't survive the network's merger with UPN, but soon enough Steven would be on the new CW.

In addition to taking acting classes, Steven tried to learn from the great actors he had worked with, like Treat Williams in *Everwood* or James Gandolfini in "Club Soda" (a short film in *Stories USA*, 2006). "I've kind of always asked for advice and tried to take in as much as I could whenever working with them." The strategy worked; Steven won the Beverly Hills Film Festival Audience Award for Best Actor for his work in "Club Soda." Next up for Steven was the Disney Channel movie *Minutemen* (2008) about three high school boys who build a time machine; that year also saw him on three high-profile primetime TV shows, *CSI: Miami*, *Numb3rs*, and *Without a Trace*.

Though he never met his famous grandfather, who passed away in 1980, Steven feels that sharing his name is both a blessing and stressful. "It leans both ways. People are excited to meet with me, and that helps, but then when you get into the meeting or audition, they expect you to be great. So it adds a little bit of pressure. But it makes things more interesting." Steven purposely chooses roles that aren't ones Steve McQueen would have been cast in. "I've gone more for the loner, side characters than the bad-ass characters." His grandfather was known as "The King of Cool," and appeared in classics like *Bullitt*, *The Getaway*, and *The Thomas Crown Affair*; he also loved racing cars and motorcycles. That trait was passed down to his son Chad, who was a competitive racer, and even to Steven, who said in one interview that he was on the verge of buying a Triumph Bonneville motorcycle. Of his namesake, Steven says, "I know he was a great actor, a cool guy, very down-to-earth. Sometimes when I watch his movies, I'm like, 'Whoa, that's cool. I'm related to that guy!'"

The audition for *The Vampire Diaries* pilot came up and Steven "loved the character" of Jeremy Gilbert. After landing the part, Steven told his little sister and cousins, who were fans of the books, about his role: "They were so excited, they started jumping up and down on their beds. It was really cute." What they told him was that, in the book series, his character was a four-year-old girl named Margaret, a change that Steven feels gives him and the writers a lot of leeway to develop Jeremy. "My character has this great freedom where it can go anywhere. He can make an extremely dark choice; he can make the right choice. Nothing's really set in stone for me. It's just kind of a mystery." He was also excited for the opportunity "to learn to adapt a character over a long period of time," should the series become a success. And there was one friendly face already on set: he and Nina Dobrev had met while auditioning for *Percy Jackson and the Lightning Thief* (neither actor got a part in it) and they had become friends. "She's like an actual sister to me. I love Nina. In the beginning [of the series], when we were busting each other's balls a little bit, we enjoyed that 'cause normally we're just nice to each other."

In the time between shooting the pilot for TVD and beginning the rest of the season, Steven filmed another big project, *Piranhas 3-D*. Reading the script, Steven "thought it was awesome. It had that *Snakes on a Plane* feel, but in 3-D." In the movie, Steven plays Jake, son to the sheriff who's played by Elisabeth Shue (she worked with his father Chad in 1984's *The Karate Kid*), and he's smitten with Kelly (*Gossip Girl's* Jessica Szohr).

Though Steven was 21 playing a 15-year-old Jeremy in *The Vampire Diaries'* first season, the actor relished the part. "Playing Jeremy is great. He's a teenager with a lot of pain, a lot of anger, and it can be a therapeutic role to play. And I can let all that anger out. You know, [as Jeremy] I fight people, I do drugs; rather than be self-destructive in real life, I get to pretend to do it on film." Of his performance style as the troubled teen in the first few episodes, Steven quipped, "Keep the angst up."

Sara Canning
(Jenna Sommers)

Sara Canning began her life on the eastern most part of Canada — born in Gander, Newfoundland, on July 14, 1987 — but began her career on the country's west coast, studying at the Vancouver Film School.

Growing up in Newfoundland, Sara was a competitive figure skater, and still counts a beach she played on as a child as her "favorite place on earth." She and her parents moved to Edmonton, Alberta, and Sara loves the perspective that granted her: "Living in the two provinces were completely different experiences and shaped me in different ways." Her first forays into acting weren't altogether successful. Recalls Sara, "I fainted on stage in my fifth grade Christmas pageant. I was a star. A falling star." She didn't let that stop her. In high school, Sara was a self-described "huge drama and musical theater nerd"; her happiest moments were "spending time with people who enjoyed and encouraged that side of me." Upon graduation, Sara enrolled at the Vancouver Film School in a program she feels "really focuses on preparing acting students for the realities of our industry." But it was still a hard slog for Sara as she began auditioning for roles in Vancouver, which is home to a lot of U.S. television series and film productions. "I went through a crazy time when I first started working in Vancouver. I was working in a restaurant [the Cactus Club] seven days a week, sneaking behind the kitchen to learn my lines for every audition I did. I really went through a stressful time."

In 2006, she had her professional debut in Citadel Theatre's production of *1984* in her hometown Edmonton, and she landed her first onscreen role in *Paparazzi Princess: The Paris Hilton Story*, which aired in 2008. Her part? The infamous heiress's little sister Nicky. Of the role, Sara says, "I put all of my media-instilled judgments about the Hiltons aside. . . . I really tried to focus on the fact that she and Paris are sisters, and they trust and rely on each other more than any other people in the whole world." In 2008, Sara got roles in two television series, both of which had a connection to Sara's future gig on *The Vampire Diaries* and both filmed in Vancouver: *Kyle XY*, which was Julie Plec's project, and *Smallville*, a cw show. Sara also starred opposite *Dawson's Creek* alum James van der Beek in a Lifetime tv movie called *Taken in Broad Daylight*; once again Sara would be playing a real-life person, this time kidnapped teen Anne Sluti. She also appeared in *Slap Shot 3: The Junior League*, and tv movies *Come Dance at My Wedding* and *Black Rain*.

Canning's lead role in *Taken in Broad Daylight* brought her another project: Kent Ulrich, the producer of the film *Black Field*, a historical drama set in the 1870s, suggested Sara for the meaty role of Scottish-Canadian homesteader Maggie McGregor. Said Ulrich, "Sara really commits herself to a role, and that showed up on [her] audition tape. [The director] loved her." Shooting in the winter in Manitoba meant "pretty freezing weather," as Sara put it, but it added to the realism of how "hard it would be to live in that area in the 1800s." The film premiered well at the 2009 Vancouver Film Festival, with Sara's performance singled out for praise.

When casting began for *The Vampire Diaries*, Sara auditioned for three different roles. She feels the stars aligned for her to get the part of Jenna Sommers: "I'd been banking on another job, which ultimately didn't work out, and I was really disappointed. But along came this pilot with an awesome cast and production team, and the possibility for a great opportunity. It was the ultimate reminder that things happen for a reason." The part required grad-school-age Sara to play the guardian to her traumatized niece and nephew portrayed by actors who are just one or two years her junior; Nina Dobrev is one year younger and a few of the show's other high-schoolers are actually older than Sara. "It's definitely a very strange thing," she says of the age discrepancy. "Taking care of her deceased sister's kids is a really noble job, so yes, she's playing a parental figure, but at the same time, she's growing up herself. She's still really young and has rough patches with guys and she's still in school, so it's been a really fun character to approach that way." Canning credits her experiences when she was juggling acting and waitressing for her understanding of Jenna. Like Sara, Jenna is "growing up very quickly" and feeling the "weight of responsibility." As well, Sara credits the disparate acting roles that led her to Mystic Falls. "I think people learn the most by doing; I'm so grateful for the different roles I've played over the past couple of years. . . . I've had the privilege of playing numerous strong women. That's really prepared me for what's going on in Jenna's life and the choices she has to make."

She and fellow Canuck Nina Dobrev share a place while in Georgia, and the two get along well: "Nina is such a great roommate. . . . We're both really easygoing. We try to help each other stay healthy, but I usually cave and bring chocolate into the apartment." She's taken to life in Atlanta, a "much different culture than the west coast of Canada," and plans to drive across America during the season 1 filming hiatus. But sometimes *The Vampire Diaries*' locales are a bit too realistically spooky: "Some of the locations are really, really creepy. You don't have to use too much of your imagination. In fact, one night when I was driving with Kayla [Ewell], the fog started coming in out of nowhere and we were like, 'Ooooooohhh, when is Damon going to pop out?'"

Zach Roerig
(Matt Donovan)

Zachary George Roerig, born February 22, 1985, in Montpelier, Ohio, isn't afraid of coming across as being "too country." He talks about fixing up his family's old barn and repainting it "barn red"; driving with his grandpa in a truck and "knowing that the coffee can beneath my feet was filled with his urine from the first few hundred miles [of his drive]"; and racing hogs for 4H while he was growing up. In the way he talks about his childhood and family — mother Andrea, father Daniel, and younger sister Emily — Zach exudes the same wholesome charm that makes his *Vampire Diaries'* character, Matt Donovan, so immediately endearing.

Zach lovingly describes the town he was raised in as having "about 3,000 people, two stop lights, pretty small town. . . . Grew up Catholic with catechism every Wednesday. I had horses . . . bailed hay every summer." He helped out with the family business, Fackler Monuments, "since I was able to tie my own work boots," working with his grandfather and father making gravestones. Preteen Zach had already showed some interest in performance. He signed up for tap dancing lessons at the age of 10 and stuck with it until he was 13 before quitting "due to ridicule from peers. That has always been a regret of mine — so I'm righting my wrong: I recently started taking class again."

At Montpelier High School, Zach ran track, played football, and wrestled. At age 16, his interests turned to acting: "I heard something on the radio about 'Do you want to be an actor?' And I was like, 'Yeah. I think I do.' My dad was always an actor at the county playhouse so I was just trying to follow in his footsteps." Zach drove into Cleveland every weekend to study at Stone Model and Talent Association in Shaker Heights (where, coincidentally, *The Vampire Diaries'* guest star Sean Faris also studied). But slowly Zach realized his heart was in acting, not in the family business: "It was always set up that I was going to be the guy to take over the business. Then in high school, I told my folks that I might want to give acting a shot." And he did; three days after graduation, he left for New York City.

Roerig landed commercials for St. Johns' University and Footlocker as well as catalog modeling jobs for Sears and Kmart, before being cast in most New York actors' first TV series, *Law & Order*, in 2004. He appeared in the short film *Flutter Kick* (2005) and two pilots, *The Prince* and *Split Decision*, in 2006, neither of which were picked up. But Zach wasn't too worried: he had a steady gig on the CBS soap opera *As the World Turns*. Playing Casey Hughes (a role that six other actors have also portrayed), Zach appeared in 247 episodes from 2005 to 2007. His character struggled with online gambling, navigated romantic intrigues, and went to prison. It was a part that allowed the young actor to gain invaluable experience. Zach got used to being recognized, but "during one vacation trip, we stopped at a truck stop to refuel. I was alarmed to hear a deep voice shout, 'Casey Hughes!' At this point my fans were generally middle-aged females so I was a little shocked when it turned out that the voice belonged to a burly trucker who happened to be a big fan of the show." Zach also appeared in one episode of *Guiding Light*, and in 13 episodes of *One Life to Live* as Hunter.

After two years of soap opera acting, Zach landed some film roles in *Dear Me* and *The Assassination of a High School President* opposite Bruce Willis and Mischa Barton. Both movies were released in 2008. That year he was back on TV — in primetime as the volatile Cash on *Friday Night Lights*. Back when that show was auditioning actors for its pilot, Zach tried out for the roles of Jason Street and Tim Riggins. In preparation for his role as a rodeo cowboy who gets involved with Tyra Collette (Adrianne Palicki), Zach had the opportunity to brush up on his horse-riding skills, hang out with real cowboys, wrangle cattle, and attend rodeos. That was the fun part; less enjoyable was the dark turn his character Cash takes. Says Zach, "It's not easy to slip into a character who's violent to women because it's so foreign to who I am as a person." But Zach loved filming in and around Austin, Texas, and made lasting friendships during the three months he was there. And unbeknownst to Zach, one of his future showrunners, Julie Plec, was glued to her screen, a devoted fan of *Friday Night Lights*.

Zach also had a fan in Kevin Williamson, who kept bringing him out to audition for various pilots he was working on. They didn't find the right fit until *The Vampire Diaries*. Though he originally auditioned for the Damon part (says Zach, "Ian has the best role on the show"), it turns out the Ohio native was more suited to play the all-American, good-natured human. While landing the role was "a process to say the least," Zach was happy to play a good guy who didn't turn bad. "Most of the characters I've played in the past started out as nice guys, but it turned out that was only an act and they became nasty guys. I thought for once I'd like to play a genuinely nice guy, which Matt is." He didn't read the book series before his audition or after he landed the part. The actor reasons, "All my girl cousins had read them and were all into the Twilight books and The Vampire Diaries, and they told me Matt was like the nice guy but not the masculine nice guy that they made him in the show. So I don't want that [characterization] to deter how I play him; I want to bring a little swag into Matt." Being on a show with at least one bloodthirsty vampire always hanging around makes Zach a little worried about his character's safety: "Every time I read a script and it says, 'Matt enters the room and Damon follows,' I'm like, 'Oh my God . . .'"

Zach understood Matt's character, saying "there are guys like Matt all over where I'm from. They always put the woman first and family comes first. Matt is small town and I grew up in a small town." Still, it is sometimes challenging to be *so* good-hearted. "I think that no matter how often we try to be selfless, we sometimes end up being a little selfish in the process, and Matt is never selfish. He is selfless all of the time; every decision he makes is selfless. I would say that's been hard to adapt to." When, or if, Matt Donovan ever discovers what lurks in the shadows of Mystic Falls, Zach expects a strong reaction: "I think Matt's got some hidden rage, I mean look at his life, he's never exhibited any ounce of anger or emotion, and so I feel like it's going to be a Ned Flanders kind of explosion."

When he's not on set, Zach is "addicted to the outdoors" — camping, hiking, even reading outside. After his time on the two soap operas, Zach bought an R.V. and toured America's national parks, blowing two tires in the Badlands of South Dakota and accidentally backing into "a buffalo in Yellowstone. It was a sleeping buffalo that turned mad quick." In the summer of 2009, Zach tried his hand at producing, something he's interested in doing more of: the independent film *Strawberry Wine* is a "kind of a love story" in which Zach also stars. Other than that, he's working on that family barn. Says Zach, "This is going to sound really country, but I'd like to get it in an Ohio barn magazine or something. I don't know if there is an Ohio barn magazine — I might even try to get one published."

Kayla Ewell
(Vicki Donovan)

"A beach girl at heart," Kayla Ewell was born on August 27, 1985, and grew up in Seal Beach, California. At Los Alamitos High School, Kayla was on the surf team and was voted prom queen in her senior year. By then, she was already a working actress. "Since I was a little girl, I always knew I wanted to be an actress," says Kayla. "The thing about this career is each job is a turning point, you never know what is coming."

Kayla studied tap, jazz, and ballet dancing at Orange County Song and Dance Company in Westminster, and it was there that she was scouted. In an interview in 2000, Kayla said, "There was an agent walking around [the dance studio] looking for dancers, and . . . he saw me in this acting class, because my dance teacher also teaches acting. And he was like, 'I'd like you to try out for some people.' I was all excited. That was a year ago and here I am." "Here" was on the set of *Freaks and Geeks*, Judd Apatow's acclaimed TV series that managed to become an enduring favorite despite only lasting one season. Kayla played Maureen in three of the series' 18 episodes, and, a decade later, it's still the show she's asked about most often: "It's such a cult hit, no matter what I do people always want to hear about it." *Freaks and Geeks* was Kayla's first TV gig, and she calls it "such an amazing learning experience."

After roles on *Profiler* and *Boston Public*, Kayla landed the part of Caitlin Ramirez on *The Bold and the Beautiful* and played that character from January 2004 to July 2005. "It's basically actor's boot camp because you have so much dialogue: you do one episode a day. But it was so much fun," said Kayla. After a three-episode arc as Casey on *The O.C.* in 2005, Kayla kept racking up the roles with parts in *Veronica Mars*, *Just My Luck*, *Material Girls*, *Close to Home*, *Senior Skip Day*, *Impact Point*, *Fired Up!*, and

Bones. On *Entourage*, Kayla played Amy in three episodes. "All the lead guys are such goofballs," she said. "You can tell they really enjoy what they do for a living. There are times it feels as if I am working with a bunch of rowdy little boys in grown-up bodies."

When Kayla read the script for *The Vampire Diaries*, she knew exactly which part she wanted to play, despite it not being the lead role. "When I first read the pilot, I was like, 'This show is so awesome and it's gonna go and I want to be a part of it. . . . Of all the characters, I really want to play Vicki.'" Kayla was attracted to Vicki's character because of how much the role would require her to stretch: "I like the role because it's the total opposite of who I am, and who I was in high school, and I get to go places I don't usually go in real life." After her audition, she met with Kevin Williamson and Julie Plec to talk about the character, and they were all on the same page about who Vicki is. For her screen test with Michael Trevino, Kayla had to perform the scene from the pilot where they are "against the tree going at it." Kayla joked that, after doing that kissing scene, she turned to him and said, "'Hi, what's your name?' That's what so weird about this job." Kayla landed the part, and she loves playing Vicki because "she stirs up trouble." Kayla feels that Vicki and Matt Donovan have had to "grow up on their own, really. I think Vicki is trying to find love, and she finds it through sex and other things like that . . . which is really sad. It's the only way that Vicki feels loved." Kayla has a strategy for playing someone who she feels has given up on being good: "The trick is just to let loose completely."

In Atlanta while filming *The Vampire Diaries*, she and Nina Dobrev shared an apartment, and the girls have become close friends — they even spent some of their time off watching *Dawson's Creek* on DVD. (Kayla's parents wouldn't allow her to watch the show when it first aired because it was "too racy.") Like the rest of her castmates, she thinks shooting outside of Hollywood has really helped create on-set camaraderie. "I personally think that [friendship] helps when you have scenes together, because you hang out all the time. It's really bonded our cast and crew a lot." Much loved and admired by her castmates and crew for both her performance and her personality, Kayla feels the same way about her *Vampire Diaries* family: "I'm definitely making some of the best friends I'll ever have right here."

Michael Trevino
(Tyler Lockwood)

Born January 25, 1985, to Mexican parents and raised in Valencia, California, Michael Trevino never witnessed the changing of seasons until he lived in Atlanta to film *The Vampire Diaries.* "I'm actually seeing leaves fall," said Trevino in the winter of 2010, "and when we were in Atlanta in July it was humid and hot, but now it's really, really cold over there. Just to experience that, for me personally . . . is something really nice."

After deciding to pursue a career in acting, Michael enrolled at the well-respected Playhouse West for theater studies. He landed some commercials and then TV gigs. The young actor appeared in *Summerland, Charmed, Cow Belles, Commander in Chief, Without a Trace, Cold Case, CSI: Miami,* and *Bones.* He was cast as Jaime Vega on *Cane* (2007), playing the son of Jimmy Smits' character; that series only lasted 13 episodes. "I was bummed when the show got canceled," said Michael of the experience. "It was my first time as a series regular. I wanted it to keep going, because I was working with quality actors and having so much fun. I learned a lot from them." Michael was back on TV with a five-episode stint on *The Riches,* the TV movie *Love Finds a Home,* and episodes of *CSI, The Mentalist,* and *CSI: NY.* He made his CW debut in 2008 on *90210,* playing Ozzie, a love interest for Naomi, in a three-episode arc. Though he had more screen time on *Cane,* Michael had his first experiences of being recognized with *90210* fans: "It was weird! I was in Hollywood, walking down the sidewalk with a couple of my buddies, and these girls on the sidewalk were waiting to cross the street with us. One girl said, 'Can I take a picture with you?' That doesn't necessarily happen a lot to me, to be honest." Michael also appears in *The Factory,* a film slated for 2011 that stars John Cusack and Mae Whitman (*Parenthood*).

About his *Vampire Diaries* character, Tyler Lockwood, Michael says, "I know it seems on the surface that he's someone who has a high temper and snaps at everybody and has a mean streak in him and that's it, that he's just that bully guy that everybody knew in high school. . . . [But] you're going to see a different side of him. He can't control himself, and although he comes from a family that is well-off, with his father being the mayor and being one of the founding families . . . , it seems like he's on his own. He doesn't have much of a support group." Michael doesn't see very many similarities between himself and his onscreen counterpart. "I played high school football like Tyler, all four years, but other than that, not really. Even when I was in high school, I definitely wasn't going around picking fights. I wasn't the big man on campus in high school. I wasn't popular, but I was well known. I always went by my last name — nobody ever called me Michael, and that was just kind of a football thing."

When he's not working, Trevino loves sports, especially snowboarding on Big Bear Mountain, which is a short drive outside of Los Angeles. He had a fair amount of free time to fill with his various athletic pursuits while in Atlanta shooting season 1; Tyler wasn't given a major storyline in the first season. But Michael was still happy to be a part of *The Vampire Diaries*: "We have an amazing crew in Atlanta and our producers and writers here in Los Angeles who work day in and day out to the wee hours of the morning writing these amazing scripts. I am just happy to be a part of it." As Michael waits for his role on the show to develop into something larger in season 2, he demonstrates a calm approach that's worlds away from Tyler's hot-headed nature, and he asks the same of the viewers at home: "Fans of Tyler are just going to have to be a little patient."

Episode Guide

Season One

RECURRING CAST: David Anders (Uncle John Gilbert), Benjamin Ayres (Coach Tanner), Dillon Casey (Noah), Melinda Clarke (Kelly Donovan), Sean Faris (Ben McKittrick), Jasmine Guy (Sheila Bennett), Kelly Hu (Pearl), Chris Johnson (Logan Fell), Malese Jow (Anna), Mia Kirshner (Isobel Flemming), Bianca Lawson (Emily Bennett), Marguerite MacIntyre (Sheriff Elizabeth Forbes), Chris William Martin (Zach Salvatore), Tiffany Morgan (Ms. Gibbons), Robert Pralgo (Mayor Richard Lockwood), Sterling Sulieman (Harper), Susan Walters (Carol Lockwood)

> *Bonnie: . . . I have this feeling.*
> *Elena: Bonnie, what?*
> *Bonnie: That it's just the beginning.*

1.01 *Pilot*

Original air date: September 10, 2009

Written by: Kevin Williamson and Julie Plec
Directed by: Marcos Siega
Guest cast: Steve Belford (Darren Malloy), Cindy Busby (Brooke Fenton), Marci T. House (Mrs. Clarke)

Elena and Jeremy Gilbert return to Mystic Falls High School after their parents' death the previous spring, and there's a new student — Stefan Salvatore — whose real identity is even more astonishing than his extraordinary knowledge of the town's Civil War history.

Before the title card for the first episode of *The Vampire Diaries*, we see a happy couple murdered. That brutality stands in stark contrast with the scenes that follow it: a grieving teenage girl writes in her diary, hoping she can get through her first day back at school. The pilot of any TV series has a lot of backstory to explain in short order, and *The Vampire Diaries* manages to give us the gist of the show in those few scenes: love, loss, bloodshed, and the supernatural. Without wasting any time, the episode introduces the cast of characters and their relationships; establishes the tone, look, and setting of the show; gives viewers a hint of what's to come in terms of plot; and, of course, sucks us in deep enough so we'll tune in again next week and give up another hour of our time. The opening scene, which feels plucked straight out of a Kevin Williamson horror movie, gives another hint of what's to come: first impressions can be deceiving — as it was for the couple tricked and murdered by a vampire, so it is for the *The Vampire Diaries* viewer as the plot hurtles forward at vampire speed with unexpected twists and turns along the way.

The writers open up the world of Mystic Falls to the viewers on a day of fresh starts for its characters. Elena Gilbert is determined to "be someone new" on her first day back to school, a day that, every September, promises a new beginning but rarely delivers. Elena's grief has consumed her since her parents' death in the spring, and it's no different for her younger brother, Jeremy. The Gilbert children are struggling to hold it together, as is their grad-school-student guardian, Aunt Jenna, who seems less organized than her niece. Elena's coping mechanism has been to withdraw into herself, write in her journal, and hang out in the place designed for quiet contemplation of grief: at the foot of her parents' tombstone in the cemetery. Jeremy, on the other hand, is acting out in a stereotypical way: smoking up, drinking, and sleeping with Vicki Donovan, an older girl who doesn't want their hook-ups

to be public knowledge. Summer is over and Vicki's looking for a fresh start, too — with grade-A jerk Tyler Lockwood.

It's hopeless for Elena to shake off the past and pretend that everything's fine, especially as she worries about her little brother. Hard-ass history teacher Mr. Tanner promises Elena that the leniency period is over, and, at the party by the falls, she echoes his speech to Jeremy. Their grief is far from over, but no one else really cares anymore. The siblings face the harsh fact that, eventually, grief becomes private, not public, as the community refocuses on living and expects the grieving to pick up where their lives left off. Unfortunately for Jeremy and Elena, they've lost the two people who could best guide them through this, their mom and dad. The writers use this honest emotional moment to highlight what is one of the show's crucial concerns: how we battle our demons. *The Vampire Diaries* may be a supernatural soap with an incredibly good-looking cast and frequent shirt-lessness, but human struggles and emotions, however ugly or difficult, are at its heart. And also . . . hot vampires!

In voiceover, Stefan Salvatore confesses he is a vampire and is taking on the risk of reentering human society because he has to know Elena. The question Stefan faces is common for any teenager — where does he belong?

Uncle Zach insists it's not in Mystic Falls. Can Stefan fit in at Mystic Falls High? The girls are on his side instantly — small town, cute new guy — and he wins over other fellow students by outsmarting Tanner. But it is his connection to Elena that most fascinates us — and him. From their first run-in outside the boys' room to the double entendre line "we have history together," the chemistry between Stefan and Elena is palpable, making us root for this vampire-human pairing. As they talk on the bridge about passion, it's clear these two won't lack in that department. They share a seriousness, thoughtfulness, intensity, and love of journaling that sets them apart from their classmates (and makes them more than a little bit broody). Nina Dobrev and Paul Wesley already seem to own their characters. Stefan feels compelled to be with Elena, but already, on day one, he's had trouble hiding his vampirism as he tries to live in a human world.

And just as Elena's past — her ex-boyfriend and the loss of her parents — complicates her potential happiness, Stefan's fresh start in Mystic Falls quickly runs foul in the form of his bloodthirsty, wise-cracking older brother, Damon. Portrayed by Ian Somerhalder, who clearly delights in the role, Damon lets the audience in on what Stefan hasn't told Elena: she's a "dead ringer for Katherine," a girl who met a bad end and whom Stefan still cares enough about to keep a photograph dating from 1864. Who was she to Stefan? Why are she and Elena doppelgängers? And why did Damon promise his brother "an eternity of misery"? With Damon come the fog, the fangs, and the fun as his character simultaneously lightens up and darkens the mood of the episode.

Elena's friends also help to balance the episode and make Mystic Falls come alive. Like you'd see in any well-written TV show, these characters are set up with narrative economy so viewers get the basics in an instant, but *TVD* isn't interested in trotting out stock characters. Matt, the athletic ex-boyfriend, makes a generous gesture by officially welcoming Stefan, shaking his hand and introducing himself, as the new guy arrives at the Grill with Elena. And yet Matt's still in love with Elena. In that one move, Matt's revealed to be a gracious guy, as he puts others' happiness and comfort ahead of his own feelings. After a seemingly superficial display of sympathy in the hallway, Caroline morphs from a one-dimensional, cookie-cutter character to interesting and nuanced thanks to the vulnerability she shares with Bonnie, drunk after the party. (Why does everyone pick Elena? *Because* she doesn't try.) We meet Bonnie as the bubbly bestie trying to reassure Elena that everything *will* get better, but after she gets a shockingly real and haunting feeling from her playful "crystal ball," it looks like Bonnie has her own dark journey ahead of her.

Between the scares, the romantic complications, the sibling dynamics, the questions about the Salvatore brothers' past, the threat of Damon exposing Stefan's true nature, Bonnie's psychic abilities, Caroline smirking at Damon, and Vicki waking up in the hospital with one word — *vampire* — on her lips, the pilot delivers more than enough juicy reasons to return for the next episode. Its strengths overshadow the moments of cheesiness, like the "dear diary" duet that closes the hour. Intrigued by the inhabitants of Mystic Falls, the viewer is left, as Elena writes in her journal, "ready for the good."

COMPELLING MOMENT: The brothers facing off for the first time in 15 years, letting the viewer know this series has a sense of humor about itself.

CIRCLE OF KNOWLEDGE:
- The opening sequence is reminiscent of Kevin Williamson's *I Know What You Did Last Summer*: a lonely road at night and a car hitting a man who comes back to kill the car's occupants.
- Lots of pop culture references are packed into this episode; President Obama, Heath Ledger, Pete Wentz, Carson Daly, and soft-rock band Air Supply all get shout-outs.
- Stefan has a Mac computer and an old-fashioned typewriter on his desk, but he handwrites his journal.
- Bonnie called it when she got a Seattle vibe from Stefan's "hot back"; Damon tells Stefan he didn't pull off the '90s grunge look.
- Given the presence of the fog and the crow, it's safe to assume that it was Damon creeping behind the tombstone watching Elena, not Stefan.
- In the cemetery, Elena refers to Alfred Hitchcock's 1963 film *The Birds*, in which a series of violent bird attacks (featuring crows) plague a young woman (Tippi Hedren).
- Matt and Elena's backstory — best friends since childhood who attempt romance in their early teen years — calls to mind the Dawson Leery–Joey Potter dynamic from Williamson's *Dawson's Creek*.

THE RULES: The introduction of Stefan and Damon to the audience provides a crash course in this series' vampirism mythology, and most of it is familiar from other vampire fiction. Vampires are strong and fast, have heightened senses and no pulse, and can seemingly appear out of nowhere. Anger, arousal, or the scent of blood brings out the vampire face: fangs and blood-filled eyes rimmed by dark veins. Vampires can compel a human with mind control but can't cross the threshold of a residence without an invitation. Without the rings the Salvatore brothers wear, they would burn in sunlight. Damon is the stronger of the two brothers because he consumes human blood. He also has the ability to summon fog to creepy effect, and he can command a crow that seems to spy on people for him . . . and totally gives them the willies.

THE DIABOLICAL PLAN: Stefan seems to be the good brother who wants nothing more than to go to high school and get to know Elena — but what's with the photograph of Katherine, dated 1864, and how could she look identical to Elena? And why did Damon promise his brother "an eternity of misery"?

HISTORY LESSON: In class with Mr. Tanner, the students are learning about the Confederacy during the Civil War (1861–1865), and in particular the (fictional) Battle of Willow Creek in 1865 where, in addition to military losses, 27 civilians died after Confederate soldiers fired on a church.

BITE MARKS: Damon kills the couple (Darren Malloy and Brooke Fenton) coming from the James Blunt–wannabe concert in the opening sequence. Damon attacks Vicki in the woods and she loses a lot of blood, ending up in the hospital. Stefan and Damon fight.

MEANWHILE IN FELL'S CHURCH: More than any other episode this season, the pilot episode resembles L.J. Smith's first Vampire Diaries novel, *The Awakening*. In addition to what was discussed in the adaptation chapter (see page 19), a good deal of the vampire mythology (the threshold rule; daywalking with the help of a ring) comes from *The Awakening*. The main action of the pilot begins as that novel does with Elena writing in her diary (blue in the book, green on TV), her aunt is flustered in the kitchen on the first day back to school, and a crow watches Elena as she makes her way to school. In the novel, Stefan arrives at school in a leather jacket and sunglasses, with one giggly girl noting the "nice rear view," which translated into Bonnie's "hot back" comment. Also taken from *The Awakening*: Stefan compelling the secretary to let him register as a student, and Stefan correcting Mr. Tanner on his historical facts (changed from Renaissance era in the books to Civil War era in the TV show) after the teacher picks on his students. Bonnie's playful attitude toward her "psychic" abilities (which are linked to her grandma) turns serious when she reads Elena's palm on the first day of school in *The Awakening*, which became a beer bottle standing in for a crystal ball in the show. In the novel, Tyler tries to force himself on Elena rather than on Vicki, and Stefan, not Jeremy, shows up to stop him; Vickie Bennett is also attacked in *The Awakening*, left dazed and covered in scratches. As in the pilot, Caroline has her eye on Stefan, but in the book she actually succeeds in getting a date with him. While Caroline expresses her feeling of being in competition with Elena in this episode, it's a more hostile relationship between the girls in the novels (Caroline is determined to overthrow Elena as queen of school). In *The Struggle*, Elena's diary goes missing, but it isn't found and returned by Stefan the same day; it falls into more nefarious hands. In the novel series, Damon actually transforms *into* the crow (and other animals) rather than simply controlling it. In *Dark Reunion*, the bloody Civil War battle that took place in Fell's Church during which the old church was destroyed becomes significant as it does in the show.

OFF CAMERA: The pilot was the only episode of *The Vampire Diaries* shot in Vancouver, British Columbia, so the town of Mystic Falls and the locations seen in the pilot, like the Mystic Grill and Elena's house, are different than the ones you'll see during the rest of the series, which was shot in and around Atlanta, Georgia. Julie Plec and Kevin Williamson's main concern with the pilot was that it wouldn't come across as being too much like *Twilight*.

FOGGY MOMENTS: Why aren't there birthdates listed on the tombstone for Elena's parents? How exactly is "Uncle" Zach related to the brothers Salvatore? Did they have another brother or sister who he's descended from? Is he a more distantly related Salvatore? Or can vampires procreate?

MUSIC: Brooke and Darren are listening to "Sort Of" (Silversun Pickups) as they drive home. At the Gilbert residence on the first day of school, Mat Kearney's "Here We Go" plays. The stoners hang out to The Raconteurs' "Consolers of the Lonely." Elena walks to the cemetery after school to "Say

(All I Need)" by OneRepublic. Stars' "Take Me to the Riot" plays at the Mystic Grill as Vicki waits on Tyler and Matt's table. Matt asks Bonnie about Elena with "Thinking of You" by Katy Perry in the background. Caroline quizzes Stefan at the Grill to "Kids" by MGMT. Zach asks Stefan why he came back to Mystic Falls to Placebo's cover of the 1985 Kate Bush song "Running Up That Hill." Stefan arrives at the party by the falls to "Death" by White Lies. Matt approaches Elena as she looks for Stefan to "Back to Me" by the All-American Rejects. At the Grill, Caroline sobers up with Bonnie to "Siren Song" by Bat for Lashes. Stefan and Elena write in their journals in the closing scenes to The Fray's "Never Say Never."

Elena: He didn't tell me he had a brother.
Damon: Well, Stefan's not one to brag.

1.02 *The Night of the Comet*

Original air date: September 17, 2009
Written by: Kevin Williamson and Julie Plec
Directed by: Marcos Siega
Guest cast: Terri James (Nurse), Elizabeth Keener (Girl), Peyton Lee (Guy)

As a comet passes over Mystic Falls, Stefan tries to cover up his brother's attack on Vicki.

Despite the heavy-handed comet metaphor and the brief return of the diary duet voice-over, "The Night of the Comet" proved that *The Vampire Diaries* was nuanced and enjoyable to watch — far from being the *Twilight* knockoff most critics anticipated it would be. From one moment to the next it's scary, romantic, playful, bloody, earnest, and . . . epic. Caroline's moans turn to screams as Damon bares his fangs, and the writers show an impressive mastery of the cliffhanger in only the show's second episode.

The morning after Stefan and Elena get to know each other, they each begin their day more optimistically than is usual for either of them, happy to have the promise of a new relationship. But Stefan and Elena are also wary; each feels the constant presence of a terrible loss, reminding them that they can lose again. Elena feels that in allowing herself to experience happiness she is betraying her grief and her parents' memory. What if she lets herself be happy and her world crumbles again, like it did in the spring when her parents died? Stefan's fear is of being exposed as a vampire. As Stefan worries about covering his brother's bloody tracks, he inadvertently pushes Elena away. She understandably reads his brush-off as disinterest rather than a desire to protect her from his homicidal vampire brother. And Stefan's right to be alarmed: Damon dangles Vicki over the roof's edge, compelling her to believe it was Stefan, a vampire, who attacked her, just to see if his brother will take a bite to protect his secret identity.

Vicki has secrets of her own — she doesn't want Tyler to know about her relationship with Jeremy. The love triangle of Tyler, Vicki, and Jeremy contrasts nicely with the Matt, Elena, Stefan triangle. Matt gives Elena space for her new relationship but lets Stefan know he'll always be by her side should she need him. Matt's observant and honest — he sees Stefan skulking at the hospital and asks him about it, but he also thanks him for finding Vicki. On the other side of the coin is Tyler and Jeremy who take the "eye for an eye" approach. Tyler and Jeremy butt heads over Vicki and hurt each other in the process by exposing secrets — Jeremy's a pill pusher, Vicki slept with Jeremy, Tyler forced himself on Vicki — just as Damon threatens to do to Stefan.

Like Emily Brontë writing under the pseudonym Ellis Bell, Stefan has chosen to hide the part of himself that's unacceptable to human society. Damon's counsel to his little brother to "be himself" perversely echoes Elena's to Jeremy in the pilot episode: she's on her brother's case for behaving badly; Damon's on Stefan's case because he's too goody-goody for a vampire. Damon calls Stefan out on his doomed plan, telling him he will never be human again. He urges him (with Vicki's bleeding neck before him) to remember who he is — a vampire that feeds on humans and does not impersonate them. The idea of finding and being your "true self" is a theme that carries across the season, especially with Stefan who faces a daily struggle between being a man or a monster. The temptations are real and powerful for Stefan; his face gets vampy when he's in the blood donor room at the hospital, and he considers biting Vicki before his will power beats out his hunger.

Damon tells Elena he's a fatalist, and Stefan echoes this idea when he talks about the comet "trapped on a path that it can't escape and once every 145 years it gets to come home." Are the Salvatores like the comet, returning to Mystic Falls only to repeat the past? Are we powerless to change the course

Dark Shadows

When asked in interviews about what intrigued him most about *The Vampire Diaries* project, Kevin Williamson almost invariably brings up a television show that ended its run almost 40 years ago: *Dark Shadows*. "I loved it. . . . It's a sort of sexy soap opera. And that's what we're going to do . . . the town of Mystic Falls [will] have a lot of things that go bump in the night. And it's not just vampires."

Created by Dan Curtis, *Dark Shadows* aired on ABC from June 27, 1966, to April 2, 1971, and in its first six months featured few supernatural elements. The gothic soap opera began with a young woman, Victoria Winters, on a train going from New York City to a small coastal town, Collinsport, Maine. Victoria is an orphan, hired from the foundling home by Elizabeth Collins Stoddard to be the governess to her nephew young David, who is nothing if not creepy. Elizabeth is clearly keeping secrets from Victoria about how she's connected to the Collins family legacy. She hasn't left the cliff-side estate in over a decade, and the dramatic music score as well as the setting — where waves crash on craggy rocks as characters stand dangerously close to the precipice — provides much of the atmosphere in the first few episodes. In the town of Collinsport, there's even more mystery as a handsome, brooding stranger, Burke Devlin, returns home with a taste for revenge, and Elizabeth's seemingly uncomplicated, blonde daughter Carolyn Stoddard takes an interest in him.

The supernatural element of the show began with a ghost story but is most famous for its vampire, Barnabas Collins, who was introduced on *Dark Shadows* in 1967. While terrorizing the town, Barnabas searches for the love of his life, Josette, who he believes has been reincarnated as a local woman. Collinsport saw all manner of supernatural elements during the show's 1,225-episode run: werewolves, witches and warlocks, a Frankenstein-style monster, time travel, and the Devil himself.

The show aired at 4 p.m. on weekdays, mostly to a young audience just home from school — Kevin Williamson was in kindergarten when he saw it. The show spawned two films, a short-lived revival series in the early 1990s, and a TV pilot commissioned by The WB in 2004. Johnny Depp, another one of the kids who grew up glued to his TV set watching the show, has signed on to star as Barnabas Collins in a *Dark Shadows* film with Tim Burton attached as director.

Kevin Williamson considers *The Vampire Diaries* to be a "modern take" on *Dark Shadows*. The older show's influence is felt in *TVD*'s embrace of all types of supernatural elements, its use of flashbacks, and in its soap-operatic serial format. Mystic Falls is Collinsport reimagined in present-day Virginia, a town with a rich and dark history and families who've known each other for what seems like forever. The Salvatore mansion bears more than a little resemblance to the Collinwood mansion with its relatively remote location, old-fashioned furniture, decanters and crystal tumblers full of ice and amber alcohol, strange artifacts and slightly creepifying paintings, and a gloomy basement that might be holding secrets. The vampire Barnabas Collins (portrayed by Jonathan Frid) has also left his imprint on the Salvatore brothers. Consumed by a need to reclaim his lost love (by finding either her or a surrogate) and wracked with guilt for the deaths his vampirism has caused, Barnabas was arguably the first TV vampire with a soul, paving the way for more recent lovelies like *Buffy*'s Angel and Spike, *True Blood*'s Bill, and *The Vampire Diaries*' Stefan (and maybe, one sunny day, Damon).

Jonathan Frid as vulnerable vampire Barnabas Collins
in the original 1966–1971 ABC-TV daytime drama version of *Dark Shadows*.
(Photo courtesy of Dan Curtis Productions, Inc. All rights reserved.)

of our lives, stuck on a path like an orbiting comet, no point in denying the inevitable? The women of Mystic Falls don't think so. Encouraged by Bonnie and Caroline, Elena pursues Stefan rather than giving up or waiting for him to make the first move. Caroline purposely and confidently strides across the town square to approach her handsome stranger. Jenna, after she gets

"Tannered," realizes she has to step up her game as guardian to Jeremy. And Elena, in her pep talk to her aunt, says she has to keep fighting the fear and not believe, as Damon says he does, that all relationships are doomed to failure before they even begin. Stefan also rejects fatalism, thwarting Damon's plan to tempt him into drinking human blood again. Damon may have lost this round but his devilish grin and pursuit of Caroline suggest he's a vampire who believes the stars are aligned in his favor.

COMPELLING MOMENT: Stefan and Elena's gentle first kiss contrasted with Damon and Caroline hot, heavy . . . and bitey.

CIRCLE OF KNOWLEDGE:
- *Night of the Comet* is a campy 1984 horror film where a comet, whose previous pass through Earth's orbit made dinosaurs extinct, turns almost every human to dust. Teenage sisters from California's San Fernando Valley (a.k.a. Valley girls) survive and have to battle zombies and an underground group of evil scientists interested in draining them of their blood.
- For the second time in the opening sequence murders, Damon kills the man first, then the woman.
- The comet passing over Mystic Falls is a short-period comet (meaning that its orbital period is less than 200 years), and Stefan is partially right: comets are made up of ice as well as dust and rock particles. Throughout human history, comets have been seen as omens. Bowdoin Van Riper in *Science in Popular Culture* writes that, in fiction, comets "signal imminent, world-altering events. They are . . . maddeningly vague omens."
- Stefan lends Elena his first edition of *Wuthering Heights*, which Emily Brontë published under the pseudonym Ellis Bell in 1847. The gothic novel, narrated by Mr. Lockwood (no known relation to Tyler Lockwood), centers on Catherine, a woman torn between two suitors, one passionate but dangerous, the other devoted but ineffectual. Since its publication, *Wuthering Heights* has had a huge influence on popular culture, from Kate Bush's 1978 song of the same name to Stephenie Meyer using it for inspiration in writing *Eclipse*. Brontë's novel was also discussed by Pacey Witter and Ms. Jacobs in the second episode of *Dawson's Creek*.
- Reports of supernatural activity from Bonnie's grandmother and from Vicki are ignored because both women were drunk when they made the claim that witches and vampires, respectively, are real. Vicki's right;

it was a vampire who attacked her. Does that mean Bonnie is an actual, factual witch? What did Bonnie feel when she touched Stefan?

- One of the reasons Stefan, Elena, and a lot of other people keep journals is to preserve their memories. A vampire has the power to make others lose pieces of their past, or even to create false memories. A scary thought, considering the already fragile sense of self some of these characters possess.

THE RULES: A well-fed vampire has more power than one who doesn't feed on humans. Stefan compels Vicki to believe an animal attacked her, but because he feeds only on animal blood, his "powers of persuasion" are weak and the exertion takes more out of him than it would his brother.

THE DIABOLICAL PLAN: Damon hints at a master plan: he's going to stick around Mystic Falls because the town "could use a wake-up call." Sounds unpleasant. He's also interested in messing up Stefan's budding romance with Elena, dropping not-so-subtle hints to her about Stefan not being over Katherine. (Is he?) Damon leaves viewers, and Stefan, hanging with his classic line about his true motives: "That's for me to know and you to dot dot dot."

HISTORY LESSON: The comet last passed over Mystic Falls in 1864, which, according to Grams Bennett, was a time of blood, carnage, and paranormal activity. On the blackboard in history class are notes on the Gettysburg Address, given by President Abraham Lincoln on November 19, 1863, on the occasion of the dedication of the Soldiers' National Cemetery for those killed in the bloody battle at Gettysburg, a turning point in the Civil War. Lincoln's speech, arguably the most famous in American history, urges citizens to not let the bloodshed be in vain but instead to honor the principles of freedom and democracy that their country was founded on.

BITE MARKS: Another couple is murdered in the opening sequence; this time the unlucky twosome is camping, worrying that rain will ruin their night. Nope. A vampire will. Vicki suffers from the aftereffects of Damon's attack, nightmares and a screaming fit. Damon also nabs Vicki from the ladies room at the Grill, dangles her off the roof, and reopens her neck wound. As "The Night of the Comet" ends, Caroline's fate is up in the air as Damon goes for blood.

When *The Vampire Diaries* is filming in Covington, GA, fans (like Jennifer Ridings who took this photo) can walk through town and spot the locations. The building that stands in for the Mystic Grill actually houses offices.

MEANWHILE IN FELL'S CHURCH: Tanner mentions that the Gilberts' car accident was on Wickery Bridge; that's also the location of Elena's car accident in *The Struggle*. Whether Vicki Donovan of TV or Vickie Bennett of the book series, this character is much abused. She suffers from nightmares and hallucinations after she's attacked in *The Awakening*. In the first three novels, Elena and Stefan believe Damon is the one tormenting her. The comet was discovered five centuries ago, roughly the same time the Salvatore brothers became vampires in the novels. When Stefan uses his vampire skills to get onto the roof in no time at all, Damon says, "Not bad. Have you been eating bunnies?" a reference to Stefan's taste for rabbit in the books. He makes his very first appearance in *The Awakening*, feeding on a bunny.

OFF CAMERA: The rose tattoo visible on Paul Wesley's arm is real; Julie Plec tweeted that it was difficult to get clearance from the powers that be to show it. In the scene with Elena at the Salvatore house, the brothers are in matching outfits (dark V-neck T-shirts and jeans). Following this twin moment, the wardrobe department began distinguishing the brothers' individual styles. Jennifer Bryan, costume designer, told EW.com, "Damon's style is very narrow. With Stefan, I can do a little bit more because he's in high school. I do a little bit more color on him because at one point, we felt that we needed to separate them so they didn't start to look alike."

FOGGY MOMENTS: Since both Stefan and Damon can freely enter the Salvatore house, can we assume Zach invited them in at some point in the past? Did Stefan really need to throw Vicki to the ground when he was resisting his need to feed? The poor girl's been through enough . . . even if she won't remember it. When Tyler and Vicki kiss at the Grill, he's holding her neck on the wound side. Even when he doesn't mean to, he's hurting her.

MUSIC: Metric's "Help I'm Alive" opens the episode. Jenna realizes Jeremy lied to her to "Closer to Love" by Mat Kearney. The Dead Weather's "Hang You From the Heavens" provides a suitable soundtrack to Jeremy's confrontation with Tyler. The girls talk about comets and Stefan at the Grill to Gossip's "Heavy Cross." Jenna tries to lay down the law with Jeremy to "I'm an Animal" (Neko Case). The residents of Mystic Falls gather to watch the comet while Dragonette's "I Get Around" plays. Vicki and Jeremy talk at the Grill to We Were Promised Jetpacks' "Conductor." Peaches' "Mud" is on when Tyler calls Jeremy a pill pusher in front of Elena. More music at the Grill with Earlimart's "Interloper" as Matt helps Vicki with her bandage and thanks Stefan for finding her. A selection suggested by Julie Plec, Sara Bareilles' "Gravity," plays as Elena and Stefan talk outside his house.

> *Stefan: I was worried that you had no humanity left inside of you.*
> *That you may have actually become the monster that you pretend to be.*
> *Damon: Who's pretending?*

1.03 *Friday Night Bites*

Original air date: September 24, 2009

Written by: Barbie Kligman and Bryan M. Holdman
Directed by: John Dahl
Guest cast: Chris Thomas Hayes (Student)

Elena tries to be more than "gloomy graveyard girl"; Stefan joins the football team; Damon takes a bite out of Caroline; and Bonnie gets more freaked out by her psychic powers.

With the Mystic High Timberwolves football and cheerleading teams as the setup, the writers give Stefan and Elena a choice in "Friday Night Bites" — join a team or accept their loner status. "The Night of the Comet" raised questions of identity, and here Elena continues to explore her own. She realizes she's not a cheerleader anymore, a truth that Damon can see with just a glance at her as she halfheartedly practices. The death of her parents changed who she is and what matters to her. In a hilariously insensitive moment, Caroline describes Elena as being in a "blah phase." But part of Elena's grieving process is recognizing who she is now and how her loss has fundamentally reshaped her. No one's identity is fixed or static, and Damon encourages Elena not to force herself to be someone she isn't any longer.

It's appropriate advice for Elena but dangerous advice when Damon takes it himself. Damon has appropriated a rather traditional vampire identity — the ruthless predator hungry for blood — and he's thrown away his humanity. Damon toys with Stefan, giving him the "I want to reform" speech he knows Stefan is desperate to hear, before laughing at the absurdity of him reclaiming his humanity. Damon behaves as he believes Stefan should do, warning him, "I'll do whatever I want to do to your little cheerleader because *that* is what is *normal* to me." After Damon brutally kills Mr. Tanner, Stefan comes to believe that his brother really is only a monster. But is Damon's total monstrousness an act? Despite his flip and flirty behavior with Elena in the kitchen, she expresses her sorrow at his loss of Katherine, and it seems to genuinely touch Damon to see her empathy. As the episode closes, Damon acts in opposition to Stefan's narration as he harmlessly (if a little creepily) watches Elena sleeping, touching her cheek gently. There is tenderness and love in Damon, but for whom? Is he seeing Katherine when he looks at Elena? Or did Elena get to him by ignoring the sexy dream he planted in her mind and by standing up to him in their parking lot encounter?

Like his brother, Stefan straddles the divide between the human and vampire worlds, but he is on the other end of the spectrum from Damon;

trying so hard to be normal, he joins the football team, just like a human teenager would. Pretending not to be a supernatural creature by hiding his full abilities and taking a hit to appease his teammates hardly seems like a healthy way for Stefan to "be himself." But his options are rather limited: he could embrace his monstrous potential like Damon does, he could keep faking it, or he could go back into hiding. For Stefan, there's only one choice. He values his connection with Elena and the possibility of friendship with Matt and Bonnie too much to retreat or, worse, to subject them to harm.

With Bonnie's realization that she *does* have psychic powers (ones that go beyond guessing which commercials will air during *90210*) her sense of self and her understanding of Bennett family history shifts suddenly, and this scares her. Matt sees his identity slipping away from him — in terms of both his position on the team and his girlfriend, he is replaced by Stefan — and he briefly tries on a Tyler-style bad attitude for size, tired of being an ineffectual "yard troll," as Tyler calls him. Of all the *TVD* characters, Matt may alone know best who he is and he doesn't spend long trying to be someone else. Even though he resents Stefan, he makes peace with him, apologizing for acting like a jerk on the field.

While some characters try on different personas or embrace a complex shift in their identity, their struggles are a world away from Caroline's experience of having Damon impose his will on her. As Elena says, Caroline may be a wee bit annoying, but seeing her turned into Damon's puppet and plaything is frightful. Bonnie's reservations about Elena's new boyfriend would be better directed at Caroline's. Meanwhile, Jeremy proves it is possible to lose your self-control without a powerful vampire controlling your mind. When Vicki passes him over for Tyler, Jeremy is without an anchor — he's not the kid he was before his parents died and he's lost the one thing he had to hold on to since then. Like her brother was, Elena is relying on her romantic relationship to keep her feeling "good" and "normal." But already she has suspicions that Stefan's hiding something from her. Elena's not stupid, and Stefan will have to keep up his stream of white lies to keep his secret safe, at least as long as Damon's around to stir up trouble.

COMPELLING MOMENT: Elena holding her own against Damon in the parking lot, defending Caroline, Stefan, and herself.

CIRCLE OF KNOWLEDGE:
- No Aunt Jenna this episode.
- The title of this episode is a play on the title of H.G. Bissinger's 1990 book *Friday Night Lights: A Town, A Team, A Dream*, which chronicles a real high school football team in Odessa, Texas. The book was adapted into a film in 2004 and an NBC TV series that premiered in 2006. Julie Plec is a dedicated fan of the TV incarnation of *Friday Night Lights*, and Zach Roerig (Matt) appeared in its third season. Like vampires on *The Vampire Diaries*, football is the way into *Friday Night Lights*, but at its heart are stories about compelling characters and their relationships in a small town.
- This episode marks the first time Damon's victim in the opening sequence isn't a stranger.
- Among Bonnie's doodles are a broom, crystal ball, burning candle, and cross.
- Since Tanner cut Stefan off before he could name the winner: the Baltimore Colts beat the Dallas Cowboys in the '71 Super Bowl.
- Damon says Stefan's diary is "very Emerson" with all its adjectives. American essayist and poet Ralph Waldo Emerson (1803–1882) kept

Benjamin Ayres as Coach Tanner

Raised in Kamloops, British Columbia, Benjamin Ayres was already a busy actor by his teens, appearing in every one of his high school's productions. After traveling Asia and the South Pacific, Benjamin returned to Canada to begin his professional acting career with a number of renowned theater productions and has since found success with television work in shows like *Stargate SG-1*, *Battlestar Galactica*, *Da Vinci's Inquest*, *Smallville*, and *Dan for Mayor*. He picked up a nomination for a Leo award for his role as the chain-smoking death-obsessed sex addict "Cancer Cowboy" Casper Jesperson on *jPod*, the CBC series based on the novel by Douglas Coupland. In an interview with Vampire-Diaries.net, Benjamin said of Coach Tanner that, while the guy is a jerk, "He definitely knows what's going on with his students. And you know, those hard-ass teachers are doing it for your best interest, too. As much as he kind of gave 'em the gears, they gave him reason to." (See page 197 for an interview with Benjamin Ayres.)

journals for the majority of his life and espoused Transcendentalism, a belief that people were born with an innate moral compass. Unlike Stefan, who respects Elena's privacy, Damon has no qualms about reading someone else's journal.

- Jeremy pushes away everyone who reaches out to him; in this episode, he brushes off Matt's attempt. Vicki is the only person whose attention he wants.
- Just like in Kevin Williamson's *Teaching Mrs. Tingle*, where students torture a mean teacher, Tanner's vicious murder is a cathartic but disturbing moment for the audience.

THE RULES: An unexpected application of being a vampire: Stefan's speed, strength, and accuracy make him an almost too amazing football player. He's also armed with an encyclopedic knowledge of history, which suggests vampires have excellent memories. A common theme in vampire fiction is their ability to heal quickly; Stefan's broken finger and cut hand heal in mere seconds. Once invited into a residence, a vampire can reenter whenever he pleases — meaning Damon can return to the Gilbert house without another invite. It matters which human invites a vampire into a home; Caroline's request for Damon to enter the Gilbert house didn't work, but Elena's did since she lives there. The crow on Elena's windowsill when she wakes from her dream (in which Stefan turns into Damon) combined with Damon's confidence that she's involuntarily thinking about him suggest that he has the ability to influence people's dreams as well as compel them when they are awake. Bonnie is quickly realizing that her abilities may be more than a joke: she has psychic instincts, and she gets creepy feelings and visions when she touches people. What else can she do?

THE DIABOLICAL PLAN: Looks like Damon had a longer purpose in seducing Caroline: to gain entry to Elena's house. His plot to compel Elena has been thwarted; will he carry through on any of his threats — to seduce her the "old-fashioned" way, or to eat her, or to kill "anyone, any time, any place"?

HISTORY LESSON: Stefan calls the Salem witches "heroic examples of individualism and nonconformity." The Salem witch hunt of 1692 to 1693 led to the prosecution of over 100 women and men in colonial Massachusetts, 19 of whom were hanged, one of whom was tortured to death. Convicted under the religious fervor of Puritanism, the accused were mostly women, often unmarried or widowed. Today, the witch trials are used as a historical argument for the importance of a fair, impartial judicial system and, on a community level, show the danger and power of rumor and fearmongering in a small town.

BITE MARKS: After Caroline unsuccessfully tries to fend him off, Damon vamps out on her. Stefan's finger is broken playing football. Jeremy and Tyler fight, and Stefan's hand is sliced breaking it up. Elena slaps Damon. Damon murders Coach Tanner to prove a point to his brother.

MEANWHILE IN FELL'S CHURCH: In *The Awakening*, Matt asks Stefan to try out for wide receiver for the football team, the same position Stefan says he plays in "Friday Night Bites." Just like she does in this episode, Elena finds herself not as enthusiastic about school activities as she once was in *The Awakening*. Bonnie's witchy ancestry leads back to the Celtic Druids in the novels, and they get a shout-out from TV Stefan over dinner. Damon gets to Elena before Stefan has a chance to protect her with vervain, coming to her in a dream in *The Struggle* just as he does here. At the beginning of *The Struggle*, Elena confronts Damon and gives him "a good hard slap," which is also her move in the parking lot. The moment of friendship between Matt and Stefan after the Tyler–Jeremy fight brings to mind the bond between the boys in the novels. Maybe one day this Matt and Stefan will be best friends, too. Mr. Tanner meets an untimely end in *The Awakening*, killed by Damon at a school event, and he has a similar demise in this episode. Just as Stefan tries to get through to his brother in "Friday Night Bites," in *Dark Reunion*, Stefan tells Damon, "You can pretend you don't care. You can fool the whole world. But *I* know differently."

OFF CAMERA: The star on Candice Accola's foot (visible in the opening scene) is a real tattoo; she also has a swallow on her wrist (more easily seen in "162 Candles"). To find the right look for "vamp mode" many trials were required but, says Ian Somerhalder, it became a relatively easy process: "The contacts are what really sell it. You have these huge, full-eye contacts with the color of the eye visible. Those are a bit difficult to get in. You cry for about five minutes. You feel like you've been scolded by your mother. Get a nice little airbrush of red around the eyes and you pop in the fangs and . . . there's a shift — I become a completely different person. It helps. A lot. And also people react to you differently. You can't just walk up to someone and just have a normal conversation with them. It is that scary. It makes people uncomfortable." The painting above Elena's bed is by Georgian artist Mary Leslie. "Lock and Load" shows Leslie's horse Darby, and prints are available for purchase at FineArtAmerica.com.

FOGGY MOMENTS: Caroline wakes up wearing different lingerie; did she change after Damon finished feeding on her? Bonnie drives a white Toyota Prius; it was blue in the pilot.

MUSIC: The Bravery's "Slow Poison" plays as the gang arrives at Mystic Falls High School. Damon drops off Caroline at cheerleading practice to "Blue Day" by Darker My Love. The girls do their routine to 3OH!3's "Starstrukk." The Black Keys' "Strange Times" provides the soundtrack for Stefan's first Timberwolves practice. Bonnie tries to convince Elena of her psychic abilities in the Gilbert kitchen to "Can't Fight It" by Oh Mercy. Jeremy watches Tyler flirt with Vicki at the Grill to Sea Wolf's "You're a Wolf." The Airborne Toxic Event's "Papillon" plays as the students gather for the kickoff party. The closing scenes are to Moby's cover of New Order's "Temptation."

Zach: Blood only runs so deep when you're related to vampires.

1.04 *Family Ties*

Original air date: October 1, 2009
Written by: Andrew Kreisberg and Brian Young
Directed by: Guy Ferland
Guest cast: Leland Jones (Pastor Bill)

Elena doesn't know what to believe as the Salvatore brothers amp up their plots against each other at the Founder's Party.

Every town has its original settlers, and the descendents of the founding families of Mystic Falls won't let anyone forget who's been around longest. The elite of Mystic Falls gather for the Founder's Party, giving us a chance to meet the parents. Caroline seems the opposite of her sheriff mother, at least superficially. She's dismissive and cruel to her, making quips about her father's boyfriend and her mom's uniform. Clearly Caroline doesn't admire her mom or want to follow in her footsteps. Rejection of the family's legacy isn't a popular choice in Mystic Falls; in fact, to Elena's surprise, Jeremy feels particularly connected to the Gilbert legacy. The pocket watch is Jeremy's link to his father, and to his family's history. Elena decides to honor Jeremy's wishes over her mother's promise, giving the watch back to her brother rather than allowing it to be displayed with the other artifacts at the Lockwood mansion. This gesture shows that, despite their recent fights about his behavior, she realizes that he would never go so far as to destroy part of the Gilbert family history. Bonnie had written off her family's legacy involving witchcraft as nonsense, but as her powers continue to astound her, episode after episode, she'll have no choice but to reconnect with her history in order to understand who she's becoming. With parents like the Mayor and Mrs. Lockwood, it's no surprise that Tyler turned out to be such a jerk. Though we see the occasional glimmer of a good guy in Tyler, especially when he's just as mortified by his parents' cruelty as we are, he treats Vicki exactly the way his mother describes her, like trash.

In scene after scene in "Family Ties" the women are mistreated: Vicki is made to feel unworthy of Tyler's attention, Jenna reveals that she left Mystic Falls with a broken heart thanks to Logan Fell, Elena is lied to by both Salvatore brothers, and Caroline is attacked and manipulated and attacked again. Candice Accola puts in a touching performance in this episode; seeing

It turns out there's way more vervain in Mystic Falls than Stefan thought. Vervain, or verbena, is a real genus of plant; the specific variety that's identified as being useful against vampires in *Dark Reunion* is *verbena officinalis*, which has a more straggly, weed-like appearance than the plant shown in Zach's grow-op in "Family Ties." A sacred plant, vervain was used as a herbal remedy and as a ritual offering by the ancient Romans, ancient Egyptians, and by the Druids. It was believed to repel the demonic influence of both vampires and witches, and is sometimes known as "herb of the cross" because early Christians believed vervain was used to staunch Jesus's wounds. Today it's used in tea and as an essential oil for herbal remedies, by Wiccans in spells, and by enthusiastic *TVD* fans looking to protect themselves from Damon's compulsion.

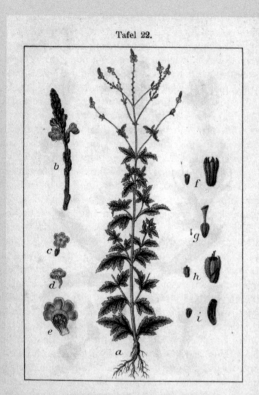

Tafel 22.

Eisenkraut, Verbena officinalis.

Caroline shaking and repeating, "I'm fine," as Elena pulls her into a hug is a heartbreaking moment. But the writers on this show are clearly not interested in creating women characters who are simply victims; they use the final acts of "Family Ties" to show them regaining control. Vicki leaves Tyler behind and chooses the guy who actually cares about her. Jenna decides to let go of the past and give Logan a very tentative second chance (but only after his apology, and the promise of cheese fries). Elena confronts Stefan about his elusiveness and, stepping in for Caroline who is literally without a will of her own, Elena marches straight up to Damon to warn him to stay away from Caroline, threatening to get the Sheriff involved if the abusive relationship continues. Elena realizes that while she may or may not be able to trust Stefan, she certainly cannot trust Damon.

Interview With the Vampire

"I miss Anne Rice. She was *so* on it." So says Damon Salvatore in "Family Ties" after flipping through one of the tomes in Stephenie Meyer's Twilight Saga where vampires don't burn in the sunlight but sparkle. New Orleans native Anne Rice published her first novel, *Interview With the Vampire*, in 1976 in what would become The Vampire Chronicles series. *Interview* has since sold roughly eight million copies and, in 1994, was adapted for the screen, directed by Neil Jordan and starring Brad Pitt as Louis, Tom Cruise as Lestat, and Kirsten Dunst as Claudia.

Interview With the Vampire begins with Louis, a vampire, being interviewed by a reporter who records people's life stories. Louis' tale, which begins in the late 1700s in Louisiana, is sort of one giant flashback with his recollection punctuated by brief conversations between the two in present time. The rules of vampirism in this world are not unlike those in *The Vampire Diaries*. A vampire can feed on animal blood to survive but the lust for human blood is strong. Sunlight will kill a vampire but crucifixes, holy water, and garlic are ineffectual. Vampires are fast and strong. With age comes power. A vampire's face doesn't change from one state to another; they always have piercing eyes, fangs, and unusually pale skin.

There are similarities between Lestat and Louis on the one hand and Damon and Stefan Salvatore on the other: their beliefs, their differences. They are individuals despite their common bond and that creates a tension that fuels the narrative. "There are profound differences between vampires," says Louis in *Interview With the Vampire*. When Lestat found Louis and turned him, Louis was a broken man, struggling with grief (in the novel, the death of his brother, for which he felt responsible; in the movie, the death of his wife in childbirth). Lestat bites Louis and leaves him halfway between human and vampire, between life and death; he then offers to "pluck out the pain and give [him] another life" (to quote Anne Rice's screenplay). But, as it turns out, there actually is no escaping the guilt, the loneliness, or the search for meaning that plagued Louis during his human life. Now he has to wallow for eternity. Unlike Lestat who delights in killing and uses the advantages of vampirism to attain material goods, Louis reads, writes in a journal, and cares about mortals. But as different as they are, the two are "locked together in hatred" (as Claudia describes them in the film), bonded through death and by blood, and, for the first part of the novel, without any other vampire companions. That central dichotomy of Lestat (amoral but full of delight) and Louis (moral but angst ridden) is replicated in L.J. Smith's Damon and Stefan Salvatore and brought to the forefront of *The Vampire Diaries* TV series.

Louis refuses to ease his own suffering or give up the regrets that plague him, because despite his immortality and power all he has of value are these shreds of humanity. Louis has respect for human life, more than he had when he was mortal, but he can only find peace one way: "When I kill there is no longing." For a time, Louis subsists on the blood of animals, like Stefan does, while Lestat plays with his food, so to speak, in front of him. Lestat takes pleasure in his victims' fear and in tormenting Louis, who reacts indignantly while not-so-secretly desiring human blood. In only its second episode, *The Vampire Diaries* showed that same game being played by the Salvatore brothers as Damon teased Stefan with Vicki, her wound reopened, on the roof. Unlike Stefan in "The

Night of the Comet," Louis eventually caves in to his need to feel the life drain from something more substantial than a rat, to feel their heartbeat fade away as their blood fuels him.

Like vampire fiction as a genre, *Interview With the Vampire* is preoccupied with death and grieving, the pain of mortality, and the inescapability of human suffering even if one has great power and eternal life.

Is Stefan trustworthy? Bonnie, the "doubt planter," suggests that Elena has a right to know if Stefan is a "calculating, manipulative liar," and, in this episode, that's exactly what he is. He's plotting against Damon and using Caroline as bait, and he's lying to Elena about big things (like what's going on with Damon and Caroline) and small (fibbing about never attending a Founder's Party before). From where Elena stands, which is in the dark, it's impossible to see that Stefan's untrustworthiness doesn't comes from being a bad guy, it's because he's trying to protect Caroline, Elena, and the whole town . . . from Damon. Until Stefan opens up to Elena and earns her trust, their relationship will strain under the weight of his secrets and lies, no matter how justifiable they are.

From Stefan's perspective, building that trust must take a backseat to protecting her from Damon. Stefan's singlemindedness is fueled by his knowledge of what his brother is capable of, and the nightmare Damon created for him didn't help the situation. The question Stefan asks himself — "How do I stop a monster without becoming one myself?" — shapes his plan to take his brother down. While the rest of the founding families pass their history down through the generations, the Salvatores *are* their own legacy. As Damon tells Elena, they are brothers cursed by rivalry.

Just when Stefan succeeds in capturing Damon, the founding families step in with their clandestine meeting to thicken the plot. In a town so obsessed with its own history, the secret of vampirism turns out to be less well kept than the Salvatore brothers thought.

COMPELLING MOMENT: Bonnie turning around to see all the candles in the room lit.

CIRCLE OF KNOWLEDGE:
* Since Matt is not a member of a founding family, he doesn't get an invite to the party and is absent from this episode.

- For many TV shows, "Family Ties" is a popular choice for an episode title; it's also the name of the 1982–1989 NBC sitcom. The comedy and tension in *Family Ties* comes from how members of the same family can be so different: Alex P. Keaton (Michael J. Fox) played the Republican son to hippie parents (Michael Gross and Meredith Baxter).
- With Damon in Elena's bedroom at the end of the previous episode, the audience is led to believe she's in real danger in the opening sequence — but it's just Damon giving his little brother nightmares.
- Mountain lions are considered extinct in Virginia but there are frequent unconfirmed reports of sightings. The last confirmed cougar in Virginia was in 1882.
- Damon is likely reading *Eclipse* since Caroline tells him he has to start with the "first one" (*Twilight*), Edward is absent for the majority of *New Moon*, and the book doesn't have the bulk of *Breaking Dawn*.
- The Jack-and-Jill bathroom connecting Elena's and Jeremy's rooms brings to mind the original *90210* series where Brenda and Brandon shared a bathroom at Casa Walsh.
- Not much has changed in the Salvatore brothers' romancing methods since they competed for Katherine in 1864: Stefan plays the gentleman while Damon is overtly sexual.
- The rich boy–poor girl dynamic between Tyler and Vicki is a common trope in small-town stories. John Hughes (who is one Kevin Williamson's strongest influences) built the movie *Pretty in Pink* around that class tension, and Williamson explored it in *Dawson's Creek* with Joey Potter, the waitress from a broken home.
- It's a nice change of pace to see Jeremy win for once; he gets the girl *and* the pocket watch.

THE RULES: With Stefan's nightmare, we learn that vampires sleep and dream — at least in the world of *The Vampire Diaries*. And because Stefan is weak for a vampire, Damon can manipulate his mind as he would a human's. Damon provides Caroline, and the audience, with the basics on how to become a vampire: feed on vampire blood, die, then feed on human blood. Presto, change-o. With a little concentration, Bonnie can light candles with her mind — but she lacks control over her gift. Her intention seems to be to light just one candle but she lit every one in the room (saving that berated waiter some work).

Rob Pralgo as Mayor Lockwood and Susan Walters as Carol Lockwood

The role of Mayor Lockwood adds another credit to Rob Pralgo's already impressive resumé. A graduate of the University of Georgia's film and TV production program, Rob became a professional actor shortly after college, pursuing acting work in the Atlanta area. Since then, he's appeared in TV shows like *Prison Break*, *Army Wives*, and *One Tree Hill*, as well as in a number of feature films. When he's not on the set of a major production, Rob produces and acts in his own independent films.

Cast as the missus to the mayor is Susan Walters. Born and raised in the Atlanta area, Susan began her professional career as a model before transitioning into acting in the '80s on the soap opera *Loving*. Some of her notable roles include Priscilla Beaulieu Presley in the miniseries *Elvis and Me*, Diane Jenkins on *The Young and the Restless*, Christine on the original *Melrose Place*, and Principal Rimkus on *One Tree Hill*. Her role as one of Jerry's girlfriends on *Seinfeld* is also well remembered — though some viewers think of her character as "Mulva" rather than Dolores.

THE DIABOLICAL PLAN: Damon covers his attacks with the mountain-lion story, then uses Caroline to get to Elena, Stefan, and the "very important" crystal in the Founder's archives. Why did he hide it there in the first place? What does it do? Stefan's master plan goes off without a hitch and the "deadly beast" is captured. But not before the Founder's Council has wised up to the return of vampires in Mystic Falls. Why are the Mayor and Mrs. Lockwood, Logan Fell, and Sheriff Forbes after the Gilbert pocket watch? Is Logan just using Jenna in order to get to it? If Elena's mother was so involved with the Founder's Council, did she know vampires are real?

HISTORY LESSON: Damon gives a firsthand account of the Battle of Willow Creek: the civilians in the church were Union sympathizers rounded up by members of the founding families and burned alive. Stefan and Damon were shot to death trying to rescue Katherine. (Presumably this was the incident that ousted the Salvatore family from the council and made them less than the town royalty they once were.) Union sympathizers in Confederate states like Virginia were common during the Civil War, and divided loyalties turned neighbors against each other.

BITE MARKS: After his nightmare, Stefan stabs Damon with a letter opener. Damon stabs him back. Caroline has bite marks all over her body from

Damon. Damon bites vervain-spiked Caroline and is incapacitated and incarcerated by his little bro.

MEANWHILE IN FELL'S CHURCH: Fell's Church gets its name from the Fell family, and in this episode Logan Fell is introduced. (In the novels, there are no Fells still living.) In *The Awakening*, Stefan and Caroline don't just dance together once, they attend the homecoming dance as a couple. What the what?!

OFF CAMERA: Taylor Swift is a favorite of Kevin Williamson but Ian Somerhalder had no idea who she was, so he downloaded a song to understand Damon's reference. The shirt that Stefan stabbed a hole through really was a John Varvatos, a designer the wardrobe department favors for Ian.

FOGGY MOMENTS: Who did Jenna mean when she said "Grandma Beth" to Elena? Elena's grandmother would be Jenna's mother or her sister's mother-in-law, neither of whom she's likely to call "grandma." Maybe Grandma Beth is Elena's great-grandmother? Mayor Lockwood's first name is Richard but his wife calls him "Charles" at the Grill.

MUSIC: Damon tells Caroline what to wear to the Founder's Party to Union of Knives' "Opposite Direction." Tyler has an uncomfortable meal with his parents to "I'm a Lady" by Santigold. Carolina Liar's "I'm Not Over" plays as Bonnie and Elena get ready for the party and Mrs. Lockwood calls. Lots of music at the party: Caroline arrives on Damon's arm to Thievery Corporation's "Shadows of Ourselves"; Elena looks at the display and Jenna insults Logan to VV Brown's "Back in Time"; Damon apologizes to Elena to Sofi Bonde's "Fallout"; Tyler and Vicki argue to Glass Pear's "Wild Place"; Elena asks Stefan to dance to Matt Nathanson's "All We Are"; and The Submarines' "Brightest Hour (Morgan Page Remix)" begins as Bonnie and Elena talk. Viva Voce's "Believer" kicks in as Jeremy and Vicki kiss, and that song continues as Damon attacks Caroline.

Damon: You caught the bad guy. Now nothing can come between you and Elena. Except the truth.

1.05 *You're Undead to Me*

Original air date: October 8, 2009
Written by: Sean Reycraft and Gabrielle Stanton
Directed by: Kevin Bray
Guest cast: Bob Banks (Old Man), Brandi Coleman (Tiki), Desmond Phillips (Tony), Javier Carrasquillo (Jared), Amber Wallace (Summer), Jackson Walker (Franklin Fell)

With his brother locked in the basement, Stefan tries to repair his relationship with Elena. Caroline wants nothing more than for her life to be normal again, and, for her, that means the Sexy Suds Car Wash.

Another exciting episode, "You're Undead to Me" comes to a skidding halt at a turning point in the season's arc: Elena's discovery that Stefan is a vampire. Even with the "deadly beast" locked up until near the end, this was a particularly scary episode: Damon wasting in his cell but able to grab Zach in a chokehold in the blink of an eye; the crow stalking Caroline; Damon calling her name in a whisper; Caroline all alone in the darkened school hallway, drawn to Damon, like a zombie; Zach's worst fears realized with the snap of a neck; and the chase through the Salvatore house, Caroline narrowly escaping into the safety of sunlight. Damon's reign of terror in this episode peaks at its most horrifying moment: his frenzied feeding at the end filmed with a shaking camera that captures Vicki's limp fingers squeaking off the side of the truck as Damon drinks long and deep. *The Vampire Diaries* is not a show for the squeamish.

Caroline not only has to deal with the literal haunting of Damon, she's trying to get back to who she was before Damon began terrorizing her. But she's been left with muddled and conflicting memories, and bite marks that she tries to hide with makeup. Her insistence that the car wash be super sexy plays like desperation, and it's clear that, despite how he wronged her, she is hurt by Damon "leaving" without saying goodbye. Even though Bonnie and Elena see that Caroline's in denial as she flits about the school like nothing's wrong and Sheriff Forbes attempts to reach out to her daughter, Caroline is ultimately left alone, a chatty girl gone quiet in her bedroom, trying to figure out what exactly happened to her.

Jeremy also confronts the nature of his relationship with Vicki, and though he doesn't like that they mostly just get high together, he's scared that pushing it beyond that will drive Vicki away, leaving him alone again. Their confrontation in the woods is harshly honest; Vicki has just as many assumptions about Jeremy's likely future as he does about her "waste-of-space, small-town lifer" friends. It seems that, for Jeremy, partying over the summer was about getting close to Vicki, but for Vicki, drug use and drinking are a big part of who she is. Like Stefan in his attempts to reform Damon, Jeremy is helpless to change Vicki if she doesn't want to resolve her addiction issues.

Stefan is again split between his two priorities: Damon and Elena. With a false sense of security that his brother is contained in his cell, he tries to win back Elena. With no viable choice but to lie to Elena about all things vampire, Stefan realizes he can open up to her about the other sides of him in order to help mend their relationship. His romantic "get to know the guy you're dumping" dinner works. Elena is temporarily satisfied by Stefan going beyond his usual "vague non-answers." But she needs to go deeper than his favorite books and movies; she needs to know why the old man recognized him, why his face gets all weird and veiny around blood, and why she saw a deep gash on his hand that was gone the next second. Elena proves to have an unrelenting nature as she sleuths out a fact and then goes straight to the source for confirmation. Nina Dobrev plays this moment of confrontation at Stefan's door perfectly: Elena is obviously scared of what Stefan is capable of but stands there bravely asking him for the truth. Bonnie shares Elena's need for answers, no matter how troubling they are, and finally turns to her grandmother for help. Both girls are well on their way to becoming believers.

COMPELLING MOMENT: Elena putting the pieces together and confronting Stefan: "What are you?"

CIRCLE OF KNOWLEDGE:
- If Zach is just the groundskeeper of the Salvatore boardinghouse, as Damon jokes, maybe the vampire brothers never required an invitation to come in.

Chris William Martin as Zach Salvatore

British Columbia native Chris William Martin, born January 17, 1975, has been acting since the early '90s when he was cast in *Fifteen*, a teen drama that costarred Ryan Reynolds (*The Proposal*). Since then he's performed in a slew of TV shows like *Madison, Felicity, Veronica Mars, The L Word, Heartland, Lincoln Heights, CSI: Miami, Bones, The Mentalist, Dollhouse*, and in the title role on *Tom Stone*. He's also appeared in TV movies and in both independent films like *Johnny* (1999, shot in the Dogme 95 style) and mainstream films like *Aliens vs. Predator: Requiem* (2007). He plays Officer Brezik in Chris Carter's *Fencewalker* (2010). Martin has also gone by the name Corky Martin, and as Chris Martin (without the William), something he changed just around the time that other Chris Martin hit the big time with his band, Coldplay. While Chris William Martin doesn't have a band of his own, he does play piano and guitar, and he appeared in two Alanis Morissette music videos, "Everything" (2004) and "Crazy" (her 2005 cover of the Seal song).

- Caroline uses her pillow to shoo away the crow just like she threw one at Damon when he attacked her in "Friday Night Bites." The pillow attack proves more effective with the bird than the vamp.
- Tiki, the mean girl at the car wash, was mentioned in "Friday Night Bites"; Caroline sent cheerleaders to help her when she had trouble holding up the banner.
- When Jeremy checks in on his sister, their usual roles are reversed. She's moping on her bed with her teddy bear, and he's trying to get her out of her funk.
- Stefan's favorite *I Love Lucy* episode, "Lucy and the Loving Cup," first aired on January 7, 1957. In it, Lucy puts a trophy on her head and can't get it off.
- As in the novels, the Salvatore brothers' rings are set with lapis lazuli, the striking dark blue semi-precious stone that was among the first gems to be used for jewelry in ancient cultures. Lapis lazuli is often imbued with the meaning of friendship and truth, and has been used as a protective stone.

THE RULES: Without blood, a vampire will turn into a living corpse. The length of time it takes to desiccate seems to depend on the initial strength of the vampire. Damon's strong connection to Caroline enables him to appear before her as an apparition, and he can direct his crow to her as well. Two commonly held conceptions about vampires are debunked: an aversion to garlic would just be a matter of an individual vampire's taste, and a vampire does have a reflection (since Elena sees Stefan's in the kitchen window). Bonnie is able to manipulate the elements — fire and water so far — but still lacks control over her witchcraft.

THE DIABOLICAL PLAN: Stefan plans to mummify Damon by starving him, then move him to the family crypt, and "reevaluate" in 50 years. The Founder's Council is searching for the vampire's lair and for the Gilbert watch, which Logan steals from Jeremy's room. Now that Damon is free, he may notice he's no longer in possession of the crystal, which projects a pentacle (a pentagram enclosed in a circle) onto Caroline's bedspread when light passes through it.

HISTORY LESSON: According to Stefan, in the Dark Ages (also known as the early Middle Ages, roughly from the fifth to tenth centuries), vampires governed their own kind and protected the secret of their existence from humans by punishing those who drew attention to vampirism with 50 years in solitary confinement.

BITE MARKS: Imprisoned, Damon is starving. He chokes Zach and later snaps his neck, killing him. Damon heals quickly after sizzling during his brief exposure to sunlight. Desperate for blood, he feeds on his crow and, after nightfall, lures Vicki away from her friends to feed on her.

MEANWHILE IN FELL'S CHURCH: In this episode, Stefan tells Elena his ring bears the Salvatore family crest that dates to the Italian Renaissance; in the novels, Stefan and Damon are from Renaissance-era Florence. The Salvatore house is referred to as a boardinghouse in "You're Undead to Me"; in Fell's Church, Stefan stays in a boardinghouse run not by his "uncle" but by the seemingly dotty Mrs. Flowers. In *The Awakening*, some Fell's Church teens go to the old cemetery to party after the homecoming dance; Vickie is attacked there. Also in *The Awakening*, Elena knows that Stefan is keeping "some secret he's afraid I'll find out." Elena discovers in *The Fury* that some of the town leaders are aware of the vampire problem and they are looking for the vampire's hideout, unaware that there's a vampire right under their noses.

OFF CAMERA: Recognize the red-haired stoner girl? That's Atlanta-native Amber Wallace, who played Lila in season 2 of *90210* and Glenda in season 4 of *One Tree Hill*. For the car-on-fire shot, a stunt double stood in for Kat Graham as the trail of fire led to the car. Damon's creepy crow came to a bitey end this episode, perhaps because waiting "37 minutes for the crow to caw," as Julie Plec described it, made the bird impractical to work with.

FOGGY MOMENTS: Why didn't Stefan hear Elena talking to Jenna and Logan? Seemed like he was within super-vampire earshot when she looked over at him washing a car.

MUSIC: Lots of appropriately titled songs in this episode. Elena wakes up while Imogen Heap's "Wait it Out" plays. S.O.Stereo's "When a Heart Breaks" is on at the Grill as Matt and Elena shoot pool. Stefan makes dinner and talks about his likes and dislikes to "Be There" by Howie Day. The Sexy Suds Car Wash kicks off to 3OH!3's "Don't Trust Me." After her conversation with Tiki's grandpa, Elena asks some innocent-seeming questions of Stefan to Gabriella Cilmi's "Save the Lies." Bonnie lights the car on fire to "Boom" by Anjulie. Caroline is cruel to her mother, Stefan finds Zach dead, and the stoners party in the cemetery to Mads Langer's "Beauty of the Dark."

Vicki: I don't want this.

1.06 *Lost Girls*

Original air date: October 15, 2009
Written by: Kevin Williamson and Julie Plec
Directed by: Marcos Siega
Guest cast: Kevin Nichols (Deputy), Desmond Phillips (Tony), Amber Wallace (Summer), Javier Carrasquillo (Jared), Jasmine Burke (Emily)

After Elena confronts him, Stefan finally tells her the secret he's been hiding — complete with flashbacks to 1864 — while Vicki learns firsthand what it means to become a vampire.

A standout episode, "Lost Girls" delivers what we've been dying to see: Katherine. And on top it gives us an unexpected turn for Vicki. With a slight variation on the "Elena figures it out" sequence from the end of "You're Undead to Me," the pace and excitement pick right back up, only to transport us back to 1864 to see Stefan meeting Katherine for the first time. Stefan reveals to Elena what many fans guessed and what readers of the books assumed: Katherine is the vampire who turned the brothers. The flashback scenes (which are distinguished by an overexposed look that director Marcos Siega also used to great effect in similar scenes on *Dexter*) reveal Stefan and Damon "before the fall," friends and brothers, playful and innocent, both instantly smitten with Katherine. Bold, unapologetic, sassy, and coquettish, Katherine's manner is starkly different than Elena's, which is a testament to Nina Dobrev's range.

Elena's understanding of the world and the people around her undergoes a dramatic shift, and "Lost Girls" is in part an episode about transition. After she confirms that Stefan is a vampire, her first instinct is to check on Jeremy; and Stefan also protects the one he cares for, making sure Elena knows the danger of this secret and standing outside her house all night in case Damon shows up. Elena gives Stefan a day to explain and faces him bravely: her

The Lost Boys

"Lost Girls" takes its title from *The Lost Boys*, the 1987 vampire movie with a comedic bent directed by Joel Schumacher. In it, two teenage brothers move with their mother to a Californian beachside town, the murder capital of the world. Terrorizing the place on their motorcycles is a gang of bad-ass teenage vampires led by David (Kiefer Sutherland). Infatuated with the pretty girl who runs with the "lost boys," the older brother, Michael (Jason Patric), is soon lured into the gang's hideout where they play tricks on him and make him unwittingly drink blood, initiating the change from human to vampire. Luckily Michael's kid brother, Sam (Corey Haim), realizes what's happening to Michael and enlists the help of some informed comic-bookstore kids to take down the vampire leader before his brother completes the change.

The original "lost boys" are from J.M. Barrie's *Peter Pan or, The Boy Who Wouldn't Grow Up* (1904), a group of boys lost by their parents, left unclaimed, and whisked off to Neverland where they spend their lives making mischief with Peter Pan, the boy who refuses to grow up. As Peter does for Wendy Darling, the boys who never grow old in *The Lost Boys* hold a certain allure for Michael. They get to do whatever they want; the tagline for the film sums up the appeal: "Sleep all day. Party all night. Never grow old. Never die. It's fun to be a vampire."

In "Lost Girls," Vicki is in the same position as *The Lost Boys'* Michael — she's a "half-vampire" who enjoys the wild ride with Damon, feeling alive and power-ful, dancing, and ransacking Stefan's room. But after her human death and as her physical discomfort grows, Vicki feels just as trapped and panicky and desperate as Michael is for a reprieve. Unfortunately for her, in the world of TVD there's no reversal option: it's either dead or undead. In the flashback, Damon and Stefan become the "lost boys." Katherine, the leader of their little gang, shows the same disregard for rules and convention as David does in *The Lost Boys*: joining the football game when, at the time, it wasn't a suitable pastime for a woman; rejecting monogamy by seducing both Stefan and Damon; and disregarding the jealousy her choice would inevitably bring up between the brothers. Seeing Vicki's transformation juxtaposed with Stefan and Damon's final days as mortals adds pathos to her storyline: the Salvatore brothers have long ago lost the innocence they had when they were mortal, but Vicki's only just lost hers.

defenses are up and she asks a lot of questions. A recurring theme in what he tells her is the importance of choice. Stefan ensures that Elena is free to make up her own mind: protecting her with vervain, arming her with information, and giving her space to decide.

As we see the beginning of the end of the Salvatore brothers' previous lives, so we see Vicki thrust into the same position Stefan once was in with Katherine — enjoying the foreplay but being turned involuntarily. Vicki's transition from human to vampire moves from the most raucous fun we've seen on the series to its saddest moment so far — Vicki crying, on the precipice of either death or vampirism, pleading with Stefan, saying, "I want to go home." Kayla Ewell's performance in "Lost Girls" ranges from manic to playful, desperate to hilarious, violent to broken. Truly a standout on the series, Ewell brings a character to life that in lesser hands, and with lesser writing, could have played as clichéd. Siblings are an important part of *TVD*, and in the scene where she is slow-dancing with Damon, the dynamic between "Vick" and "Matty" plays out as a parallel to that of Damon and Stefan — the older sibling's the screwup, the little brother is the golden boy. Their partying is interrupted by moments of sullen introspection, Damon's to look at Katherine's portrait. Vicki and Damon are, in a lot of ways, two of a kind.

In "Family Ties," Jeremy says to Vicki, "You know you're making the wrong choice and yet you make it anyway." Here Vicki makes what could potentially be the worst choice of her life, from Stefan's perspective at least. Stefan didn't choose to begin his transition into a vampire, but he made the choice to complete it by feeding on human blood (a detail Elena picks up on). In the old cemetery outside the crypt, Stefan almost convinces Vicki to choose death over a life as a vampire, revealing that he would not now make the same choice he did in 1864. But Vicki is unable to resist the bloodlust and feeds on Logan. Her plaintive "I'm sorry" as she looks up, mouth bloodied, is one of many apologies in an episode full of empty reassurances.

COMPELLING MOMENT: Vicki and Damon's dance-and-destroy party.

CIRCLE OF KNOWLEDGE:
- No Jenna, Caroline, Tyler, or Bonnie in this episode.
- Too bad Sheriff Forbes and Logan didn't look up at the name on the crypt for a clue to the vampire's identity: Salvatore.
- Wooden bullets, like the ones Sheriff Forbes and company use, do exist but they are usually hollow and used as blanks; the wood splinters and turns to ash when the gun is fired. A solid wooden bullet doesn't have a very long firing range and lacks the accuracy of a regular bullet.

THE RULES: Elena and Stefan run through a few more vampire rules at the Grill: garlic, crucifixes, and holy water are no problem for *The Vampire Diaries'* undead. Wood bullets slow vampires down but don't kill them. During Vicki's transition from human to vampire, she's sensitive to light and noise, has incredible strength, and confuses her appetites — hunger, lust, and anger. As her human side dies, a vampire-to-be regains those memories she's lost through mind control; Vicki can remember being compelled on the rooftop and in the hospital, and Stefan remembers Katherine compelling him. Every transitioning vampire has a limited amount of time to make the choice — feed on human blood or die.

THE DIABOLICAL PLAN: The pocket watch is part of a vampire-detecting compass, which quickly falls into the hands of Damon. The brothers now know the town leaders are on the hunt for vampires. What did Stefan leave out of the story he told Elena? Damon's doubt that she heard enough backstory to understand their dynamic is intriguing.

HISTORY LESSON: Just as in present-day Mystic Falls, in 1864, the town leaders knew that vampires exist and sought to eradicate them. Damon was a Confederate soldier in 1864, but he did not return to battle — is he a deserter or a Union sympathizer?

BITE MARKS: Damon kills Tony, Summer, and Jared and burns their bodies. Vicki and Damon engage in some consensual biting but Damon's decision to turn her into a vampire is all his own. Stefan is shot with a wooden bullet, Damon bites Logan to stop him from staking his brother, and Vicki feeds on Logan. In the flashback, Katherine feeds on Stefan.

MEANWHILE IN FELL'S CHURCH: L.J. Smith uses flashbacks in the novels to show the Salvatore brothers falling in love with Katherine in *The Awakening*. Stefan helps Vickie (Bennett) in *The Struggle* when she has a violent episode at school; he uses compulsion to calm her, as Stefan does in this episode at the Gilbert house. Though the mechanism for becoming a vampire is slightly different in the novels, in *The Fury*, there is a vampire whose body was not strong enough to complete the change without human blood. Vampire hunters in *The Fury* are armed with wooden bullets. In *The Fury*, after Damon prevents someone from killing his little brother, he says to Stefan, "if anyone's going to have the satisfaction of killing you, it will be me," a line echoed in this episode in the cemetery when Damon saves Stefan from Logan's attack.

OFF CAMERA: "Lost Girls" is one of Nina Dobrev's favorite episodes and it is Ian Somerhalder's favorite. In an interview at the end of season 1 with the

L.A. Times' ShowTracker blog, Ian said, "It's still my favorite. I read it, and I called Kevin and Julie to thank them. Me and Kayla Ewell had so much fun shooting that episode." Jasmine Burke plays Emily in this episode only; in future episodes, the role is played by Bianca Lawson.

FOGGY MOMENTS: Couldn't Damon just overpower Stefan and take *his* ring? Why did the original Salvatore home fall into disrepair? In the flashback scenes, there is a house directly across from it and a road running in front of it. Seems to have been smack dab in the middle of early Mystic Falls, but in present day, Elena and Stefan have driven to the middle of nowhere.

MUSIC: Elena meets with Stefan at the Grill to A Fine Frenzy's "Stood Up." Damon impatiently calls Stefan, asking about his ring, while "Weight of the World" by Editors plays. Damon explains to Vicki how she got to the Salvatore house after her enjoyable shower with The Temper Trap's "Fader" in the background. Damon and Vicki dance and destroy to Anberlin's cover of "Enjoy the Silence" (originally by Depeche Mode). They slow dance to Green Day's "21 Guns." Elena makes her choice and finally falls apart to "Down" by Jason Walker.

> Damon: *None of this matters to me. None of it.*
> Elena: *People die around you. How could it not matter? It matters, and you* know *it.*

1.07 Haunted

Original air date: October 29, 2009
Written by: Kevin Williamson and Julie Plec (teleplay); Andrew Kreisberg (story)
Directed by: Ernest Dickerson

It's Halloween in Mystic Falls. Vicki decides whether she wants to be on the Stefan or the Damon diet while Elena keeps the truth from those she cares about.

Where "Lost Girls" was about the importance of having a choice, "Haunted" deals with the importance of what choice you make. The right choice is often the less fun, more difficult one — hard to accept when there's an easier, more satisfying, seductive path. Vicki's choices are personified in

"Count Deepak" Stefan, who preaches a moral life filled with drinking animal blood but getting no satisfaction, and in Damon, who offers a lifestyle where the id gets what it wants when it wants it — "snatch, eat, erase." Trying to convince a new vampire with addiction issues to behave with restraint puts Stefan in a pretty unenviable position, but he shoulders the responsibility for Vicki, once again cleaning up his brother's mess.

The choice Stefan has made to subsist on animal blood is the more honorable one but it means he's weaker than a human-blood-drinking vampire. Physical power has been a problem before: he was overpowered by Damon in the pilot; he was unable to effectively put the mind whammy on Vicki in "The Night of the Comet"; and, now, in "Haunted" he can't erase Jeremy's memory for Elena. The conversation between Vicki and Stefan, with Elena sitting right beside him, about when he last drank human blood is delightfully awkward. But Stefan replies with one of his "vague non-answers." When and why did Stefan decide to go vegetarian?

Even as this episode ends the Vicki chapter of the season, "Haunted" keeps the rest of storylines racing along: the secret council has a new ally, Damon Salvatore, who can supply them with vervain and Bonnie's discovering her legacy. As Stefan and Damon show Vicki the ropes of vampirism, Bonnie is studying witchcraft with Grams and is, like the other newbie to the supernatural, itching for the fun part — she wants spells and tricks more than history books. Grams is like Stefan, lending a gravitas to the situation so Bonnie understands how serious being a witch is.

Bonnie and Vicki both show up to the Halloween party in costumes that reveal their new identities, with no one the wiser. Bonnie's a witch, Vicki's a vampire . . . and Elena's a nurse? Though she wears last year's costume, it fits her persona now. Her first instinct is to protect Jeremy from both immediate physical threats and major psychological damage. She saves him from Vicki by making herself Vicki's target and she takes away Jeremy's suffering by having Damon erase his memory of Vicki dying. Elena's choice to keep Stefan's secret has already had fallout: she spends the episode lying to the people she cares about most. When she suggests Jeremy not join the search party for Vicki, Jeremy sees her as callous and uncaring, just as she herself had misconstrued Stefan's attitude before she knew his real motivations and worries.

The writers remind us of the ongoing connection between Matt and Elena, former best friends now exes, when they show up to the Halloween

Paul M. Sommers, Director of Photography

Paul Sommers was just 18 years old when he started his career in the film and TV business. In the early '90s, he worked as a grip and a dolly grip mostly on film projects. From there he evolved into a Steadicam operator, a job he performed for about 10 years on TV shows like *Without a Trace* and *Cold Case*. As that latter series progressed, Paul transitioned into the role of cinematographer. In addition to continuing with cinematography work on TV shows *Viva Laughlin* and *Valentine*, Paul shot *Walmart Soundcheck*, a special series of performances with artists like the Black Eyed Peas and Demi Lovato, as its camera operator. On *The Vampire Diaries*, Paul is the director of photography and his role is to "have an opinion" on everything in front of the camera, primarily overseeing the camera and lighting departments. He works with the episode's director to decide how each shot will be crafted, from blocking the actors' positions to lighting to other factors that contribute to the look of the show, like the set dressing and wardrobe. Though he enjoys being in the thick of the action as a camera operator, Paul loves his job on *TVD* and is responsible for executing the signature look of the show.

party in their coordinated costumes from last year. That reminder helps drive home how incredibly difficult it is for Elena to look Matt in the eyes and lie to him about his sister — having just seen her staked in the heart and killed. After experiencing that pain, Elena's final act of the episode — to take away Jeremy's memory — is a dangerous choice but it makes sense from an emotional perspective. She wants to keep him from feeling the way she does. Seeing someone you love and feel protective toward looking inconsolable, in pain, and overwhelmed by the senselessness of death . . . if you could take away that pain, would you? Jeremy tells Elena that Vicki is responsible for every single moment of happiness he's experienced since their parents died, so she understands that Vicki means to Jeremy what Stefan means to her. To help him, she accepts the aid of the person responsible for Vicki's death.

While Stefan drove the stake through Vicki's heart that ultimately ended her existence, it was Damon who deliberately created the whole mess in the first place. Elena turns her "judgey little eyes" on Damon, imploring him to own up to his choices and the tragedies he's left in his wake. And in a small way, he does — he can't undo what he did to Vicki but he can take away Jeremy's haunting memories. Ironically only Damon has the power to smooth over the tragedy he himself created.

The Vampire Diaries has been deadly since its opening images, but "Haunted" marks the first death of a major character. Kayla Ewell turns in another strong performance for her last as Vicki, and Steven R. McQueen proves he can hold his own in tough emotional scenes as he breaks down with Elena and delivers one of the most heartbreaking lines — "Why does everyone have to die on me?" Just like Elena is to Jeremy, Vicki was a big sister to Matt, protective of her little brother, and both he and Jeremy lose Vicki without the closure of knowing she's gone for good. Elena chooses to hold on to her memories — she'd rather keep the pain than lose what she feels for Stefan, a sentiment that helps to close some of the distance that's grown between them.

COMPELLING MOMENT: Vicki learning about vampire speed . . . and ditching the Salvatore brothers.

CIRCLE OF KNOWLEDGE:
- Aunt Jenna is absent for the second episode in a row.
- Damon says Stefan is "singing 'The Rain in Spain'" with Vicki, a reference to *My Fair Lady* (1956) in which do-gooder Professor Higgins attempts to make a respectable lady of Cockney flower-seller Eliza Doolittle.
- F. Scott Fitzgerald's *The Great Gatsby* (1925) is mentioned for the second time: in "You're Undead to Me," Stefan named it as one of his favorite books, and here Carol Lockwood dresses as Daisy Buchanan, the object of Gatsby's affection, for Halloween.

THE RULES: Stefan teaches Vicki a vamp trick to help her fit in with humans: caffeine warms a vampire's blood so the skin isn't cool to the touch. Stefan is able to track Vicki, using his heightened vampire senses. The crystal, which Grams reveals was once Emily Bennett's, burns Damon's hand. Why?

THE DIABOLICAL PLAN: The compass is now in Damon's possession, and he recognizes it. When did he see it before?

HISTORY LESSON: There are six generations of Bennetts between Emily and Bonnie, and the family has been in the Mystic Falls area since 1692 when they fled Salem. Grams confirms that the girls persecuted in Salem were not real witches. (Bonnie refers to them as having been burned but they were actually hanged.) The Salvatore family was originally part of the council.

BITE MARKS: The roles are reversed as Vicki becomes the aggressor and Tyler wants her to stop. Tyler punches Damon who throws him across the parking lot. Vicki chokes Elena and threatens to rip her head off. Vicki bites Jeremy's lip and starts to attack him before turning her attention to Elena. Stefan stakes Vicki as she bites Elena. Elena slaps Damon hard.

MEANWHILE IN FELL'S CHURCH: In *The Fury*, Damon mocks the Stefan diet as Stefan trains a new vampire not to feed on or hurt humans. In the show, Stefan's concern is that Vicki's addictive personality will complicate her transition. In *The Struggle*, he explains that personality plays a role in how deeply affected by supernatural forces a person will be; of Vickie he says, "Some people are more easily influenced than others." Just like Matt's house in the book series is rundown, the Donovan house in the show is shabbier than those of the wealthier founding families. A key scene in *The Awakening* takes place at the high school's Halloween haunted house, and "Haunted" recreates that scene complete with a Druid Room and a "sacrifice" on an altar. In *The Awakening*, Stefan dresses up as Dracula for Halloween (at Bonnie's suggestion), and in this episode, Vicki also wears a costume suited to her new identity. In *The Struggle*, Elena deals with the burden of her knowledge of Stefan's and Damon's secrets, of lying to her friends and hiding the truth about the violence in Fell's Church.

OFF CAMERA: The makeup effects department, led by Connor McCullagh, makes its own fake blood for the show, a few gallons at a time, with edible corn syrup, food coloring, salt (as a preservative), and peppermint extract to make it more palatable. A batch of blood lasts two to three months, and it's used carefully since it's hard to clean up, especially if it gets on wardrobe. The bite wounds are made of prosthetic pieces glued down and then blended in with makeup and finished off with blood. The fangs, which are made from a mold of each actor's mouth, just sit on the teeth, explains Ian, "so they don't affect your speech patterns at all. I could recite the Gettysburg Address like it was nothing."

Killing a major character this soon in the season was a shock to many fans. "By killing her," explained Kevin Williamson, "I thought it set a precedent that we will go there, and it was so early in the show that I felt we could

"When I'm around her,
        I completely forget what I am."

— Stefan, "162 Candles"

"*. . . it was epic.*"

Mystic Falls, 1864

Ian Somerhalder as Damon Salvatore, the self-proclaimed
"better, hotter, superior choice."

get away with it. I don't want to turn off the audience by killing off a popular character, but you have to do it. It's a vampire show."

Kayla Ewell revealed to *EW*'s Michael Ausiello that Vicki's death scene was actually filmed twice: "Funny story: in the original script, Jeremy kills Vicki. And that's what we shot. Jeremy is forced to choose between saving the love of his life or his sister, and he chooses his sister. We shot the whole thing and I [moved back to] L.A. Then about a week and a half later, I got an email from Kevin and Julie Plec asking me to come back to Atlanta to reshoot my death scene — only this time Stefan kills me."

MUSIC: Elena wakes up to Gary Go's "Open Arms." Tyler talks to Matt in the hallway at school with Final Flash's "Fading Light" in the background. "No One Sleeps When I'm Awake" by The Sounds plays as Vicki asks Damon why he turned her. The school's Halloween party kicks off with White Lies' forebodingly titled "To Lose My Life." "Open Hearts" by The Longcut is playing as Elena and Jeremy arrive at the party and the crowd makes Vicki hungry. Damon and Mrs. Lockwood talk about vervain to The Dodos' "Fables" (from the album also portentously titled *Time to Die*). Elena looks for Jeremy at the Halloween party while he makes out with Vicki between the buses as Bat for Lashes' "Sleep Alone" plays. "The Weight of Us" by Sanders Bohlke provides the plaintive soundtrack to Jeremy crying in his room, Stefan listening on the Gilberts' porch, and Matt coming home to an empty house.

Bonnie: I need to swear you to secrecy.
Elena: It's kind of a bad week for that kind of stuff.

1.08 *162 Candles*

Original air date: November 5, 2009
Written by: Barbie Kligman and Gabrielle Stanton
Directed by: Rick Bota
Guest cast: Arielle Kebbel (Lexi), Bridget Evelyn (Girl), John Gilbert (Guy), Kevin Nichols (Deputy), Jason Giuliano (Deputy #2), John Michael Weatherly (Bartender)

Even the undead celebrate birthdays, and Lexi, Stefan's oldest friend (at 350 years), comes to Mystic Falls for his annual one day of fun. Bonnie shares her supernatural secret with Elena.

Another strong, fast-paced, emotional rollercoaster of an episode, "162 Candles" manages to let the characters catch their breath after Vicki's death before hurtling the plot forward when Stefan's seemingly infinite patience with Damon comes to an end. It's a testament both to the writers and to Arielle Kebbel's performance that the audience connects to Lexi so quickly. She's likeable, playful, and brings out a previously unseen side of Stefan. Even though she's only around for one day, her death has a strong emotional impact — the audience cares about her because of how much she meant to Stefan.

Before "162 Candles" goes doom-and-gloomy, there's some fun to be had. Damon may be the most-hated vampire around but he's great at banter with Lexi and with Elena. And from Caroline's hilarious one-liners — "Are you wearing polyester?" — to her fear that the hurtful things Damon says are absolutely true, this is also a great episode for her character. She finds herself back under Damon's influence and at odds with Bonnie as she tries to get the crystal back. Caroline undergoes a fairly common struggle — a guy pushing two best friends apart as the girlfriend loses part of herself in the relationship — in a uniquely Caroline way. Being deep may not be her thing, as Matt gently affirms, but Caroline gets drunk and confesses her profound feelings of isolation to him. By reaching out for him, Caroline unknowingly gives Matt what he needs too: companionship. He's without a mother or sister, he doesn't know his father (as Vicki told Damon in "Lost Girls"), he's lost his closeness to Elena, and his best friend is *Tyler*. Matt and Caroline is an unexpected pairing, but it feels right for them to take a break from being alone, together.

Stefan also gets a (short-lived) reprieve from his isolation. If Elena finds it hard to only have Stefan to talk to, Stefan must find it incredibly difficult to be alone with Damon. Lexi's friendship is important to Stefan as she not only understands him and gets him to quit brooding for one day a year but she's a powerful ally, physically stronger than Damon. It's hard to fathom how well you could get to know someone given more than a century (or how devastating it would be to watch that person die). Lexi's sympathetic ear also gives the writers an opportunity to have Stefan describe his feelings for Elena in a swoon-worthy scene.

Elena's asked him to stay away from her because of the hurt and death inextricably linked to the Salvatore brothers. She's decided the risk is too high for her and her family, but Elena still suffers from the break-up, and, for the

The Newton County Courthouse (pictured above) in Covington, GA, was completed in 1884, and in the square across from it is a monument honoring Confederate soldiers killed in the Civil War. The courthouse and square are the defining locations of Mystic Falls.

first time, we see her give up. She stays in bed and doesn't return phone calls — a refreshingly normal response to a break-up, a death, and a complete perspective shift on the supernatural. Just as Lexi brings some levity to Stefan, Bonnie helps Elena by showing her that the supernatural isn't only about darkness and death; it can also be awe-inspiring and beautiful. As much as Elena wants to talk to her friend, to be as open as Bonnie is being with her, her promise to keep Stefan's secret holds her back. And Bonnie will be glad to have Elena to talk to since her nightmare as the episode closes suggests that, in addition to vampires and witches, there are spirits in Mystic Falls.

"162 Candles" changes tone with Lexi's death, pushing Stefan over the edge. Out for his brother's blood, Stefan still listens to Elena's counsel and refrains from killing Damon (and rather just shows his brother that he could). Because of Elena, Stefan has stayed in Mystic Falls despite the danger to himself with the council knowing about vampires. Now he tells her, "You were right to stay away from me"; he seems set to leave town to protect her from Damon. But will Lexi's words to Elena hold true? If their love is real, will Stefan be able to walk away?

COMPELLING MOMENT: Bonnie and Elena encircled in white feathers.

CIRCLE OF KNOWLEDGE:

- No Tyler in this episode.
- Directed by John Hughes in 1984, *Sixteen Candles* is a quintessential '80s teen film and this episode's title is a nod to it. Molly Ringwald plays Samantha, a girl whose entire family forgets her 16th birthday since it happens to fall the day before her older sister Ginny is getting married. Sam is in love with Jake Ryan (Michael Schoeffling), a senior who's dating the prom queen and who doesn't even know she exists. Or so she thinks. A freshman geek, Farmer Ted (Anthony Michael Hall), is trying to win her affections with awkward attempt after awkward attempt. In the end, Jake finds Sam, and they celebrate her birthday in what became a classic scene — sitting on the dining room table, b-day cake between them, sharing their first kiss. Kevin Williamson loves John Hughes, and that director's influence is clear in *The Faculty* (which reinvents the *Breakfast Club* characters) and in *Dawson's Creek*. There's a season 2 episode where everyone forgets Pacey Witter's 16th birthday ("Crossroads").
- Stefan and Lexi's theme song is Bon Jovi's "Wanted Dead or Alive" from the 1986 album *Slippery When Wet*, a cowboy anthem about the itinerant lifestyle of an outlaw, equally applicable to vampires whose immortality forces them to never settle in one place for long.
- Compare Stefan's description of Katherine in "You're Undead to Me" to his description of Elena here. He focuses on Elena's admirable qualities, without mentioning her physical attributes, and, most importantly for Stefan, how real his feelings are for her. They are his own, not manipulated.
- It's unnerving to hear Elena's words about Vicki coming out of Jeremy's mouth when he's speaking to Sheriff Forbes. When Damon repeats to Elena that he "took away his suffering," it implies that he took away *all* of Jeremy's suffering.
- After the initial moment of misunderstanding, Elena and Lexi quickly become allies. It's an unusual and refreshing depiction of women getting along without jealousy or competition. Thank you, *TVD* writers!
- With a nearly passed-out Caroline in his arms, Matt flicks on her bedroom light with her foot. It's a humorous moment but it also subtly shows just how accustomed he is to putting drunks to bed, experience

gained taking care of his sister and (extrapolating from his comment to Stefan) his mother.

THE RULES: The older the vampire, the stronger she is. The Salvatore brothers' rings are nontransferable: Stefan's ring would not protect Lexi from the sun. Not surprisingly, the one quality all vampires seem to possess across the board holds true in *The Vampire Diaries* world: they're great in bed. Alcohol curbs the cravings for human blood. Lexi demonstrates another application of compulsion: tricking humans into giving you free stuff. A witch's talisman is a powerful tool, says Grams, and Bonnie's doesn't want to leave her.

THE DIABOLICAL PLAN: Damon cozies up to Sheriff Forbes by pretending to be Zach's go-between and learns who in Mystic Falls knows about vampires. Damon's "diabolical master plan" involves earning the trust of the council by solving their "vampire problem" and throwing them off the Salvatore trail. But killing Lexi was an opportunity seized, not Damon's ultimate reason for returning to Mystic Falls. His plot to get the crystal back from Bonnie by using Caroline fails. Bonnie's ancestor Emily seems to be using the crystal to communicate with Bonnie in her dreams, but what does "It's coming" mean? And why did Bonnie wake up in the old cemetery?

BITE MARKS: Lexi shoves Stefan to the ground (and gives him a good snarl). Damon bites the boy in the alley. Lexi throws off the deputies, Sheriff Forbes shoots her four times, and Damon stakes her. Stefan attacks Damon, and they fight. Stefan stakes Damon in the gut.

MEANWHILE IN FELL'S CHURCH: Just as Elena wrestles with not telling Bonnie about Stefan in "162 Candles" so does Elena in *The Struggle*: "She wanted nothing more than to tell Bonnie and Meredith everything. To tell them the whole terrifying story. . . . But she couldn't . . . it wasn't her secret to tell."

OFF CAMERA: When Lexi and Damon are lying on Stefan's bed, the tattoo on Ian Somerhalder's arm is visible. It reads *hic et nunc*, Latin for "here and now." John Gilbert (who definitely belongs on the show with that name) plays Damon's victim in the alley and is also a stunt double for Paul Wesley and a few of the other actors on *The Vampire Diaries*. Arielle Kebbel, who plays Lexi, had her first major TV role on *Gilmore Girls* as Lindsay; she has appeared in *American Pie Presents Band Camp*, *John Tucker Must Die*, *The Grudge 2*, *Forever Strong*, and *The Uninvited*; and she costars with Sean Faris (who shows up on TVD in "Unpleasantville") in *Brooklyn to Manhattan*.

FOGGY MOMENTS: In the pilot, Caroline reports to Bonnie all the details she's learned about Stefan, including that he's a Gemini. Either Stefan fibbed or Caroline doesn't know her astrological signs because, with an early November birthday, Stefan's a Scorpio. Really wish Caroline didn't say "Indian giver" — even with her disclaimer. It may be realistic to have a character use a racist expression but it's totally unnecessary in this case. There are plenty of other ways to show how desperate Caroline is.

MUSIC: Stefan and Lexi catch up to The Birthday Massacre's "Happy Birthday." Lexi comes out of the shower to "Thinking of You" by Pete Yorn. Caroline's party at the Grill kicks off with "Feel It in My Bones" (Tiësto featuring Tegan and Sara), and she tries to get the crystal back from Bonnie to "Escape Me" (Tiësto featuring CC Sheffield). Lexi and Stefan play pool, and Damon and Elena banter to "Tokyo" by Telekinesis. Lexi dazzles the bartender and gives Elena a pep talk to "Too Close" by Mike Sheridan and Mads Langer. Fauxliage's "All the World" plays as Elena approaches Stefan and Caroline stumbles over to Matt. Lexi tries to find out Damon's plan to The Black Box Revelation's "Love in Your Head." Matt puts Caroline to bed while "Yet" by Switchfoot plays.

> Damon: *Seriously, what game do you think you're playing?*
> Stefan: *That's a funny question, considering the fact that I've been asking you that for months. It's frustrating, isn't it?*

1.09 *History Repeating*

Original air date: November 12, 2009
Written by: Bryan M. Holdman and Brian Young

Directed by: Marcos Siega
Guest cast: Maria Howell (Mrs. Halpern)

Bonnie is haunted by the spirit of her ancestor Emily. Stefan tries a different tactic with Damon to learn why he wants Bonnie's crystal. A new history teacher arrives in Mystic Falls.

A séance opens up a channel of communication between the world of the living and the spirit world, and beyond the literal séance that the girls hold at Elena's house, "History Repeating" features lines of communication opening up between characters. Matt and Caroline changed their relationship with their cuddling-only sleepover, and with her guard up post-Damon, she misinterprets Matt's brevity as a brush-off. Once Matt decides to be more expressive, he comes over to tell her that he understands how lonely she feels because he feels that way, too; only then can the two of them build on their friendship. When a forced apology about the necklace evolves into a meaningful conversation, Caroline and Bonnie repair their friendship, which was damaged by secrets that were kept both voluntarily and involuntarily. Caroline promises to listen to Bonnie and understands that witchcraft is not to be made light of anymore. A friendship shared between three people is

Chris Johnson as Logan Fell

Originally from Massachusetts, Chris Johnson has been working as a professional actor in Los Angeles since 2002. His TV credits include *CSI, NCIS, JAG, Without a Trace*, and *South Beach* (on which he plays Vincent). His film credits include *xXx: State of the Union* (2005) and a bit part in Kevin Williamson's *Cursed* (2005). Chris describes Logan Fell as a guy who "wasn't a very good boy back in the day but [is] trying to make good now" and wants to rekindle romance with Jenna. Chris worried for his character's longevity because in horror movies the journalists "usually go down" but hoped Logan wouldn't be killed off right away. Chris got his wish when Logan came back from the dead and his character arc lasted five episodes instead of just the one he was originally hired for. He and his wife, actress Amy Laughlin, were expecting a child when Chris came to Atlanta to film *The Vampire Diaries* and he joked that if the show needed a baby vampire, he'd have a little actor for them in nine months' time.

always complicated: two of the three may share a slightly different bond than either does with the third and that's certainly true of Caroline, Bonnie, and Elena. As Caroline openly says, Bonnie is her first best friend, and the same holds for Elena.

In a surprising turn after Stefan nearly killed Damon at the end of the last episode, in this episode, Stefan decides to play nice with Damon, and Damon attempts to apologize to Stefan, vowing not to attack humans for a whole week. There is a complete lack of trust between the brothers, and they're both right to second-guess the other's true motivation. Damon wants to keep a low profile so the council thinks its vampire problem is solved, and Stefan wants to finally discover Damon's reason for returning to Mystic Falls. Even though they are both on guard and half faking it, the brothers revert back to their pre-vamp mode, and there is an easiness and playfulness between them as they drink, play darts, and toss the football around. (Vampire football? Way cooler than vampire baseball.) Stefan's plan works, even though Damon sees right through it: he tells Stefan his plot to get into the tomb, only to see it destroyed along with the crystal.

Love and revenge — that's why Damon came back. Not only is Katherine alive (though desiccated) but Damon's love for her was real; she never compelled him. She only compelled Stefan. Damon loves Katherine as much as Stefan does Elena. Just as Damon's final act as a human was to save her from the fire, now, his sole purpose is to free her from the tomb. The Salvatore brothers are two sides of the same coin — each brother's primary concern is the woman he loves. Stefan wants to leave Elena to protect her, but to do that, he'll have to isolate himself again and lose the meaningful connection he's found with her. In his breakdown at the end of the episode, Stefan throws his journal in frustration. He can't express himself through journaling anymore; he's accustomed to Elena being his confidant.

One of the major motivators for the current inhabitants of Mystic Falls — protecting loved ones — applies to its spirits as well. With the line of communication opened by the séance, Emily Bennett possesses Bonnie in order to save her and the rest of the town from the fury of 27 vampires released after nearly a century and a half of entombment. Though Damon's attack on Bonnie was no doubt traumatizing for her, that act opens up one last blocked channel of communication. Now that Bonnie's seen vampires and has been both fed on and has fed, Elena finally gets to open up to her best friend, after feeling trapped by secrets and lies since "You're Undead to Me." It's a cathartic moment for Elena, when she can share what has happened, how her world has changed, and the violence she's seen.

COMPELLING MOMENT: The brothers mimicking each other.

CIRCLE OF KNOWLEDGE:
- Again, no Tyler in this episode.
- Damon says he'll try the Stefan diet for a week but won't eat anything with feathers, a reference to the last time he was forced to drink the blood of an animal: his crow in "You're Undead to Me."
- Emily says "incendia" and the pentacle she's drawn in the dirt lights on fire. Incendia comes from Latin verb *incendere* meaning "set fire to"; in the Harry Potter series, "incendio" is the spell that sets things aflame.
- There was a distinctly *New Moon* vibe to the scene where Stefan walks away into the woods, leaving Elena to call after him. (Of course, Elena doesn't then fall into a four-month brokenhearted coma because her boyfriend is leaving.)
- Is Alaric a vampire? There was a very deliberate pause at the threshold of the Gilbert house and he wears a Salvatore-esque ring. But he's shown eating human food twice. Puzzling.

THE RULES: Emily takes possession of Bonnie through the séance. Celestial events can be used to power spells. In "Lost Girls," we're told Damon's blood healed Vicki, but it's shown onscreen in this episode when Stefan's blood heals Bonnie's neck wound.

THE DIABOLICAL PLAN: Damon's plan is finally revealed and it's been in the works for 145 years: he made a deal with Emily to protect the Bennetts in exchange for Katherine's safety. Damon protected Emily's children and has kept his word since then (not hurting Bonnie) until Emily breaks the deal. He wants to release the entombed vampires, get revenge on Mystic Falls, and be reunited with Katherine. Since Emily gave the crystal to Katherine before her capture, Emily must have had some inkling that Katherine would need to be saved before that last night.

HISTORY LESSON: Jenna says the original Gilberts came to America on the Mayflower, a ship that carried English Separatists (called Pilgrims) from Plymouth, England, to Plymouth, Massachusetts in 1620. The journal of Johnathan Gilbert begins with an entry dated — well, what do you know — June 1864. Our favorite year was a time when the town of Mystic Falls was filled with fear and hysteria, that is, before the vampires were rounded up. Alaric (c.370–410), a fearsome Visigoth whose name means "king of all," was a (perhaps the) catalyst for the decline of the Roman imperial power.

BITE MARKS: On a diet of animal-blood only, Damon feels more pain than usual when Stefan tackles him on the football field. In Bonnie's body, Emily throws Damon into a tree, where he's impaled by its branches. Damon attacks Bonnie in anger, nearly killing her. Stefan bites his own wrist to feed Bonnie his blood.

MEANWHILE IN FELL'S CHURCH: The math teacher in Bonnie's dream is named Mrs. Halpern, after the math teacher in *The Awakening*. Alaric Saltzman, the cool, handsome teacher with a boyish smile who replaces the deceased bully Mr. Tanner, arrives in *The Struggle*. Stefan's school attendance is pretty spotty both on the show and in the novels. The ruined church is an important setting in the novels, and in "History Repeating" Bonnie calls it Fell's Church, the name of the town in the book series, which in turn got its name from the Fells, the founding family. Under the ruined church in the novels is a tomb belonging to Honoria and Thomas Fell. In *The Struggle*, Elena doesn't want to leave Bonnie by herself so she suggests a sleepover.

In this episode, as in the pilot, Caroline expresses a passing interest in dating Stefan, which was a serious bone of contention between the girls in *The Awakening*. In *Dark Reunion*, Caroline, Bonnie, Meredith, Vickie, and Sue Carson hold a séance to try to contact a spirit that seems to be reaching out to Bonnie through her dreams. In *The Awakening*, *The Struggle*, and *The Fury*, Bonnie is possessed on different occasions by the spirit of a good witch who used to live in Fell's Church — usually as she stares into a candle (as Bonnie does during the séance in "History Repeating"). In *The Fury*, it's revealed that Katherine worked with her maid, Gudren, to escape the death the brothers think she suffered; here she's helped by her maid Emily.

OFF CAMERA: As much fun as it was for the audience to see Stefan and Damon imitate each other, the actors had just as much fun filming those scenes. "That was fantastic! We had a blast," said Paul Wesley. "We spend 24 hours a day together, so I didn't have to look at him anymore: I knew exactly what he did. I knew exactly how to make fun of him. I get all his little quirks. We had so much fun that day. Everybody was laughing. It was one of the days on set where the crew was like, 'Oh my god, Ian and Paul are not taking themselves so seriously.' I'm usually like, 'I need another take.' I'm always about it being good and perfect, to the point of detriment, and that day we just wanted to have fun."

FOGGY MOMENTS: What did Emily mean at the end of the previous episode when she said, "It's coming"? Was that just a creepy cliffhanger or is there an "it" still to come?

MUSIC: Caroline and Elena arrive at school to Echo & The Bunnymen's "Think I Need It Too." Pablo Sebastian's "Lies" plays as Bonnie and Elena talk about Damon in the car. Jenna and Jeremy have dinner at the Grill to Idlewild's "Post-electric." When Jenna's introduced to Alaric, "The Spectator" by The Bravery is on. Jenna and Alaric get to know each other at the bar and the Salvatore brothers play darts with Great Northern's "Houses" in the background. The closing montage that begins with Jenna destroying the photo is to Barcelona's "Come Back When You Can."

> *Elena: You don't get to make that decision for me. If you walk away, it's for you. Because I know what I want. Stefan, I love you.*

1.10 *The Turning Point*

Original air date: November 19, 2009
Written by: Kevin Williamson and Julie Plec (teleplay); Barbie Kligman (story)
Directed by: J. Miller Tobin
Guest cast: Melissa Ponzio (Daphne the Jogger)

Logan Fell's return to Mystic Falls delays the Salvatore brothers' departure. Elena and Stefan's relationship takes a major step forward and then one huge, shattering leap backward.

In the season 1 finale of *Dawson's Creek*, Dawson and Joey have one of their usual meta-commentary chats about cliffhangers. Joey says, "a cliffhanger is merely a manipulative TV standard designed to improve ratings" to which Dawson argues that it works from a narrative standpoint to keep audiences interested. Not if it's a fake-out or a tease, Joey counters; a cliffhanger is only interesting if the plot or characters actually change in its aftermath. For the fall finale of the *The Vampire Diaries*, the writers throw a cliffhanger at the audience bigger than any in the season so far and one that promises to have lasting effects on the characters. Elena knows she looks like Katherine. And she's trapped in a crashed car as the man she hit stands back up.

Rewinding to the beginning of "The Turning Point," the episode gives us another look at the supporting characters' families, who haven't been a focus since "Family Ties." It's notable how absent the parents are in Mystic Falls. The Gilbert children are orphans living with their Aunt Jenna who is more of a friend than a mother figure, Bonnie's parents are divorced and as yet unseen, and Matt's mom is off with her boyfriend. Caroline's father hasn't made an appearance in Mystic Falls yet, and while Sheriff Forbes clearly loves Caroline, her scoffing reply to her daughter's interest in broadcast journalism shows where Caroline got her ability to be dismissive. Tyler seems to have the worst of it: it may be better to not know your father at all (like Matt) than to have an aggressive, self-important jerk like Mayor Lockwood as a role model. Alaric steps in as a sort of protective father figure

Marguerite MacIntyre as Sheriff Forbes

Marguerite MacIntyre began her career on the stage and lived in New York working on Broadway and off. "It's the most fun you'll ever have," said Marguerite, "but at some point you want to buy a house, so I started getting TV work to augment it." To do that more easily, she relocated to L.A. Her TV credits include *Seinfeld, Two Guys, a Girl, and a Pizza Place, The Shield, The Days,* and *Bones.* Marguerite had worked with Julie Plec before *The Vampire Diaries* on ABC Family's *Kyle XY,* playing Nicole Trager. As mom to Josh and Lori, and psychologist and stand-in mother to Kyle, Nicole was a much-loved character, and Marguerite was surprised by how quickly the fans and critics responded to the show. During *Kyle XY*'s second season in 2008, the actress said: "It was very sweet and it was nice to see people respond to what you're trying to do and [at the Television Critics Association Awards] I realized it was a very special thing. It took me a while to understand but I finally got it." After *Kyle XY* was canceled, Marguerite didn't have to wait long before she had another recurring role on a TV series, landing the part of Caroline's mom and the town's sheriff, Elizabeth Forbes.

to Jeremy, and he later proves to be quite capable of handling himself in a fight in a parking lot, should it come to that. His kindness to Jeremy and flirtation with Jenna make Alaric an easily likeable character, but one who clearly knows what's hiding in the shadows of Mystic Falls. Not that *The Vampire Diaries* was short on handsome and troubled men, but Matt Davis's Alaric is an appreciated addition.

Logan Fell returns as a vampire with abandonment issues; he feels discarded by Liz and the Founder's Council as well as by the vampire, whoever it was, who turned him but left him alone to figure out the mechanics of his new life. Logan's not the only one with abandonment issues. Elena wants Stefan gone if he's going to go, and career night at the high school brings up questions about the future that have no easy answers. How can she plan long-term with a vampire? For Stefan, the wandering lifestyle of a vampire isn't easy. He can never commit to a place or a course of study or a career because he doesn't age like the people around him. His one constant is his room at the Salvatore boardinghouse but in "The Turning Point" he embraces the more meaningful connection he's made with Elena. Stefan opens himself up to her in an intimate way when he decides to stay in Mystic Falls, lets Elena see his vampire face, and invites her into the sanctuary of his bedroom, a very personal place for him.

The Vampire Diaries is an intensely romantic show, and Elena and Stefan's first time does not disappoint. It begins with her explanation to him that there already was death and sorrow and immeasurable loss in her life, that he isn't responsible for it, and her speech culminates in a moment the audience has been waiting for: she tells him she loves him. Elena makes sure Stefan understands that it's *his* fears that are driving him to leave. She realized in "The Night of the Comet" that she had to "fight the fear," and she helps Stefan do just that. As his face turns vampy as they kiss, she doesn't let him hide it. He's more scared in that moment than she is. Set to a song about finding connection and letting go of fear, the scene is appropriately epic for a romance that's been building in intensity all season.

The problem with spontaneous sex, as Stefan realizes, is there's no opportunity to hide the incriminating portrait of the ex. Just as they both come to accept the new intensity of their relationship, Elena sees the photograph of Katherine, the secret Stefan has kept from her. She takes off her vervain necklace in a symbolic act; Elena feels betrayed and no longer wants the token of his affection, or his protection. But judging by the way that contorted man in the road straightened himself out and came toward her, she could use a friendly vampire's assistance.

COMPELLING MOMENT: Alaric the Vampire Slayer!

CIRCLE OF KNOWLEDGE:
- Matt and Caroline hang out together eating junk food, watching *So You Think You Can Dance*, and cuddling? Best relationship ever.
- Jenna and Jeremy call Johnathan Gilbert a lunatic and a drunk, discounting his writings about the supernatural. This makes him the third character, after Vicki and Grams, to be dismissed as unreliable when he's actually correct.
- Logan Fell as a vampire on the loose in Mystic Falls without a mentor played out like a frenzied serial killer from a Kevin Williamson movie. Truly frightening.
- There's a poster for a school production of *Hamlet* in the background when Elena offers to give Stefan a ride home. If Stefan stays in Mystic Falls, he should totally audition for the lead; he could play the brooding Dane in his sleep.

- That was a lingering shot of the full moon after Tyler is baffled by his own violent outburst at Jeremy.

THE RULES: Every sense and feeling is magnified in the transition from human to vampire, which is why Logan finds himself overly emotional. It seems to be an unwritten rule that a maker must train his new vampire convert in how to control the hunger for blood. Stefan explains to Elena that he can only stay in one place for a few years, then he must leave before arousing suspicion because he hasn't aged.

THE DIABOLICAL PLAN: With the crystal destroyed, Damon was briefly without a plan, except to continue harassing his little brother for all eternity (and/or appear with Stefan on *The Amazing Race*). Now he knows someone else wants to get into the tomb. Who turned Logan? Who is in the road?

HISTORY LESSON: The Founders recorded the details of vampirism in the journals and passed them down through the generations, preserving the secret history of Mystic Falls and protecting their descendents.

BITE MARKS: Logan shoots Damon seven times. Tyler and Jeremy fight in the hall and later, outside, Mayor Lockwood shoves Tyler. Logan smashes Caroline's head into the car window. Damon shoots Logan four times. At Damon's suggestion, Logan hits him before "escaping." Tyler sucker-punches Jeremy. Alaric stakes Logan, killing him. Elena is involved in a car wreck, hitting a man in the road who stands back up. . . .

MEANWHILE IN FELL'S CHURCH: Stefan suggests to Elena in *The Struggle* that they should break up to make it easier on her; she says she will only break up with him if he doesn't love her, and his response is a passionate kiss. The difficulty of protecting people outside the "circle of knowledge" is shown when Elena urges Jenna to never let Logan in the house just as, in *The Struggle*, Elena tries to make it clear to Bonnie and Meredith how imperative it is that they never invite Damon in.

OFF CAMERA: The exterior and some of the interiors of the Salvatore boardinghouse are filmed at Glenridge Hall in Sandy Springs, Georgia, a Tudor-style private estate built in 1929 with a mile-long driveway. It's used as a filming location fairly often, in TV shows, commercials, and films like *Driving Miss Daisy* and *Remember the Titans*.

FOGGY MOMENTS: Wouldn't Damon have smelled the pile of bodies in the warehouse before Logan pointed them out? How did Elena leave the Salvatore house without Stefan noticing? Did his superior vamp hearing deactivate because he was blissfully post-coital?

MUSIC: Jeremy reads the Gilbert journal and takes out his sketchbook to Five for Fighting's "Chances." Tyler and Matt play basketball to "Coast of Carolina" by Telekinesis. Career night begins with The Features' "Off Track." Stefan kisses Elena, and they finally sleep together to "Cut" by Plumb. Matt confronts Tyler about his "bromance bitch act" to Tyrone Wells' "This Is Beautiful."

> *Elena: What am I to you? Who am I to you?*
> *Stefan: You are not Katherine. You are the opposite of everything that she was.*
> *Elena: And when did you figure that out?*

1.11 *Bloodlines*

Original air date: January 21, 2010
Written by: Kevin Williamson and Julie Plec (teleplay); Sean Reycraft (story)
Directed by: David Barrett
Guest cast: Gina Torres (Bree), Brandon Quinn (Lee), Nancy Montgomery (Juanita)

Damon saves Elena from the car wreck, and she returns the favor after he brings her to Georgia to catch up with an old acquaintance. Stefan helps Bonnie as she tries to get her powers back. Jeremy meets a pushy but charming homeschooled girl at the library.

The winter premiere episode after a nine-week break, "Bloodlines" takes the action out of Mystic Falls for the first time as Damon goes on a road trip and brings Elena with him. When Damon asks her to just press pause on

"Matt has fit in so well with the cast. He came aboard and just settled right in. He's hysterical. We are just always laughing, whenever we're working together. He's great. He's a lot of fun. We're just so goofy." — Sara Canning on Matt Davis

her life for five minutes (which turns out to be more like 24 hours), he gives Elena an excuse to not deal with the question of why she looks so much like Katherine — well, not yet, anyway.

Before Elena gets back in the car with Damon, she asks him if she can trust him, and in large part this is an episode about trust — building it, breaking it, and regaining it. Stefan continues the cross-generational relationship between the Salvatores and the Bennetts by building trust with both Bonnie and Sheila. With Bonnie, Stefan is supportive and encouraging as she tries her locator spell, and he is reassuring after he gets her out of the tomb. In a variation on the trust game where one person falls backward into the other's arms, Bonnie closes her eyes and trusts Stefan to use his vampire skills to leap them out of the tomb to safety. With Sheila, Stefan extends his hand as a show of trust, allowing her to read him, and he also brings her granddaughter home safely. In return, Sheila extends trust to Stefan but with reservations; she will "protect [her] own before anybody else," knowing that if a lynch mob comes for the vampires, the witches aren't safe either.

With no trust in his brother, Stefan fears that Damon is holding Elena against her will, since she is without the protection of her vervain necklace. Since this risk is also on her mind, Elena asks Damon to promise not to compel her — and he sticks to his word. The bond between Elena and Damon grows as he shows uncharacteristic concern for her well-being: at the scene of the car accident with his impossibly cute "upsy-daisy" line; at the roadside when he zips to her side of the car; after her call with Stefan when he asks her if she's okay; and outside the bar when he tracks her after she disappears (and thereby falls into Lee's trap). Both Bree and Lee assume that Elena is Damon's girlfriend, and she plays along since it's easier than explaining the truth — and it's a choice that comes in handy. When Lee threatens to kill Damon, she advocates for him as if she loved him, as if he were her Lexi. Elena again proves herself to be good in a crisis, and she is justifiably proud of herself for saving Damon's life with words alone.

In avoiding her trust issue with Stefan, Elena manages to upset her relationship with Jenna, worrying her aunt by not calling and then fibbing to her when she does. But, luckily for Elena, Jenna has kept the secret of Elena's adoption from her, thanks to a promise Jenna made to her sister and brother-in-law. But Elena's main focus is what she perceives as Stefan's betrayal of her trust. Damon tells Elena that it's "kinda creepy" that Stefan is dating her when she's Katherine's doppelgänger, and frankly, it has been an uncomfortable undercurrent in an otherwise sweet courtship. What were Stefan's initial intentions when they met? How much of their relationship has been a lie? Elena's questions in the hours after seeing Katherine's photograph are answered in a completely unexpected way that reveals Stefan to be an even more heroic character. Stefan and Elena were only separated for a day, but the fast pace of *The Vampire Diaries* provides resolution within the hour. "Bloodlines" ends with Stefan and Elena back together, closer than before, as Stefan tells her he loves her.

From Elena letting loose during her time-out with Damon to her discovering the truth about Stefan and about her own parentage, Nina Dobrev delivers another nuanced performance. This episode is not just about plot twists and entertaining character pairings but about *The Vampire Diaries'* core concerns of love and loss. Elena learns in the same moment that her father died making sure she lived and that he's not her birth father; it's clear that bloodlines are not the only ties that bind people together. Since Elena's not born of a Gilbert and a Sommers, her bloodline likely leads back to Katherine, partially explaining for the resemblance.

Alaric's flashback scenes bookend the episode and move us from the sweet-as-pie morning scene to the events of that night when he comes home late to find Damon with his teeth in his wife's neck. Damon's preference for female victims has left a string of brokenhearted widowers in his wake. Lee sought revenge on Damon for killing Lexi; now Alaric has found the vampire who killed his wife. (Will Coach Tanner's girlfriend show up at some point?) Damon doesn't know it but he has a new enemy sitting right down the bar from him. Elena also has a false sense of security with Damon. Even though his actions in "Bloodlines" indicate that Elena is safe with him and will be protected by him, Damon remains determined to open the tomb, and he proves he can still cavalierly murder anyone, no matter how close he once was to them. Imagine being in the car with him, not knowing that the hands on the steering wheel had just been washed clean of his ex-girlfriend's blood.

COMPELLING MOMENT: Driving home from Atlanta, Damon tells Elena that she's not the worst company in the world.

CIRCLE OF KNOWLEDGE:
- No Caroline, Matt, or Tyler.
- Alaric stakes Logan, eats food, and is shown not wearing his ring in the daylight. It's pretty clear that the new history teacher is *not* a vampire despite his misleading tendency to linger at a threshold. (Plus he took his ring off at the gym, and vampires don't have to work out.)
- Jeremy tells Anna he's watched *The Lost Boys* (see page 90) and *Near Dark* "like 50 times." A cult classic, *Near Dark* (1987), directed and cowritten by Kathryn Bigelow (who won the Oscar for directing *The Hurt Locker* in 2010), stars Adrian Pasdar as Caleb, a young guy from a small town in Oklahoma who flirts with a cute stranger, Mae (Jenny Wright). She bites him and turns him into a vampire, and he must prove himself worthy of joining the gang she lives with by making his first kill. But Caleb doesn't lose his sense of morality along with his mortality and so he has a hard time stomaching the brutality. He chooses his human family over Mae, and in the end is able to save her and himself *and* destroy the vengeful vampire gang.
- Damon likes pickles. Elena doesn't.
- This is not the first time Elena has saved Damon's life. Stefan chose not to kill Damon at the end of "162 Candles" because Elena convinced him

In Love with a Monster: Team Damon

If Damon existed in the real world, even those on Team Damon would be horrified by him. He's boastful, self-important, treats women as if they are disposable and interchangeable, and — here's the biggie — kills people . . . sometimes just for his own amusement. Like, lots and lots of people over decades and decades. So why is there a Team Damon? Why is his character just as popular a romantic choice for Elena as is Stefan? On a smaller (and mortal) scale, the lushy womanizing Chuck Bass on *Gossip Girl* presents the same quandary: in the very first episode of that show, he sexually assaulted 14-year-old Jenny Humphrey; by episode seven, fans were cheering as Blair Waldorf chose him to lose her virginity to. Why are men who would be morally repulsive in real life acceptable and even alluring when they are characters on CW shows?

For starters, these guys *aren't* real people. Fiction allows us to explore vicariously all the terrible, nasty, and sometimes evil behavior that we know is wrong. Because characters like Damon Salvatore don't obey the rules the rest of do, they tend to be more fun — they say what they want, they take what they want, and they do it with a smirk. Damon Salvatore is handsome, powerful, free of responsibility, sexual, funny, and fearless. With no worries about repercussions or consequences (he can just make people forget whatever he wants them to), he's incredibly confident and self-assured.

But what makes Damon (and Chuck Bass) romantically interesting, as opposed to being simply an entertaining villain, is the idea of some counterpart or soulmate who is capable of changing this already attractive person into someone who is nearly perfect, leading him to discover the heart and goodness that's lurking beneath the surface. The specter of rehabilitation arose in Jeremy and Vicki's relationship: Vicki was the attainable bad girl. Shortly after she chose Jeremy over Tyler, she said she hoped Jeremy wouldn't try to change everything about her. She was still going to use drugs and party, case closed. And for 145 years, Stefan has been trying, on and off, to "fix" his brother, with no luck. But in the short time that Damon's known Elena, there is already a change in him, the most significant glimpse of which came in "Bloodlines." If his goal is to provide his brother with "an eternity of misery," the best way of achieving that is to harm Elena — and let's face it, he's harmed countless others. But when she is absolutely defenseless, without vervain and woozy from the accident, he's nothing but gentle and careful with her. The idea of Damon fundamentally changing who he is, striving to be a better person, to be worthy of her affection, is a profoundly romantic idea and one that seems to at work in the Damon-Elena relationship. But why Elena and not Caroline or any one of the other women who came before her? Initially his fascination with Elena was likely the same as Stefan's: she looks like Katherine. But Elena sees the human beneath Damon's vampy exterior and doesn't let him get away with anything: she slaps him for trying to kiss her in "Friday Night Bites" and again in "Haunted" when she insists that human life not only matters but matters to him. Her righteousness gets through to him because in Elena it's paired with empathy. In Elena's presence, Damon may feel judged but he also feels understood. A compelling combination for Damon and for the Damon-Elena shippers.

not to, and he tells her Damon has her to thank for his life in "History Repeating." The heart of her argument to Stefan is the same as hers to Lee: be a better vampire than Damon is.

- Stefan must have told Lee that Damon killed Lexi.
- "Damon doesn't get mad, he gets even," says Stefan in "Lost Girls." And Damon proves that true by killing Bree.

THE RULES: A witch's powers can be disabled by a mental block, like fear. A vampire's body functions almost identically to a living human's as long as he drinks blood. (A description that is somewhat contradictory to the moment in the pilot episode where Damon's victim couldn't find his pulse and assumed he was dead.) Vampires cannot procreate (but they "love to try," says Damon). Grams could sense Stefan was a vampire by touching him (just as Bonnie could in "The Night of the Comet," but she didn't know how to interpret the feeling). One spell cannot override another, but a spell can be undone by finding its reversal spell in a witch's grimoire, or spell book.

THE DIABOLICAL PLAN: Damon's idea to consult with Bree to find another way into the tomb works: she tells him to get Emily's grimoire and reverse her spell. Bonnie unintentionally gets into the outer chamber of the tomb and can hear the vampires murmuring behind the door, which is sealed with a pentacle. What made the ground give way beneath Bonnie — gravity or a mystical force?

HISTORY LESSON: According to Anna's research, there are a handful of deaths in Mystic Falls, about every 10 years, which are usually reported as animal attacks but are actually the work of vampires.

BITE MARKS: Elena escapes the car accident relatively unscathed, feeling dizzy, headachy, and with cuts on her head and hands. Bonnie also gets battered in her fall into the tomb. Lee beats the heck out of Damon. No comparison to Bree's injuries: Damon crushes her heart, killing her.

MEANWHILE IN FELL'S CHURCH: In *The Struggle*, Elena asks Bonnie to do a locator spell to find Stefan; in this episode, Stefan asks Bonnie to find Elena. Like Damon's concern for Elena in "Bloodlines," in *The Fury*, Elena is left in Damon's care in the hours after her car accident and he treats her with tenderness: "he'd kept her safe. And he hadn't kissed her while she'd been in

This private residence in Covington is used for exterior scenes of Grams Bennett's home like Stefan's conversations with Sheila in "Bloodlines."

that horrifyingly vulnerable state. He'd been . . . kind to her." In *The Struggle*, Elena is in a car that goes off Wickery Bridge and Stefan goes into the water after her in an attempt to save her. That incident was reimagined as a shocking backstory for Stefan.

OFF CAMERA: Damon tells Elena he's taking her just outside Atlanta, which is where they were actually filming. The scenes at Bree's Bar were filmed at the Depot Bar and Grill (4122 Emory Street NW) in Covington, Georgia. On Malese Jow's first day as Anna on set opposite Steven R. McQueen, they filmed the library scenes. "Steven had some really, really big words to say," recalls Malese. "He had to say the words 'allegorical' and 'folklore' and stuff and he just could not spit them out. I had a heyday with that. I would make fun of him, and he would make fun of himself — it was a hilarious day on set." New York born Gina Torres guest stars as Bree. A regular feature on sci-fi and supernatural shows, Gina has appeared in *Alias*,

Angel, Firefly (and the movie *Serenity*), *Hercules, 24, Justice League, Gossip Girl,* and *FlashForward*.

FOGGY MOMENTS: The articles Anna pulled are from the *Mystic Falls Courier*, and yet in the pilot we saw Zach reading the *Mystic Falls Daily*. When Bonnie first spoke about Grams in the pilot and in "The Night of the Comet," she was described as boozy but there hasn't been a whiff of that since.

MUSIC: The flashback to Alaric with his wife is to Florence + the Machine's "Cosmic Love." Elena wakes up in Damon's car to Editors' "An End Has a Start." Dandelions' "On a Mission" is on in the car as Damon and Elena talk about her accident. Black Mustang's "Between the Devil and the Deep Blue Sea" is on at Bree's Bar when Damon and Elena walk in. "Can't Stop These Tears (From Falling)" by The Black Hollies plays as Bree relates how she knows Damon. Bree tells Damon there's no other way into the tomb to Hope Sandoval's "Trouble." Elena finally takes Stefan's call and Damon listens in while The Steps' "Push" is on in the background. Damon and Elena eat burgers and fries to "Pepper Spray" by The Upsidedown. The Stereotypes' "The Night Before" is on when Elena shows off her drinking-game skills. Anna and Jeremy play foosball to The Dig's "Look Inside." Bree has her heart crushed to Alex Band's "Only One." Julian Casablancas' "Out of the Blue" is on as Damon and Elena return to Mystic Falls. Alaric grades some papers at the Grill to "Nothing Is Logical" by The Bell.

> *Elena: It's not like I can kill him.*
> *Bonnie: There's a thought.*
> *Caroline: I'll help.*

1.12 *Unpleasantville*

Original air date: January 28, 2010
Written by: Barbie Kligman and Brian Young
Directed by: Liz Friedlander
Guest cast: Joey Nappo (Kid in Hoodie)

It's Mystic Falls High's 1950s Decade Dance and a few uninvited vampires make an appearance. Without even bothering to wear costumes. The race to open the tomb is on.

A decidedly fun episode, where "Bloodlines" took the action out of Mystic Falls, "Unpleasantville" takes the show away from its usual look, exchanging dark for bright with the explosion of color at the Decade Dance and an era-appropriate soundtrack to match. Each episode of *The Vampire Diaries* feels fresh because of changes like this; the format is about as far from "monster of the week" as a show can get. "Unpleasantville" pulls together the various A and B storylines that have been building and knits them into promising new plot twists.

A large part of the episode's energy comes from Stefan and Damon working together against a common enemy instead of battling each other. From the planning stage at Elena's house to the stake-toss in the cafeteria, the brothers present a united force. And there's time for dancing in between — Damon grinds with some random girl ("You really can't take him anywhere," says Elena) and Stefan gives in to Elena's request and shows off some sweet moves before he plants a kiss on her. Elena continues to display her bravery; her first instinct is to protect her family from the vampire who can come into the house whenever he wants. When Noah threatens Jeremy at the dance, she puts her own life in jeopardy to protect her brother's without a second thought. She owns her choice to be with Stefan, not allowing him to feel responsible for the danger she's in. (And anyway, if Noah was after her because she looked like Katherine, he would have stalked her regardless of her involvement with Stefan.) Elena feels exhilarated after the battle in the cafeteria, not scared or upset; she faced a murderous vampire and survived; she's stronger than she knew.

Not everything was as it seemed in the '50s, as Stefan tells Elena; behind the seeming innocence of the decade lay violence and injustice. In present day Mystic Falls, the same holds true: the strange homeschooled girl, Anna, turns out to be a vampire who is after the Gilbert journal; the bartender Ben is her vampire boyfriend; Alaric fakes compulsion to throw off Damon's apt suspicion; and the deal between the brothers is a lie. There's an unavoidable risk in relationships, there's no way to be certain the person you trust and open yourself up to is worthy of it. Matt and Caroline take their first relationship misstep as she unintentionally insults him (which really is her special talent) nailing the one thing he feels most self-conscious about. For all intents and purposes an orphan, Matt's story is a sad one, but he doesn't feel sorry for himself. He's just afraid of losing the only good thing in his life — Caroline. Matt and Caroline acknowledge the unresolved feelings he has for Elena, the same way Alaric and Jenna get in some great flirting without ignoring his painful memories and unresolved issues about the death of his wife . . . Isobel.

Is Elena's birth mother Alaric's dead wife who was killed by Damon!? These plot twists add a lot of the excitement to the series with storylines impossible to predict even two episodes earlier — but answers always follow close behind. Already a great character thanks to his interactions with Jenna and Jeremy, Alaric is "real boss" and gets more interesting with each scene. Jeremy is "becoming himself again" and that's at least in part a result of the encouragement Alaric gives him. Jeremy's personality change in the wake of his mind-wipe has been dramatic but, knowing its origin, difficult to cheer for, especially as he now finds himself not far from where Elena was in the early episodes of this season. He is unknowingly hanging out with a vampire and sees her face get all veiny. Combine that with all the research into Mystic Falls' mysterious animal attacks. How long will it take Jeremy to figure out what Elena discovered in "You're Undead to Me"? If he's like his sister, he'll want the truth, good or bad.

COMPELLING MOMENT: One of the most romantic scenes on the show so far: Matt and Caroline kissing in the street.

CIRCLE OF KNOWLEDGE:
- No Tyler this episode.
- This episode's title is a play on the 1998 film *Pleasantville*. Directed, produced, and written by Gary Ross, the story follows teenage twins, the socially awkward David (Tobey Maguire) and the popular Jennifer (Reese Witherspoon), who are transported from the '90s into a black-and-white 1950s sitcom called *Pleasantville*, which David watches avidly. David and Jennifer pretend to be Bud and Mary Sue Parker and literally bring color to this "perfect" town as they expose its residents to crazy ideas like personal freedom and creative expression. *Pleasantville* shows that fixed concepts of identity can lead to various forms of oppression. In "Unpleasantville," traditional roles are also turned on their head: Bonnie takes action instead of waiting for Ben to make the first move, Caroline

confronts Matt, Elena rejects the role of damsel in distress and fights back to protect her family, the usually honest Stefan deceives his brother, and Anna and Ben turn out to be the opposite of what they're perceived to be.

- Noah's taunting and threatening phone calls to Elena were a not-so-subtle nod to the *Scream* franchise and the first movie's iconic opening scene where Drew Barrymore's character receives a terrorizing phone call. Back in the first season of *Dawson's Creek*, Kevin Williamson paid homage to his own film in "The Scare" when Jen Lindley gets scary phone calls, which directly reference *Scream* (1996).
- The fight scene between Elena and Noah was very *Buffy the Vampire Slayer* with a race down the school hallway, after hours, to find a locked exit and handy wooden objects that Elena could use as stakes. Like Buffy, Elena is exhilarated by the fight and proud of herself for being clever while under threat.

THE RULES: Bonnie makes it explicit: fire kills vampires. Vampires can't sense each other's presence. Alaric demonstrates a handy trick for humans: keep vervain on you and if a vamp tries to control your mind, fake compulsion.

THE DIABOLICAL PLAN: As Stefan calls it, Damon's "diabolical plan — the sequel" is to find Emily's grimoire, reverse her spell, and open the tomb. His efforts to befriend Bonnie are self-serving because he'll absolutely need

Matt Davis as Alaric Saltzman

Born May 8, 1978, in Salt Lake City, Utah, Matthew Davis didn't consider a career as an actor until college. At the University of Utah, Matt took some theater classes and found his calling. He says his parents were "completely supportive of me. When they knew I was serious about this, they were behind me all the way." After he moved to New York City, he started working in theater before transitioning into film with roles in *Tigerland, Urban Legends: Final Cut,* and *Pearl Harbor.* In 2001, Matt landed the part that he's still most often recognized for: "No one really knows who the hell I am — everyone thinks I went to college with them, and then they slowly dial it in and realize, 'Hey, you're that a-hole boyfriend from *Legally Blonde.*'" A string of film roles followed for him, including one in *Blue Crush*; he played a football player and love interest to Kate Bosworth's character. "I did feel the pressure I've always heard actresses talk about," recalled Matt, "in playing a supporting role as the love interest. You have to be focused on your diet and staying in shape and looking good at all times. I really came to understand those elements. It's not easy."

Cast as Adam in *What About Brian* in 2006, Matt made the transition from film work to television: "It's a great role. I'm excited about all of this. [Television] is a new thing for me, but so far I'm loving it." The show lasted two seasons, and following that, Matt appeared in *Law & Order: SVU, Limelight, Finding Bliss, In Plain Sight,* and *S. Darko.* He was back with a recurring role on a TV series in 2009, playing Josh Reston in a five-episode arc on *Damages.*

Matt came to *The Vampire Diaries* midway through the season as a guest star but the episode "Fool Me Once" made him one of the cast. He had no trouble fitting in with the actors who'd been on the show from the start. "Everyone was so cool and welcoming," said Matt. "It's such a solid group of very lovely people. They are all super professional and everyone shows up ready to work and does the best that they can. When we have time to go together to a movie, we do that. We have a very strong bond." Matt hasn't read the novels to get background on his character; he believes the key to Alaric is in the backstory specific to the show: how Isobel's death has shaped him. "His whole life changed when she vanished," he says, "and he's been searching for her ever since." With any character being susceptible to a deadly bite or wooden stake, Matt says being an actor on *The Vampire Diaries* "is like *Survivor* — you keep delivering and hope they'll still write for you."

Matt's fans can get to know his irreverent personality by following his "Ernesto Riley" Twitter account. The name was a random invention of his, and his tweets are sometimes just as random (on aliens, philosophy, Justin Bieber ...). But he's just trying to liven the place up: "the current conversation on Twitter is boring so I thought I'd make it interesting." Mission accomplished.

a witch to do the magic — as will Team Anna, which explains Ben's interest in Bonnie. Before anyone reverses the spell, they need the Gilbert journal for clues to find the grimoire. Stefan may ultimately want Damon out of Mystic

Falls but he won't let him open the tomb and let Katherine (or the other 26 vampires) out. He deceives his brother and brings Elena in on it.

HISTORY LESSON: In a break from American Civil War history, the notes on the blackboard in Alaric's classroom cover three *other* bloody conflicts. The Congo Civil War, also known as the Second Congo War, began in 1998 and lasted until 2003 (the date on the board) and it was the world's deadliest conflict since World War II. The Easter Uprising of 1916 started the Anglo-Irish War, or Irish War of Independence, which ended in a truce in 1921. Finally, Greek forces occupied İzmir, Turkey (also known as the Occupation of Smyrna) from 1919 to 1922. Elena asks Stefan what the 1950s were really like and expresses a common tendency in popular culture to romanticize the era, thinking of poodle skirts and malt shops rather than remembering it for what Stefan suggests were its defining moments — McCarthyism, racial segregation, and the nuclear arms race.

BITE MARKS: Assuming that Noah didn't pick up a part-time job, the real pizza guy came to a bad end. At the Gilbert house, Noah attacks Elena but Stefan pushes him off before he gets his fangs into her. In the caf, Elena fights off Noah with pencils and mop sticks. Stefan stakes Noah in the gut, tortures him for information, then finishes him off.

MEANWHILE IN FELL'S CHURCH: Stefan brings Elena vervain in *The Struggle*, which she plans to share with Meredith and Bonnie. In *Dark Reunion*, Bonnie has a dream set in a 1950s soda shop complete with Elena in a poodle skirt and "Goodnight Sweetheart" on the jukebox. In this episode, Damon's list of founding family members includes Honoria Fell; Honoria plays a crucial role in the novels, which is revealed in *The Fury*. When Damon, a vampire with access to her home, threatens Elena's little sister in *The Struggle*, Elena chooses to put herself in harm's way to protect her family just as she does in "Unpleasantville" when she endangers herself to protect Jeremy and Jenna.

OFF CAMERA: Matt's middle initial is "G" just like Zach Roerig's, whose middle name is George. Dillon Casey, who plays Noah, may be familiar to viewers from TV shows like *Valemont*, *Being Erica*, and *M.V.P.* In the TV movie *Too Young to Marry* (2007), Dillon and Nina Dobrev play teenagers who tie the knot. Ben is played by Sean Faris, an actor and model who's appeared in *The King of Fighters*, *Forever Strong*, and *Never Back Down* as well as *Reunion*, *Life as We Know It*, and *Smallville*.

FOGGY MOMENTS: The address Matt writes down isn't the same as the one that was on Vicki's driver's license in "Lost Girls." Her zip code was a Virginian one; Matt's is for Georgia. The brush-stroke of paint on Matt's arm changes after the first shot. As pointed out on the Vampire-Diaries.net's wiki, Elena asks Stefan what he looked like in the '50s but she's already seen him in the news clip in "You're Undead to Me." It makes sense that Dr. Gilbert would fake the medical records of Elena's birth but did Miranda Gilbert somehow retroactively fake a pregnancy? In a small town, would people not have clued in that something was fishy about Miranda not being pregnant but all of a sudden having an infant, or does everyone know that Elena's adopted and it's just the best-kept secret in Mystic Falls?

MUSIC: We Barbarians' "There's This There's That" plays as Matt chats with Ben, and Elena tells Bonnie she's adopted. Anna and Jeremy hang at the Grill to Systems Officer's "Pacer." The Decade Dance kicks off to The Misfits' cover of The Drifters' song "This Magic Moment." Rogue Wave's version of Buddy Holly's "Everyday" plays as Jenna and Alaric talk. Elena and Stefan discuss the '50s as they dance to Jef Scott's "Dreams Are for the Lucky." Caroline and Bonnie arrive at the Grill to U.S. Royalty's "Keep It Cool (Remix)." Alaric quizzes Damon while Stefan and Elena dance to The Misfits' cover of Del Shannon's "Runaway." Autovaughn's "Everybody" is on when Bonnie asks Ben out. Anna helps Jeremy at the punch table and asks to borrow the Gilbert journal to Jocko Marcellino's "Slow Dance." The Misfits cover Jerry Lee Lewis's "Great Balls of Fire" as Stefan shows Elena one smokin' dance move. The Angels' "My Boyfriend's Back" is covered by The Raveonettes as Damon dances with a random blonde girl. Caroline confronts Matt while St. Leonards' "Now That We've Grown" is in the background. To accompany the surprise ending is Oranger's "Mister Sandman" cover (originally recorded by The Chordettes), a punked-out version suited to Anna and Ben, the bad-ass vampire couple.

> *Damon: You know I really like this whole ménage à threesome team thing. It's got a bit of a kink to it. Don't screw it up.*

1.13 *Children of the Damned*

Original air date: February 4, 2010
Written by: Kevin Williamson and Julie Plec
Directed by: Marcos Siega
Guest cast: James Remar (Giuseppe Salvatore), Ric Reitz (Barnett Lockwood), Joe Knezevich (Johnathan Gilbert), Charles van Eman (Businessman), Thomas Elliott (Coachman), Phillip DeVona (Sheriff William Forbes)

In a flashback to 1864, Stefan foolishly places his trust in his father, which leads to Katherine's capture. In the present day, he and Elena trick Damon into trusting them in an effort to find the grimoire before Damon can.

As Elena and Stefan look for the Gilbert journal, she observes that though Damon's methods are wrong, he is motivated by a pure feeling — his love for Katherine. *The Vampire Diaries* opts for shades of grey rather than laying black or white on any of its characters as it explores how ambiguous being "in the right" is in "Children of the Damned."

More so than in "Lost Girls," this flashback shows Damon's perspective on the events of 1864. He swallows his fear as Katherine shows him what it means to be a hunter and we see that Damon gave up his innocence for love, a bond that was and is as strong as the bond between Stefan and Elena, or between Elena and Bonnie, who tells Ben she would die for her best friend. In the flashback, Damon says he would rather die than expose Katherine. Damon's flashes of humanity aren't only reserved for the 1860s; on family night at the Gilberts', we get a glimpse of who Damon can be. He has an easy, loose, likeable manner and, when he wants to, he gets along well with people. He's charming and open with Jenna as he makes dinner and she sips wine, and he bonds with Jeremy over video games and advice about girls ("Hot trumps weird — trust me"). While he doesn't reveal what he is or what he's done, Damon demonstrates that he can be an honest person; his conversation with Jenna about his relationship with his father is frank, and he's never hesitated to call it like he sees it with Elena. Stefan tells Elena that trust doesn't come "naturally" to Damon — but it did in his human life when he trusted Stefan. Stefan's betrayal (he chose obedience to their father over his

James Remar as Giuseppe Salvatore

Since the late 1970s, Boston-born James Remar has been making his mark in film and television with a resumé that now boasts well over a hundred credits. With memorable turns as villains in his earlier films — like *The Warriors* (1979), *48 Hrs.* (1982), and *The Cotton Club* (1984) — in more recent years Remar has been best known for his TV work. He played Samantha's billionaire boyfriend Richard on *Sex and the City* and plays Harry Morgan, adoptive father to a serial killer, on *Dexter* (for which he was nominated for a Saturn Award for Best Supporting Actor). A *Dexter* connection led to his role on *The Vampire Diaries*: "I was brought in by Marcos Siega, who has directed several episodes of *Dexter* . . . [he] thought I'd be right for this role," related the actor to *TV Guide*. In 2010, besides playing dad to the Salvatore brothers, James Remar filmed *Deathgames*, which Nina Dobrev also stars in.

promise to Damon) hurt, and Damon is genuinely hurt again by Stefan and Elena's betrayal with the grimoire. Humans and vampires alike can fake feelings and mislead each other. Damon's question to Elena in the kitchen — "Is it real?" — is a central issue for the Salvatore brothers.

Stefan digs up the past by unearthing his father's grave to get the grimoire and revisits the choices he made in 1864, seen in flashback, which broke the bond of brotherhood he had with Damon. He feels at fault for betraying Damon by misplacing his faith in his father. Always one to try to make the moral choice, Stefan struggles with the pain, hurt, and loss that can come out of making the "right" decision. Who is at fault? By honoring the sense of duty he was raised with and obeying his father, Stefan lost his best friend. Stefan makes grey choices in "Children of the Damned": he deceives his brother for the greater good (preventing the tomb from being opened, a choice Elena agrees with) but then hands over the grimoire to Damon to save Elena from being forced into a life of vampirism — despite the still-present risk that unleashing 27 vampires on Mystic Falls poses.

Though it's hard to have sympathy for a new character who betrays our Stefan and Damon, Giuseppe Salvatore believes he is in a position of moral authority, acting in his sons' best interest and to protect the town. His strict sense of duty and honor leaves no room for a moral grey area when it comes to the "demons." A father who counted on his sons to share his perspective, Giuseppe feels shame because of his children's feelings for Katherine, and he makes it clear that sympathizers are just as bad as vampires. Part of why Stefan trusted his father and felt he could turn to him is that Giuseppe treated him differently than he treated Damon. Like most siblings, Stefan and Damon did not receive the same treatment. Stefan, the good and obedient son, still has the respect of his father and consequently still has faith in his goodness. But Damon, the failure and "war deserter," knows what it's like to feel the sting of rejection and judgment from Giuseppe and knows his father can't be trusted with Katherine's secret. Just as Giuseppe cannot see Damon's decision to leave the Confederate army as an issue of principle, he cannot fathom that vampires could be anything other than evil. This episode explores the common war strategy of demonizing the enemy — it's much harder to kill someone when you know that at their core they are the same as you. It dips into issues of persecuting the Other, something that has simmered in the subtext of previous episodes with the Salem witch trial references and the backdrop of Civil War politics. As in *Battlestar Galactica* where the "enemy" Cylons sometimes behave more humanely than the humans do, supernatural and sci-fi shows have a unique ability to explore these ideas from the distance of an alternate reality. *The Vampire Diaries* does just that, especially when it gives its viewers the disturbing image of Katherine and Pearl muzzled like rabid dogs.

Trust breeds trust, Elena tells Damon, and new alliances are formed and old ones broken in "Children of the Damned" as Alaric and Stefan, Anna and Damon, Bonnie and Ben, Pearl and Johnathan Gilbert, Katherine and Pearl, and Elena and Damon navigate the murky waters of trust, not always capable of making the right decisions about who to have faith in.

COMPELLING MOMENT: The hurt on Damon's face when he realizes that Elena had him fooled, lying straight to his face.

CIRCLE OF KNOWLEDGE:
- No Matt, Tyler, or Caroline.
- The title of this episode is also a sci-fi film from 1963. *Children of the Damned* is sort of a thematic sequel to the more widely seen *Village of the Damned*; in it, children with extraordinary abilities are rounded up and studied, and when threatened they fight back. The movie culminates with the children hiding out in a church, which ends up burning — à la Fell's Church, 1864 — and killing everyone inside.

- Damon's predatory tricks were learned from Katherine: she gets a carriage to stop and then attacks when the person investigates the body in the road — just like Damon did in the opening kill-scene in the pilot. (Noah may have also learned this trick from Katherine; he used a variation on this tactic with Elena in "The Turning Point.")
- Notice how Katherine refers to the "other animals"; she doesn't consider herself human.
- Stefan asks Alaric if he's playing at Van Helsing, the doctor from Bram Stoker's *Dracula* (1897) who hunts the Count.
- While Katherine poses as an orphan, Elena is an actual orphan.
- The professions of the founding family members don't seem to change over the years: Forbes is the sheriff, Lockwood the mayor ("Family Ties"), and Fell the journalist ("You're Undead to Me").
- Stefan learned the trick he used in "Family Ties" from his father. In it, he spiked Caroline with vervain to capture Damon, which his father did to him to catch Katherine.

THE RULES: The essential oil of vervain burns a vampire's skin. The fast reflexes of a vampire make them quick studies at video games.

THE DIABOLICAL PLAN: It's a race to find the grimoire between the Salvatore brothers and Anna. Anna wants to get into the tomb to free her mother, Pearl. Stefan's plan to thwart Damon is revealed. Anna is the mystery vamp who turned Logan Fell. Alaric tells Stefan that he doesn't want revenge, he just wants to know what happened to Isobel.

HISTORY LESSON: Katherine's cover story is that she lost her family in the fires in Atlanta. Over the course of the summer of 1864, the Atlanta Campaign was waged between the Union and Confederate armies. It ended with Atlanta occupied by Union troops at the beginning of September and fires were set as the city was evacuated. (The fire scene in *Gone With the Wind* depicts that event.) In the 1860s, croquet was just becoming popular among the leisured classes in England and America; the first comprehensive croquet rulebook was published in . . . 1864. At the time, it was unusual for women to play a game in the outdoors and in the company of men. Katherine not only plays croquet but she beats Mr. Salvatore at it.

BITE MARKS: In the flashback, Katherine kills the man and the coachman. Stefan shoves Alaric into the desks. Damon and Anna exchange chokeholds. Katherine is poisoned by feeding on Stefan and is captured and muzzled. Pearl is shot in the back, muzzled, and captured. Damon force-feeds Elena his blood.

MEANWHILE IN FELL'S CHURCH: Honoria Fell supplies the apothecary with a vervain elixir; in the novels, Honoria was a sort of "town protector" of that era. Elena takes on that role in *The Fury*; when the people of Fell's Church are in danger, she feels a surge of protectiveness: "She felt somehow responsible for the town . . . [there was] something more important than her own problems now." Mystic Falls Elena feels the same way. In *The Awakening*, Stefan recalls a heated argument between Damon and his father, Giuseppe, Conti di Salvatore, about Damon's decision to drop out of university. Damon "brought out the violence" in his father who considered his eldest son a lazy ne'er-do-well. Elena convinces Stefan and Damon to work with each other in *The Fury* but not without Stefan's caveat: "I'll work with him, but I won't trust him. I can't. I know him too well." In *The Struggle*, Elena arrives home for a family dinner to find Damon an unexpected guest for a meal less pleasant than family time in "Children of the Damned." In *The Fury*, the new history teacher, Alaric Saltzman, turns out to have been brought in by the principal to solve the vampire problem in Fell's Church. The backstory for Alaric and his wife in "Children of the Damned" is adapted from details in *The Fury*: Alaric is the parapsychologist from Duke University (he is unmarried) and he's been studying the victims of vampire attacks. Though neither Alaric has personally encountered a vampire before they enter the action, the Alaric in the books is less a roguish Batman-type than his onscreen counterpart.

OFF CAMERA: The line "If I see something I haven't seen before, I'll throw a dollar at it" was written by Kevin Williamson, who heard it from a dance instructor in college after Kevin was forced to wear a leotard to class. Nina Dobrev loves playing the "two completely different" characters of Elena and Katherine: "As soon as you put in the teeth and the eyes and you're in that whole getup, you just feel more animalistic and crazy. It's cool to play that because it's so different from myself."

FOGGY MOMENTS: Why aren't the men of Mystic Falls fighting in the Civil War? They look able-bodied. Giuseppe's tombstone says he died January 23,

1864, but the first Founder's Ball — the night Stefan found out Katherine was a vampire — wasn't until September 24 of that year. Johnathan Gilbert knew Pearl as a lady of Mystic Falls, able to walk in daylight, then discovered she was a vampire — why didn't he record that important detail in his journal? Logan Fell told Damon that none of the Founders' journals mentions day-walkers, but the Founders had captured at least two (Pearl and Katherine). A little lax in your journaling there, founding fathers. Damon sees Katherine muzzled in Stefan's room, so he did know that Stefan was with Katherine that night, contrary to "History Repeating" where Damon was surprised to learn that Stefan knew that Katherine had Emily's crystal. Was Anna, or Annabelle as she was then known, already a vampire in 1864?

MUSIC: Damon flirts with Jenna in the kitchen to Kate Earl's "When You're Ready." Surfer Blood's "Floating Vibes" is playing in the background while Bonnie and Ben are at the Grill. When Bonnie calls Elena to report on her date, "Goodbye" by Elefant is playing. Bonnie realizes Ben is a vampire when she kisses him to Experimental Aircraft's "Stellar."

> *Sheila: You got some nerve knocking on a Bennett witch's door*
> *and asking her for anything. You are no friend to us.*
> *Damon: What did I do?*
> *Sheila: Spirits talk, Mr. Salvatore, and so does my granddaughter.*

1.14 *Fool Me Once*

Original air date: February 11, 2010
Written by: Brett Conrad
Directed by: Marcos Siega
Guest cast: Justin Smith (Duke)

The tomb opens.

The spirit of Jay Gatsby may live in Damon Salvatore. In *The Great Gatsby*, F. Scott Fitzgerald writes, "No amount of fire or freshness can challenge what a man will store up in his ghostly heart," words describing Gatsby's five-year

quest to regain the love of Daisy Buchanan — it also describes Damon's 145-year quest to free Katherine. Like the bitter disappointment Gatsby faces when he realizes the real Daisy can't possibly match up to his imagined love, Damon, the "love-struck idiot," is made a fool when the tomb finally opens to reveal that Katherine isn't there and never was. She's free and roaming around, and never cared enough to once in all this time reach out to him.

Damon was fooled by Stefan and Elena's double-cross in "Children of the Damned," and fooled again by Anna and, most significantly, by Katherine. His diabolical plan, and its sequel, centered on rescuing Katherine, but the joke's on him. His focus has been on her and only her for nearly a century and a half, and she is at the root of the discord between the brothers. A heartbreaking revelation that it's all, seemingly, been for naught. Though it *was* an unexpected twist, the narrative groundwork was laid for Katherine's betrayal. She's willful and selfish and had demonstrated a disregard for Damon's feelings by carrying on a simultaneous relationship with his brother — not exactly the picture of devotion. In "Unpleasantville," Noah says to the brothers that they weren't the "only ones," implying that he was another of Katherine's boy toys, that there was nothing special about the relationship the Salvatore brothers shared with her. But for Damon, it was real and it was love. In "History Repeating" Damon tells Stefan that Katherine never used compulsion with him, that his feelings were real. That authenticity is hugely important to Damon. Elena knows her deception hurt Damon, and he says as much to her when she makes her appeal to work together again. She's able to reestablish her bond of trust with Damon by being honest with him and, in a symbolic gesture, taking off her vervain necklace. He chooses not to compel her, just as he chose not to on their road trip, because he craves a real connection; he wants their fun and their friendship and their understanding to be authentic. And it is. Damon may tell Stefan that he "sincerely" hopes Elena dies but he caves to Anna's demand when she threatens Elena. Only at Elena's request does Damon leave the tomb. He does care, and it's because Elena understands his drive to do whatever it takes for love; she reaches out to him outside the tomb as Damon reels from the discovery that he's been made a fool for the past 145 years. A truly empathetic person, Elena really means it when she says she's sorry Pearl was trapped in the tomb because of Katherine, just as she is truly sorry to see Damon heartbroken.

Damon wanted to be the white knight for Katherine but instead it's Stefan who gets to play the hero for Elena. The name origin of Salvatore is savior, as L.J. Smith writes in *The Awakening*, and Stefan is named after Saint Stephen, the first Christian martyr. He lives up to his name when he enters the tomb to save Elena, knowing there's no escape for him. In that moment at the threshold — Elena safely outside, Stefan trapped inside — Elena silently recognizes his sacrifice. Both Stefan and Elena honor their promise to Damon and get him out of the tomb, and in that act they help to rebuild broken trust and demonstrate that the ties of brotherhood between Stefan and Damon remain strong in spite of their animosity.

Like Damon, Jeremy is friendless and loses his chance at connection with Anna as the tomb opens. Though "strange and lurky" Anna has used him to get at the Gilbert journal and brought him to the tomb to feed her starving vampire mother then used him as leverage, she seems to have real affection for Jeremy (which Ben picks up on). No character on *The Vampire Diaries* is ever one note and Anna displays a warmth and sweetness in her reunion with her mother not usually seen in a villain. In his desperation, Damon asks why she gets her happy ending, and in the surprisingly emotional last twist of the episode, Bonnie could ask the same question.

Grams has been Bonnie's guide as she discovers her powers. She's a strong, smart, and fearless character who holds her own and possesses a wealth of knowledge about the tenuous relationship between witches and vampires.

Grams works with Stefan but she has her own agenda: to protect her family from the vampires — at least from those less concerned with human safety than Stefan has proven himself to be. It's Bonnie who insists they lift the seal so Stefan can escape. He saved her life from Damon in "History Repeating"; she saves him from a potential eternity of entombment here. What neither witch knows is the cost of performing the spell — Grams' life. Bonnie unravels when she discovers that Grams is gone. This scene makes the list of *The Vampire Diaries'* most upsetting. Kat Graham turns in an achingly real performance as the inconsolable Bonnie now faces a significant loss of her own.

The last episode before a six-week hiatus, "Fool Me Once" marked another chapter-end in the season — the quest to get inside that creepy, creepy tomb is finally completed — and left fans eager for the next. Does Jeremy know that Anna's a vampire? Will he figure out what happened with Vicki? What will Damon do now that his purpose is lost? Grams had warned Bonnie that they might not be able to put the seal back up after bringing it down. And that tomb vampire looks like he's been freed.

COMPELLING MOMENT: With Stefan looking on, Elena comforts Damon who's just had his 145-year-old sense of purpose crushed.

CIRCLE OF KNOWLEDGE:
- No Jenna or Alaric in this episode.
- Elena tries to sneak past sleeping Ben and get out the door in an echo of the scene in "Friday Night Bites" where Caroline tried to get past Damon and out of her bedroom.
- The witches' incantation is the same for both parts of the spell — opening the door and lifting the seal — and while they may not be speaking Latin, a few words are familiar. Other than *quo* (meaning where or which), *terra* means earth or ground, *mora* means pause or delay, *incandis* relates to light or fire, and *signus* is a variation on *signum* or seal.
- Elena hugs Damon in a moment that recalls one of their early interactions in the kitchen in "Friday Night Bites" when she told him that she was sorry for him, that he lost Katherine too.
- Bonnie reaches for the grimoire when she realizes Grams is dead, hoping to use supernatural powers to undo the tragedy. After Vicki died, Elena had the same instinct and followed through on it, asking Damon to erase Jeremy's suffering.

Jasmine Guy as Sheila Bennett

From the Atlanta area, Jasmine Guy is an accomplished actor of both stage and screen but she's best remembered for two TV roles — Roxy on *Dead Like Me* and Whitley on *A Different World*. The actress first got her break on the series *Fame* in 1982 and since then has been steadily working in film and television as well as on Broadway in *The Wiz*, *Leader of the Pack*, *Grease*, and *Chicago*. Many of Jasmine's stage roles are musical; she recorded an album in the '80s and continues to perform. Jasmine calls the actors on *The Vampire Diaries* the "most beautiful cast I've ever worked with," and the admiration was mutual. Kat Graham said she was honored to work opposite Jasmine Guy, calling the opportunity "amazing." To prepare for the role, Jasmine imagined her own backstory for Sheila Bennett and believes "whoever is in between me and Bonnie is, you know — my progeny is estranged in some way because of my practices."

THE RULES: A witch can disable a vampire with a spell that inflicts pain to his mind. The power of a witch can be fueled by strong emotions like worry or anger. In their spell, Grams and Bonnie use the four elements — fire, earth, air, and tap water.

THE DIABOLICAL PLAN: The name of the game in "The Turning Point" is leverage. No one can trust anyone else so they all make sure to have a backup plan in order to get what they need. Anna and Ben use Elena and Jeremy to motivate Bonnie and Stefan to play nice. Damon takes Elena into the tomb to make sure that door isn't sealed behind him. But Grams, with a trick up her sleeve, has rigged her spell so humans can get out but vampires can't (which is why she has no problem letting Anna into the tomb).

BITE MARKS: Kidnap victims Bonnie, Elena, and Jeremy all suffer minor head injuries. Sheila inflicts brain pain on Damon. Bonnie lights Ben's arm on fire. Stefan burns Ben with daylight and later burns him to death with his flamethrower. Anna bites Elena to feed Pearl. Grams dies, over-exerted from the spell.

MEANWHILE IN FELL'S CHURCH: In *The Fury*, the gang is led to the vaulted tomb under the old church by Bonnie, who is possessed by the spirit of Honoria Fell. Though the plot is significantly different, Damon, Stefan, and Elena do meet Katherine in the tomb. Because of that, for some readers of the books, the expectation that Katherine *would* be in there was heightened.

Grams lives on Oak Street; in the novels, the streets of Fell's Church bear tree names (the Gilberts live on Maple) and oak is explained to be the "most sacred" tree to the Druids: "the spirit of the trees brought them power."

OFF CAMERA: Julie Plec explained to iFMagazine.com the showrunners' choice to make the tomb nearly pitch-black: "less is more, as far as what we show. Kevin referenced a movie called *The Descent*, which I actually haven't seen, but it's literally [someone] with a glow stick [who] can see two feet in front, [nothing] behind. . . . it's very deliberately dark and creepy and glimpses of this and hints of that, so that it doesn't suddenly turn into *Night of the Living Dead*. It doesn't look that good on television when you do it, and it takes away some of the mystery of what's really going on."

FOGGY MOMENTS: Did something happen in the bathroom with Bonnie and Ben? She comes out looking a little shell-shocked. When Elena shows up to talk to Damon, she takes her scarf off twice. Why did Anna turn Logan into a vampire and then abandon him? She could get the Fell journal without turning him, and a reckless vampire in Mystic Falls only heightened the council's response to the problem. Sheila disables Damon so easily that it raises a question about "Bloodlines": since Bree was a witch, why didn't she even attempt to use her powers to stop Damon from killing her?

MUSIC: Oh Mercy's "Can't Fight It" is playing at the Grill when Matt, Tyler, Caroline, and Jeremy talk about Duke's party. (This song was also featured in "Friday Night Bites.") Caroline launches into her first speech with Earlimart's "Before It Gets Better" in the background. Duke's party kicks off to "Answer to Yourself" (The Soft Pack). Tyler tries to hit Jeremy up for some weed to Tokyo Police Club's "In a Cave." Anna and Jeremy talk in the woods with U.S. Royalty's "Every Summer" faintly playing. Tyler steals Matt's beer to The Steps' "Out Tonight." As Matt and Caroline realize neither one wants to mess up their relationship, Black Rebel Motorcycle Club's "All You Do Is Talk" plays. The closing scenes of Damon sitting in front of the fire and Bonnie discovering that Grams is dead are to Leona Lewis's "Run."

Damon (to a fatally injured Alaric): We're kindred spirits. Abandoned by the women we love. Unrequited love sucks. Sounds like I got a lung . . .

1.15 A Few Good Men

Original air date: March 25, 2010
Written by: Brian Young
Directed by: Joshua Butler
Guest cast: Amanda Detmer (Trudie Peterson), Mike Kalinowski (Hiker), Maia Osman (Wasted Girl), Jeni Perillo (Bethanne), Dax Griffin (Bachelor #3), Michael Showers (The Man)

Elena searches for her birth mother, Isobel, but Isobel doesn't want to be found. Kelly Donovan returns to Mystic Falls just in time for the bachelor-auction fundraiser.

In a brilliant casting move, Melinda Clarke brings Kelly Donovan back to Mystic Falls where she deftly embarrasses Matt, belittles Caroline, and manages to make the audience feel for her. All Kelly has in her life is her son Matt — her boyfriend has ditched her and it sounds like he's just the latest in a string of boyfriends who've done the same. Though it's completely unfair for her to ask Matt to never leave her when that's precisely what she does to him again and again, he reassures her that he won't. In "Fool Me Once," Caroline and Matt arrived at common ground, neither one "ooged" out and no more need for preemptive speeches. While their relationships with their mothers may be equally problematic, Matt takes a more active role as a son than Caroline seems to take as a daughter. But Kelly's attitude to Caroline, notably calling Caroline his "rebound girl" to her face and in front of Elena (ouch), makes her presence an immediate and undeniable strain on Matt's new relationship.

From one absent mother to the next, Elena's birth mother turns out to be a bigger troublemaker than Kelly Donovan. Isobel is not dead; she's undead, an evil and intriguing vampire. She manages to terrorize Elena without setting a foot in Mystic Falls, controlling a man and sending him to kill Trudie (her best friend from high school) and, after delivering a message to Elena (to stop searching for Isobel), to kill himself. The actions of this dangerous and detached vampire seem disconnected from the human Isobel was once, as seen in the flashbacks with Alaric, even though we learn how

Music on *The Vampire Diaries*

Music supervisor Chris Mollere credits his parents for his love of music, counting his father's diverse collection of records as a major influence on him as he grew up in his military family, traveling the world. Chris went to the University of Texas at Austin to study psychology, business, and advertising. While there, Chris became deeply involved in Austin's music scene. He went to live performances by a diversity of artists and worked with bands in the areas of production, promotion, and management. After college, Chris moved to L.A. and began working with Emmett Furla Films as a producer's assistant in 2005 and 2006. It was slogging work but an invaluable experience: "When I moved out here, I worked as an assistant to a lot of film producers. I learned a lot, working 80- to 90-hour weeks. But I wouldn't change it for the world. It taught me a lot about breaking down scripts, production, and I learned the broad spectrum of the entire industry very quickly." During that time, Chris realized the job of a music supervisor would combine his interests in music and film, and he sought out work in that area. He worked on independent films, supervised commercials, and assisted a TV composer because "you have to pay your dues." The first series he worked on as music supervisor was *Kyle XY* alongside its producer Julie Plec. He's also worked on projects like *Greek*, *10 Things I Hate About You*, *Pretty Little Liars*, *The Haunting of Molly Hartley*, and *Dead Like Me: Life After Death*.

Step one for the music supervisor on a TV series is figuring out the musical identity of the show, and with *The Vampire Diaries*, Chris and the producers wanted the songs to create another narrative layer, adding to the storytelling in the way music does on shows like *The O.C.* and *Grey's Anatomy*. Unlike with some series, it wasn't about choosing big-name artists but about finding the right musical fit. As Chris explains, "You don't have to be signed on a major record label to actually be good for the project." With the fast pace of episodic television production, Chris doesn't have a lot of time for mulling over song choices, which means it's crucial that his sensibility for the sound of the show aligns with the director's and the showrunners' vision. Permissions to use a song are cleared about a week before an episode goes into sound mixing, earlier for more complicated situations or for songs attached to major labels. With not a lot of time to get the paperwork done, Chris's strong relationships with artists, publishers, and label representatives are incredibly important. In order to get into music supervision not only do you need a love of music but, Chris stresses, "the most important thing is to learn the [permission] clearance side. Most people think music supervisors just put music into scenes for TV and film. They don't think about the business and legal aspects. You can get into a lot of trouble if you don't know them." Julie Plec mentioned during her interview with The VRO that Chris went so far as to sleuth out the location of an artist in Sweden, Mads Langer, to request permission from him to use "Beauty of the Dark" at the end of "You're Undead to Me." These "moment songs" help make *The Vampire Diaries* emotionally powerful, and Julie hopes that the show's soundtrack, slated for October 2010, will include all of those tracks that fans identify so strongly with turning points in the narrative.

Not all of the music heard on *The Vampire Diaries* is licensed; the musical cues are often the work of Michael Suby, who has composed for films like *The Butterfly Effect*, and for TV series as diverse as *Keeping Up with the Kardashians*, *Robot Chicken*, and *Kyle XY*. Michael's interests and talents intersect with TVD. Before *The Vampire Diaries* began, he told Soundtrack.net what would be his dream projects: "I really love doing sci-fi stuff, and I'm way into anything that's mystical and dark, I love thrillers. What's occurred to me is that I seem to be able to write really beautiful, slow music really easily, so I'd be a great guy to do a slow-paced Merchant-Ivory romance, or something like *The Cider House Rules*. So maybe someday something like that, but I'm just happy to be working, to be honest!"

unsatisfied she was with her life. As Damon finally confirms for him, Alaric didn't lose Isobel to a vicious vampire attack; he lost her to her desire to be a vampire. With this revealed, and the secret of the baby given up for adoption, Alaric is cut adrift from the memory of his wife and the quest he's been on to avenge her death; he's become a kindred spirit, as Damon says, to the vampire who turned her. But to Isobel's credit, before she abandoned Alaric, she protected him with a token of love and apology: a ring that brings him back from the dead, a work of magic that even Stefan cannot comprehend.

As mediator between Damon, Alaric, and Elena, Stefan tries to keep the Isobel information under control in order to limit the fallout. He doesn't want to provoke Damon, but both Alaric and Elena have a right to know everything he knows. It's a thankless job for Buzzkill Bob but he does all he can, warning Alaric not to seek revenge while Damon's volatile. Like Elena, Stefan hopes that the Katherine Incident will change Damon for the better and bring out that humanity they know is buried somewhere in him.

Damon says he's liberated now that he's without a master plan but his actions are driven by depression, spite, and lack of purpose. He exploits women in a sorry attempt to forget that he cared, and still cares, about one of them; he flirts with the mayor's wife (again); he taunts Alaric in a public forum; he kills Alaric. . . . But he also is open about his heartache with Sheriff Forbes and he clearly identifies with Alaric. Having his "heart ripped out" by Katherine has brought out Damon's humanity, as Stefan and Elena hoped it would, but it hasn't diminished the demon in him. His only moment of remorse comes when he unintentionally hurts Elena, unaware that Alaric's wife, who was so "delicious," is Elena's birth mother.

For fans of Damon and Elena there is a set of nicely paired scenes in "A Few Good Men" that feature the two of them together as Stefan watches on — the first one sweet and intimate, the second angry and full of disappointment. Drunk Damon asks Elena for help with his buttons in an echo of him fastening her necklace in "Fool Me Once." His reaction to Elena's excited news about her birth mother so perfectly illustrates his personality. His insensitive-seeming "Who cares?" actually comes from a considerate place, revealed as he finishes his thought — "She left you. She sucks." Enter Stefan who doesn't visibly react to seeing his girlfriend help his brother get dressed (he also didn't react in "Fool Me Once" when she hugged Damon), and Stefan doesn't even flinch when Damon later delivers one of the best lines in the episode — "Where'd our girlfriend go?" In the second Damon-Elena scene, the three characters are similarly positioned, but instead of a moment of connection, Elena confronts Damon about the unexpected consequences of his actions, as Stefan looks on, worried about when Damon will hit his breaking point.

The parallels between Alaric's heartbreak and Damon's are beautifully realized in their fight scene, neither willing to let go of the woman who loved but abandoned him. Maybe Katherine sent Isobel to Damon. Maybe Isobel still loves Alaric since she protected him with the ring. Maybe, boys, it's time to let go. While Alaric and Damon are capable of dwelling for years on lost loves, *The Vampire Diaries* doesn't hold on and draw out plots — consider how quickly the birth mother storyline developed. It moves forward at a powerful pace, and anyway, there's a farmhouse full of vampires itching for an A story.

COMPELLING MOMENT: Meeting Kelly Donovan: "Not on my couch."

CIRCLE OF KNOWLEDGE:
- No Jeremy, Bonnie, or Tyler in this episode.
- "A Few Good Men" takes its title from the 1992 film (based on the 1989 play of the same name) written by Aaron Sorkin and starring Jack Nicholson, Tom Cruise, and Demi Moore. The story follows a military court trial of two marines accused of murdering a fellow marine and is perhaps most memorable for Jack Nicholson's delivery of the line "You can't handle the truth!" under cross-examination.
- Grove Hill, where Trudie lives and Isobel grew up, is a real town in Virginia.

- When the man in the road was in the background of the shot, and out of focus, it looked like he had no head. Fitting, since he was under complete mind control.
- Seeing Damon party with the sorority girls under compulsion who, he assures Stefan, will wake up the next day thinking they just blacked out draws a very strong line of comparison between Damon and a sexual predator who roofies his victims. From what was shown between Damon and Caroline, it's reasonable to assume that when Damon brings home a woman, the sex is consensual but the feeding is not.
- Matt does the same thing for his mom that he did for Vicki when she returned home in "Haunted": he cooks her some food.
- How many daywalkers were there in Mystic Falls in 1864? So far, there's been Katherine, Pearl, Anna, Harper, and the woman in the square, Bethanne.
- Mrs. Lockwood doesn't realize that Damon's suggestion for a romantic date — dining somewhere isolated in the woods — implies the date is the main course.
- The book on Elena's bedside table is *Majoring in the Rest of Your Life* (1999) by Carol Carter, an advice guide for college students.
- In the flashback, when Isobel tells Alaric she's selfish and a horrible wife but he loves her anyway, it sounds a lot like Katherine in "Children of the Damned" telling Stefan she's selfish and spoiled but she'll get her way.
- Isobel's phone number led fans to a recorded message from Stefan and Damon hinting that Stefan did his share of nasty things when he first became a vampire.
- In "Bloodlines," the writers dropped their first clue that Isobel ended up a vampire: she was *not* a morning person.

THE RULES: A very healthy diet of human blood will bulk a vampire up. Though Stefan's never seen anything like it, Alaric's ring, which he got from Isobel, protects him from "things that go bump in the night," which definitely includes Damon.

THE DIABOLICAL PLAN: Desperate for some sign that Katherine does care about him, Damon theorizes that she was the one who sent Isobel to him. The tomb vampires are gathering. . . .

HISTORY LESSON: While Harper may just be polite, it's probable that his manner with the white hiker is a subtle reminder of what it was like to be African-American in Virginia in 1864; in the flashbacks, African-Americans are the servants and maids. From Stefan's respect for Damon's objection to the Confederacy to his attendance at the anti–Vietnam War rally led by Sheila Bennett, it's likely that both Salvatore brothers have long been progressive in their politics.

BITE MARKS: Harper kills the hiker. Damon feeds on the Tri Delta girls. Under compulsion by Isobel, the creepy man kills Trudie and then himself. Damon (sort of) kills Alaric. Ms. Gibbons, who owns the house where the tomb vampires are gathering, has bite marks on her neck.

OFF CAMERA: Damon quips to Stefan about putting on a little weight with a healthier diet, something that Paul Wesley intentionally did the opposite of in preparation for playing this part. "I'm trying to lean out as much as I can," said the actor. "I feel like vampires are these svelte creatures whose nutrition is essentially animal blood, so I knew that I couldn't eat all these different carbs and sugars because it just didn't feel right, physically and mentally. So I've been limiting my intake, just because I feel like that's what Stefan does, every day. For the first time in my life, I've been doing cardio."

FOGGY MOMENTS: Jenna's search term changes from "Peterson" to "Trudie Peterson" from one frame to the next. This episode marks the second instance of product placement for Microsoft's search engine Bing. While product placement may be a necessary revenue stream for the show, it could be better integrated into the dialogue and storyline. Let's be honest: no one says, "I Binged it." Why did Isobel have Trudie killed? If it was because she didn't want Trudie telling Elena too much, why not kill her earlier before she had the chance to say anything at all?

MUSIC: Damon bites the sorority girls to Jet's "Black Hearts (On Fire)." Damon sits down next to Alaric at the bar to The Alternate Routes' "Time Is a Runaway." Carol Lockwood begins the fundraiser while Sound Team's "Your Eyes Are Liars" plays. Kelly arrives to buy some raffle tickets and "Real You" by Above the Golden State is on in the background. Carol introduces the bachelors as Free Energy's "Something in Common" plays. Sweet Thing's

"Winter Night" is on when Kelly calls Caroline a fake. Jenna wins a date with Alaric, and Carol with Damon, to Sounds Under Radio's "Portrait of a Summer Thief."

> *Stefan: I remember them. From 1864. They were in the tomb.*
> *Damon: Yeah. About that.*

1.16 *There Goes the Neighborhood*

Original air date: April 1, 2010
Written by: Bryan Oh and Andrew Chambliss
Directed by: Kevin Bray
Guest cast: Stephen Martines (Frederick), Jeni Perillo (Bethanne)

Elena tries to have one normal evening with her boyfriend . . . and her ex-boyfriend and his new girlfriend, who's one of her best friends. Damon may not have a master plan anymore but Pearl and the tomb vampires do.

Elena wants a day off from the supernatural drama to try and be "normal," and for the bulk of "There Goes the Neighborhood" everything is as normal as a town full of vampires can be. Even at the farmhouse where the tomb vamps have gathered, they're being acclimatized to the ways of 2010 — remote controls and texting and haircuts to blend in with the humans. Pearl and Anna check out some real estate . . . after laying a serious threat on Damon that makes it clear there's a new force in town that would have no trouble taking down a Salvatore.

The Matt and Caroline–Elena and Stefan double date is as awkward as the idea promised to be. Caroline gets her back up about the closeness that Matt and Elena still share. Matt is a stand-up guy and has always gone out of his way to be fair to Stefan but their car-bonding scene seems to push the boys over into actual friend territory, developing a relationship that's among the fans' favorites from the book series. Caroline and Elena deal with feelings that Caroline first expressed in the pilot episode, that she's in competition with Elena. For once, Elena seems more clueless than Caroline, not realizing what it feels like to be the second choice. It's a difficult night for Caroline

Melinda Clarke as Kelly Donovan

The daughter of a ballet dancer and a soap opera actor, Melinda Clarke followed in her father's footsteps; he was an original cast member of *Days of Our Lives* and Melinda appeared on the show in 1990. Though her credits include *Xena, Seinfeld, Charmed, Soldier of Fortune, Inc., The District, Everwood, CSI,* and *Chuck,* her defining role is as the feisty, fun, and often inappropriate Julie Cooper-Nichols on *The O.C.* Melinda brings the same energy to her role on *The Vampire Diaries* as Kelly Donovan. "It was fun to work with Ian [Somerhalder] because there's a looseness to him, to his character," said Melinda in an interview with TeenDramaWhore.com. "He definitely brings a lot to the character. It's not just lines on the page. And I think Kelly is similar to that. We don't really know why Kelly is such a bad mother, why she does what she does, like drinking, and where she's been. They definitely didn't explain that, so that leaves a lot to be explored in the future if she comes back." Whether or not Kelly Donovan returns in season 2, Melinda will be on The CW in *Nikita,* playing series regular Amanda.

— watching her boyfriend reminisce with his ex, while her ex flirts with her boyfriend's mother who thinks Caroline is fake and shallow. But Matt makes it clear that she's the only one he wants to be with. Caroline is his first choice. Kelly Donovan definitely doesn't think of Matt before she thinks of herself. Melinda Clarke is again pitch-perfect in her sizzling scenes with Damon and also as the ne'er-do-well mom to Matt who relies on her son to take care of her, instead of letting him be a kid for once. Just like Elena was, Matt is looking for a break from the hardships of his day-to-day existence.

In an episode that otherwise felt like a bridge from one major story to the next, "There Goes the Neighborhood" delivers a shock: Jeremy wants to be turned. The build to this revelation begins with Jeremy's latest theory that vampires are misunderstood outsiders. It's a romantic idea that obviously leaves him a place to fit in, where he wouldn't be as lost as Anna can see he is a mile away. Jeremy is like his sister in his need to prove or disprove his suspicions, but he chooses a more intense way to find out if he's right about Anna. When he slices his hand open and offers it to her, it marks the first consensual blood sharing since Vicki and Damon, but this scene is more intimate and intense. Why does Jeremy want to be a vampire? To find Vicki? When Elena had Damon wipe Jeremy's mind, the nightmarish reality of vampirism — the violence and the horror — went with it, and that ignorance has led Jeremy to want something he probably wouldn't otherwise. It is one repercussion of Elena's actions that she could never have anticipated.

Near the end of "There Goes the Neighborhood" the Gilbert siblings brush their teeth together, neither one mentioning that their evening was spent with a vampire. It's a humorous scene but it also speaks of the distance between them, the siblings' new normal. As Damon and Stefan launch into their usual banter, Frederick and Bethanne attack them in a great and unexpected fight scene. Afterward, Elena, all tucked into bed with her teddy bear, calls Stefan to say she's home safe and had a wonderful time on their date. Stefan is sweet as pie on the other end . . . as Damon pounds bourbon and drags the body of a dead vampire in the background. That's normal for the Salvatore brothers.

COMPELLING MOMENT: Jeremy provoking Anna, then telling her to "Go for it."

CIRCLE OF KNOWLEDGE:
- No Alaric, Tyler, or Bonnie.
- In the scene with Pearl and Anna at the boardinghouse, the pillow on the couch behind Damon is embroidered with a quotation from Alice Roosevelt Longworth (1884–1980): "If you can't say anything good about someone, sit right here by me."
- Damon refers to Katherine as his "reason for existence" and literally she is: if Katherine hadn't turned him into a vampire, Damon would have been dead a long time ago.
- One of the great things about *The Vampire Diaries* is how fast-thinking the no-special-powers mortals can be: knowing that vampires have superior hearing, Elena uses her phone to text Stefan about her encounter with Frederick at the bar.
- Jeremy's "vampire as misunderstood outsider" theory could use Stefan as a prime example. Matt accurately describes him as a loner who people stay away from . . . and why? Because he seems to have everything.
- What a subtly tragic moment when Caroline feels déjà vu at the Salvatore boardinghouse but has no idea that she has actually been there before (when she released Damon in "You're Undead to Me"). Elena and Stefan know what happened to her but Caroline herself doesn't.
- In "History Repeating," Damon revealed that only half his plan was releasing Katherine from the tomb; the other half was to let the vampires out so they could rampage in Mystic Falls. Now, the tomb vampires have

that instinct for revenge on the town's citizens that Damon seems to have moved past.

THE DIABOLICAL PLAN: The tomb vampires, led by Pearl, seem intent on staying in Mystic Falls and reclaiming their homes. Frederick wants revenge on the Salvatore brothers for getting them entombed in the first place. Why is Pearl interested in the Gilbert office?

BITE MARKS: Pearl overpowers Damon and presses his eyes in with her thumbs. Harper and Frederick fight; Pearl breaks it up by strangling Frederick. Jeremy slices his own hand open. Frederick and Bethanne attack Damon and Stefan; Stefan stakes Bethanne. Pearl stakes Frederick in the belly as punishment for disobeying her.

OFF CAMERA: Stephen Martines, who plays Frederick, had his first recurring TV role on *General Hospital* as Nikolas Cassadine from 1999 to 2003. He's since appeared on *Guiding Light*, *Monarch Cove*, and *The Closer* as well as other shows and films. Malese Jow revealed to MTV's Hollywood Crush how the vampire veiny look is achieved: "I thought they were going to draw red eyes and put in the veins, but it's actually little black dots, two above your eyes and two below your eyes, and then they CGI everything."

FOGGY MOMENTS: Jenna says to Kelly she heard she was back in town — wouldn't they have run into each other at the fundraiser in the previous episode? Stefan and Hugh Hefner on a double date in the '70s? He may have partied with Bon Jovi but Playmates seem out of character for Stefan, as does Elena's impressed reaction. If Frederick had to ask Jenna where Damon lived, then it stands to reason that Pearl didn't tell him that the Salvatore house wasn't protected from uninvited vampires. Frederick was willing to dive at the window and potentially find it barricaded by the threshold rule?

MUSIC: In the school hallway, Stefan and Elena give the audience a little recap to Keane's "Better Than This." "Cloudhead" by In-Flight Safety plays as Kelly and Damon talk at the bar. The double date begins to Tegan and Sara's "The Ocean." Kelly and Jenna listen to Damon's woes while "Cross My Heart" by Marianas Trench is on in the background. The Constellations' "Perfect Day" plays as Matt and Stefan shoot pool. Kelly shows Damon her

trick with the cherry stem to In-Flight Safety's "Crash/Land." Erin McCarley sings "Love Sick Mistake" as Elena and Caroline argue. Caroline and Matt make up and make out in Stefan's car to Parachute's "The Mess I Made."

> *Damon: How many of those vervain darts do you have left?*
> *Alaric: One.*
> *Damon: Not going to be enough.*

1.17 *Let the Right One In*

Original air date: April 8, 2010
Written by: Julie Plec (teleplay); Brian Young (story)
Directed by: Dennis Smith
Guest cast: Stephen Martines (Frederick), Molly O'Neill (Mystic Grill Hostess), Brian Ames (Billy)

A storm comes to Mystic Falls, giving the tomb vampires an opportunity to seek revenge on Stefan and giving those who knew Vicki closure of the worst kind.

Perhaps the most powerful episode of the season, "Let the Right One In" takes the show for a dark turn after the previous episode's somewhat playful attempt at normalcy in Mystic Falls. The storm gives Frederick and his vamps an opportunity to leave the house during the day, and leads Caroline to find Vicki's body. By the end of the episode, every character has been through hell, and there's more coming.

Stefan is again punished for his choice to feed only on animal blood. Weakened by the fight with Frederick and Bethanne the night before and unwilling to drink the blood Damon has in the house, he's forced out into the storm to hunt and is easily taken down by Frederick and his vampires. Harper feels that those vampires need to punish someone for their entombment and so direct their revenge on the Salvatore brothers for their role that night in 1864. Contrasting Stefan and Harper to Frederick and his nameless compatriots, it's made even clearer that all vampires are not demons, as Giuseppe Salvatore believed. Some are vengeful torturers; others speak out against such brutality and evil.

With Damon blocked from the house by the threshold rule and Elena too vulnerable in a house of angry vampires, an unlikely alliance is struck with Alaric who can both enter the house and rise from the dead. It seems that Damon enjoys fighting with Alaric at his side as much as the audience loves watching them team up, but Alaric hasn't forgotten who Damon is or that he just killed Ms. Gibbons. Alaric hates Damon but may never be able to kill him and Damon can't kill Alaric (unless he manages to get that ring off him first) — that mutual roadblock lends energy to their dynamic. In such a dark episode, a moment of humor like Damon's "It happens" after the punch in the face from Alaric provides a much needed break in tension.

Damon may make Elena cranky but she and he feel the same desperate determination to save Stefan. Her actions in this episode show just how hard Elena will fight to protect her loved ones. Damon is serious for once; telling Elena that he can't be distracted from saving Stefan by worrying about protecting her was a particularly moving moment — another flash of connection between them while she feels useless and terrified for Stefan. But Elena's not one to collapse into a heap of sobs. In Nina Dobrev's layered reaction, her eyes darken with tears but above all she shows strength and resolve.

Anna feeding on Jeremy in "There Goes the Neighborhood" and Stefan on the hunt for the first time onscreen in this episode prepared us for the high-stakes moment when Stefan, near death, reluctantly feeds on Elena so they both can escape Frederick. In the rescue operation, Elena justifies her "insane" decision to get out of the car by dealing with the vervain-soaked ropes, helping Harper, getting Stefan out of the house, and stabbing Frederick with a vervain dart. In offering her blood to Stefan, she saves his life along with hers. A brave act of trust with a frightening outcome — Stefan kills Frederick in a frenzy that rivals and perhaps exceeds Damon's darkest moment. Since the pilot episode, Stefan has been winning the war against the monstrous side of him that craves human blood. There is an undeniable awkwardness between Stefan and Elena afterward in his room despite the truth of what he says to her — their actions saved each other. At least she didn't see him sucking on the last of Damon's stash with empty blood bags littered around him . . . disturbing.

There's danger for a human getting intimate with a vampire, an always-present risk of becoming the next meal, but Pearl sees the danger in a vampire loving a human (145 years of entombment, for example). Pearl and Anna's mother-daughter dynamic has its ironies: a teenager who's taken care of herself for a century and a half being told who she can and cannot date by a mother whose only experience in that intervening time has been isolation and suffering. Anna seems to really care for Jeremy, which she demonstrates by not taking his vervain bracelet, and she pushes him to express why exactly

> ## Let the Right One In
> *Låt den rätte komma in* is a Swedish novel by John Ajvide Lindqvist published in 2004, which was adapted into a critically acclaimed and award-winning film in 2008 (with a second, American adaptation, *Let Me In*, in 2010). The story follows Oskar, a 12-year-old boy tormented by classmates, living in an apartment complex where a young girl, Eli, and her caregiver move in. Oskar and Eli begin a sweet and odd friendship, and he eventually learns what the audience has already seen: she is a vampire. A beautifully acted and filmed movie about the love between a human and a vampire, its themes resonate with *The Vampire Diaries* in general and with this episode in particular: the boundaries between people, both emotional and literal in the case of the threshold rule; the importance of choosing who to let "in" (like Elena and Stefan or Jeremy and Anna); the fierce protectiveness for loved ones (Elena and Damon's need to help Stefan finds a counterpart in Eli's actions in the film's final scenes); and the violence of revenge after the torture Oskar undergoes, and that Stefan endures, and the burden of history that is repeatedly raised as a backdrop to *The Vampire Diaries* and that is implicit in the bodies of all vampires, no matter how young they may look.

he wants to become a vampire. His answer lays bare his vulnerability and shows her the emptiness and isolation he feels, the hole inside from all the loss he's experienced. But just after Anna promises to give him what he's asked for (after her fight with her mother), his whole perspective shifts — he realizes that Vicki's dead, not a vampire out there somewhere, and he can't join her for all eternity. His hope is lost and, it seems as he tears up the newspaper clippings, so is his desire to become a vampire.

The most upsetting scene to watch (more even than the graphic torture scene) is the Donovan family learning that Vicki isn't out gallivanting somewhere, too busy partying to call home. She's dead, buried near the falls in a grave shallow enough to be washed open by a heavy storm. Like the painful circumstance that brought Damon and Alaric together, Sheriff Forbes and Kelly Donovan are united in grief, as are Tyler and Jeremy, together at the kitchen table. Seeing Matt crumple into tears in Elena's arms is an incredibly sad moment even in the context of a show filled with loss and mourning. In that embrace there's more than the grief of a brother losing his sister; Elena is hiding the truth from everyone, carrying the burden of knowing how Vicki died, and Caroline, after the trauma of finding Vicki's body, has to watch as Matt breaks down with Elena, in silent pain as she's again pushed to the side.

After an episode full of despair like this one that's emotionally powerful; beautifully filmed, acted, and written; and manages to be heartbreaking and action-packed and even humorous, it's hard to find a word that better describes *The Vampire Diaries* than epic.

COMPELLING MOMENT: Realizing who Caroline has found.

CIRCLE OF KNOWLEDGE:
- No Jenna or Bonnie this episode.
- Elena began to trust Damon for the first time during their road trip to Atlanta in "Bloodlines"; his car is back on the scene as they reestablish their relationship while rescuing Stefan.
- In the pilot, Matt says the reason Elena gave him for ending their relationship after her parents died was that she needed some time alone. That's what Matt tells Caroline — even though he doesn't break up with her, does the same fate await them?

THE RULES: Damon isn't able to override Frederick's compulsion of Ms. Gibbons. As with a spell, adding more compulsion to existing compulsion doesn't work.

THE DIABOLICAL PLAN: Frederick and company direct their need for revenge at the Salvatores. Knowing what would work (and has worked) on him, Damon lies to Alaric, telling him that Pearl has information about Isobel, in order to get him to help rescue Stefan.

HISTORY LESSON: The Lockwoods profited from the town's vampire purge in 1864 and are now the largest landowners in Mystic Falls.

BITE MARKS: Frederick kidnaps and tortures Stefan. Harper is staked in the legs, restrained for objecting to Stefan's torture. Damon kills Ms. Gibbons and a number of the tomb vampires. Alaric also kills some tomb vamps and is bitten. Elena stabs Frederick with a vervain dart and feeds Stefan her blood to revive him. Stefan kills Frederick. Pearl slaps Anna. Alaric punches Damon in the face.

Kelly Hu as Pearl

She competes in poker tournaments, runs marathons, and was Miss Teen USA 1985 — Kelly Hu is not your average actor. When Kelly was just a toddler, she showed a propensity for performance and began dancing, baton twirling, and acting in her youth. After she picked up the pageant title, Kelly modeled and began working as a professional actor in 1987 with a role on *Growing Pains*. Some of her notable TV appearances include roles on *Nash Bridges*, *Martial Law*, *CSI: NY*, and *Army Wives*. Kelly is known for her action-movie work, like in the 2003 X-Men sequel, *X2*, and *The Scorpion King* (2002). She's also done a lot of voice work in video games and animated series (*Phineas and Ferb*, *Robot Chicken*). On *The Vampire Diaries*, Kelly was pleased to be acting with Ian Somerhalder again; the two had appeared together in *The Tournament*. Of her character, Pearl, Kelly said, "I like her strength. She is so powerful but yet still very sophisticated, still a lady. You usually don't get a lot with female vampires. You usually see a vixen, but Pearl is a classy businesswoman. . . . She has realized that in order to survive for so long as a vampire, one really has to be smart and be able to exist in the world by being respectable."

MEANWHILE IN FELL'S CHURCH: Jeremy says he read somewhere that vampires don't like running water — perhaps he read it in *The Struggle*, where vampires' inability to cross running water is mentioned. In *The Fury*, Stefan is swarmed, and Damon and Elena work together to save him. Alaric's history classroom is also used as a gathering place and strategy room in *The Fury*.

FOGGY MOMENTS: What exactly is Pearl's plan? When she met with Damon in "There Goes the Neighborhood," it seemed like she wanted to destroy the townsfolk, get revenge, and take back the vamps' land. But she preaches measured action, self-control, patience, and no revenge-seeking to Frederick. Damon is able to enter the house after killing Ms. Gibbons, but in "The Turning Point," Logan said he was unable to enter his own house after becoming a vampire. Logan was technically dead: why couldn't he enter his house when there was no living owner?

MUSIC: At the Grill, Anna and Jeremy discuss vampirism to Class Actress's "Let Me Take You Out." Jeremy tells Anna the reason he wants to turn while "I Was Wrong" (The Morning Benders) plays. Matt talks to Caroline on the phone while The Silent League's "Resignation Studies" plays at the Grill. The vampires are listening to Black Angels' "Young Men Dead" when

Alaric comes in. Pearl and the mayor talk at the Grill to "Boy" by Lights On. Caroline listens to Love Grenades' "Young Lovers (Sam Sparro Mix)" while stuck in her car. Anna leaves with Pearl with Systems Officer's "East" in the background. Black Rebel Motorcycle Club's "Conscience Killer" is playing on the stereo when Frederick asks the vampire to turn it down. While Elena talks to Stefan, Sounds Under Radio's "All You Wanted" begins and then she gets the call from Jeremy about Vicki.

Elena: He's not himself, Damon.
Damon: Well, maybe his problem is he spent too long not being himself.

1.18 Under Control

Original air date: April 15, 2010
Written by: Barbie Kligman and Andrew Chambliss
Directed by: David von Ancken
Guest cast: Justin Smith (Duke)

Stefan tries to detox from human blood. It's the kick-off to Founder's Day, and Uncle John Gilbert returns to Mystic Falls, which presents a new threat to the Salvatore brothers.

Almost everybody decides to get hammered at the kick-off party, but binge drinking is the least of Stefan's problems. Paul Wesley puts in a stellar performance, showing unseen sides of Stefan while keeping true to the Stefan the audience knows. Control slips away from Stefan as the craving for blood becomes more powerful. As he kisses Elena, he finds himself wanting her blood more than he wants her and so he catapults himself across her bedroom. His attempt to control his cravings by drinking booze instead leads him to the less-than-rational behavior of a lushy vampire. Stefan uses compulsion on the DJ and with the rude guy on the dance floor; he roughs him up, there and in the parking lot; and in his frantic state, he can't stop himself from licking the drops of Kelly's blood off his fingers. The bloodlust is a powerful force over Stefan — consider the moment when he is completely sidetracked from his mission with Damon by the scent of human blood. Characterized as an addiction, Stefan's blood-struggle stands as a test of his and Elena's relationship. He confesses to Elena his fear of hurting her and the shame he feels letting her see this side of him. She stands by her vampire, unafraid of him, stressing the importance of open dialogue to fight through his bloodlust. Stefan may take strength from her in the moment but he's unable to resist the glass of blood Damon leaves for him.

When he's not playing the role of tempter, Damon raises the question of who Stefan really is — is his true self that person he strives to be, or is there some monster inside that's undeniably part of him? Elena has faith that Stefan will never hurt her, but Stefan himself and Alaric acknowledge that, as a vampire, Stefan will always have the potential inside him to act as most vampires do. "We are who we are," says Damon, but the question of identity isn't so simple for Stefan, or for Tyler.

A difficult character to sympathize with in the early episodes of the season, Tyler Lockwood has been a bully and an aggressor with Vicki, with Jeremy, and here, inexplicably, with Matt. What saves Tyler from being a

Malese Jow as Anna

Elizabeth Melise Jow — born on February 18, 1991, in Tulsa, Oklahoma, to a Caucasian mother and Chinese father — has always been a performer. Malese was a singer before she was an actor, entering in vocal competitions and singing at charity benefits. By seven years old, she was opening sold-out shows for legendary country acts and was recording jingles for McDonald's commercials that aired worldwide. She and her mother, two younger brothers, and younger sister made the big move from Tulsa to Los Angeles when Malese was nine, and in 2002 the young performer sang on Ed McMahon's *Next Big Star* where, after some stiff competition, she lost by one vote. A bit discouraged, Malese refocused her attention on acting, first appearing in TV commercials as well as *The Brothers Garcia*.

All actors face rejection as they audition for parts, so Malese developed a healthy attitude to the business at a young age: "Coming to grips with how many people are going after the same roles will make you realize that it's more like a business decision and nothing personal, and more than anything, it should make you want to fight even harder for the next opportunity that comes along." By 2004, Malese landed the role she's still best known for: Geena Fabiano on Nickelodeon's *Unfabulous*. Her teen years saw her in other popular shows geared to the younger set like *Wizards of Waverly Place*, *iCarly*, *Hannah Montana*, *The Secret Life of the American Teenager*, and *Gigantic* as well as *Bratz: The Movie*, *Aliens in the Attic*, *I Can Do Bad All by Myself*, *The Young and the Restless*, two Mitchel Musso videos, and the ABC Family movie *You're So Cupid*. As Malese grew out of her teen years, the roles she landed became more mature, like the sometimes violent, sometimes sweet Anna on *The Vampire Diaries*. Alongside Justin Timberlake and Jesse Eisenberg, Malese will appear in *The Social Network*, directed by David Fincher.

Most of Malese's existing fanbase is young, thanks to her work on Nickelodeon and Disney Channel shows, and she's often asked for advice on how to break into show business. Malese emphasizes aiming to be "successful, not necessarily famous" and to have a true passion for performing. For Malese, "Singing was always something I did for fun — and it came so naturally to me, but I found that acting was such a challenge — it keeps me on my toes and I never get bored with new scripts. Now as I've gotten older, I'm realizing that singing is much more complex than I ever imagined before. I think the writing and recording process is just as intense as acting and I can't wait to actually do an entire CD." Malese counts Pat Benatar, Paramore, and Patsy Cline as her musical influences, and says that she loves that with music there are "no rules or boundaries." She writes her own songs and loves that she uses music for creative expression, without being at anyone else's mercy.

The appeal of acting for Malese lies in the challenge of bringing a character to life, despite working with memorized lines. She loves the rush from performing and she won over *The Vampire Diaries'* producers, who had originally envisioned a much shorter character arc for Anna and Pearl, one which would have ended in "Fool Me Once." Malese brought life to the undead Anna, and fans love her character's relationship with Jeremy and with her mother. But the actress, like the audience, didn't know at first that Anna was a vampire. "There was really nothing in [the character breakdown] that made me think that she was going to be a vampire. Once I got to the producer session, they said, 'Can you read it a little more menacing?' and I was like, 'Huh, okay.' I didn't know that she was going to be a vampire until the day I got on set; they were like, 'You're going to be fitted for contacts.'" Malese loved going head-to-head with Ian Somerhalder as Damon. "Don't judge a book by its cover," said Malese to MTV's Hollywood Crush. "Don't assume that just because I'm five-foot-four I can't kick some butt. It's awesome, getting to play kind of a badass. I think that's great. I think it's time for the females to be a little threatening to people." *(See page 203 for an interview with Malese Jow.)*

one-note jerk are his abusive relationship with his father, who cares more about throwing a party than about the town's safety, and his genuine bafflement at his own behavior. Some force takes over Tyler — he loses control of himself and flies into a rage, but when he's in control, he's shown an artistic side ("The Turning Point") and a kinship with Jeremy after Vicki's death and kindness to Kelly (at least before they start making out). His regret for how he treated Vicki and his realization that he never had the chance to make it right is the most surprisingly poignant moment of the episode as Tyler says, "I don't deserve to even miss her." Kelly and Tyler aren't the first to behave inappropriately in the face of great loss, but seeing his mother and erstwhile best friend making out is the final straw for Matt. He's given his mother the chance to do right by him time and again and she consistently fails him. Though Kelly still thinks she can change who she is, Matt loses faith and kicks her out. "I'm better off without you" may be the worst thing a mother could hear from her only living child, especially when she knows it's true.

Elena faces her own familial crisis when Damon alerts her to the problem with Jeremy (while doing a hilarious impression of him). Earlier in the episode, Alaric asks Elena how she handles lying to everyone, but she explains that she feels justified in doing something she otherwise considers wrong because her motivation is right — she's protecting her family and friends. She believes her small sin prevents major damage. The issues she had with Stefan before she knew he was a vampire have now cropped up between her and her brother — he realizes she's keeping things from him and he can't trust her anymore. After rebuilding their relationship by telling him she's adopted, Elena doesn't know how to lie straight to his face, and so she falls back on the words no one ever wants to hear: "let it go" and "move on." Damon's playful snooping in Elena's bra drawer earlier in "Under Control" foreshadows Jeremy's actual invasion of her privacy later. Again the show approaches usually black-and-white subjects — lying is wrong, reading your sister's diary is wrong — and makes them profoundly grey. Who wouldn't protect their little brother? Who wouldn't need to know the truth about their girlfriend who died under suspicious circumstances? While their acts are both motivated by good intent, that doesn't mean their relationship hasn't been severely damaged. Jeremy's lost his trust in his sister.

Drawing together *The Vampire Diaries'* new dynamic duo, Alaric and Damon, Uncle John Gilbert promises to bring a whole whack of problems with his return to Mystic Falls: he has a protective ring, he knows Isobel, he knows what really went down in 1864, and, sounding like a modern Giuseppe Salvatore, he preaches values of tradition, obligation, family legacy, and duty to Jeremy. Uh-oh.

COMPELLING MOMENT: Most uncomfortable scene in the series: Stefan licking Kelly Donovan's blood off his fingers.

CIRCLE OF KNOWLEDGE:
- Bonnie and Caroline aren't in this episode.
- The title of this episode, "Under Control," is ironic. Stefan is losing control over his craving for human blood. Tyler and Kelly behave irrationally, drinking and kissing, and, in the case of Tyler, becoming violent. Elena also loses control of the Jeremy situation.
- When Damon says Elena's room is just as he remembers it, she may think he's joking, but he was in there (without her knowledge) in "Friday Night Bites."
- Elena says to Damon, "Please don't make me sorry I asked you." A familiar refrain on this show where characters are constantly treading carefully in fear of having their trust betrayed.
- The last time Stefan used compulsion for personal gain, as he does with the DJ, was in the pilot when he made the Mystic Falls High secretary accept his woefully inadequate admissions paperwork.
- Recognize the jerk at the party who Stefan roughs up? That's Duke, who threw the keg party in the old cemetery in "Fool Me Once."
- In "The Night of the Comet," Elena tells Stefan she hides her diary on the second shelf behind a "hideous ceramic mermaid," but Jeremy finds it behind the horse painting. Presumably, she moved the diary to a more difficult-to-find location after she started writing about the vampires in Mystic Falls.
- In "162 Candles," Stefan tells Lexi that if he were to start drinking human blood, he didn't know if he could stop. What happened the last time Stefan drank human blood? Seems like there's an untold story there that not even Damon knows.

THE RULES: What does the Gilbert Family Magic Ring protect the wearer from (besides Damon Salvatore)? Was Grayson Gilbert wearing his when he was in the car accident?

THE DIABOLICAL PLAN: Uncle John Gilbert successfully fires up the secret council about the fact that vampires are back in Mystic Falls. How does he know everything? Does he know Katherine? What is his connection to Isobel? Why doesn't John want Jenna to sell Dr. Gilbert's office? Does he know Pearl wants to buy it? What is his endgame? Why is he instantly unlikeable?

BITE MARKS: Damon snaps Uncle John's neck and throws him over the balcony. Matt punches Tyler; Tyler beats the crap out of Matt; Kelly gets hurt in the melee. Stefan hurts Duke's arm. Mayor Lockwood hits his son in the face.

MEANWHILE IN FELL'S CHURCH: In *The Awakening*, after Elena finds out that Stefan is a vampire, he attempts to scare her off by displaying his strength thereby illustrating the risk he poses to her. But she holds firm, as Elena does in "Under Control," telling him, "You will never hurt me." Elena's reason for confiding in her journal is explained in *The Struggle*: "I need someone to turn to, because right now there's not a single person on earth that I'm not keeping something from."

FOGGY MOMENTS: If Grayson Gilbert used to own and presumably wear the ring that is now Uncle John's, wouldn't Jeremy have noticed that Alaric's ring was eerily similar to the one his father once wore? Jeremy commented on the ring in "History Repeating." In "Children of the Damned," Giuseppe refers to his sons as "descendants of the founding families" but the boys are members of the founding families since the town was founded four years earlier in 1860. And a very nitpicky comment: Founder's Day (singular possessive) or Founders' Day (plural possessive)? Since there is more than one founder it should be Founders' Day, but after flip-flopping in this and the next few episodes, the show settles on Founder's Day.

MUSIC: Stefan works out to Black Mustang's "You & I." Tyler joins Jeremy in the smokers' corner to Golden Dogs' "Yeah!" Stefan gets the DJ at the party to change the music to "1901" by Phoenix. Alaric approaches Jenna while The Postelles' "White Night" plays. Elena bumps into Duke while dancing with Stefan to Katy Perry's "Use Your Love." Damon warns Elena about Jeremy's suspicions with "Brick by Boring Brick" by Paramore in the background. Kelly and Tyler talk to The Virgins' "Hey Hey Girl." The Airborne Toxic Event's "Does This Mean You're Moving On?" plays as Damon tells Stefan the bad news and the really bad news, then Stefan goes into a blood trance with Kelly. Damon sees John return to the party to "To Be Your Loss" by The Morning After Girls.

Elena: That wasn't you.
Stefan: Oh, that was absolutely me. A monster.
A predator. That's who I am, Elena.

1.19 Miss Mystic Falls

Original air date: April 22, 2010
Written by: Bryan Oh and Caroline Dries
Directed by: Marcos Siega
Guest cast: Spencer Locke (Amber Bradley), Stepheny Brock (Blair Fell), Autumn Dial (Tina Fell)

Stefan insists he's fine but his bloodlust takes control of him at the Miss Mystic Falls competition.

A great episode of *The Vampire Diaries* where no one dies and no one takes their shirt off, "Miss Mystic Falls" explores the Jekyll-and-Hyde role reversal of Stefan and Damon — one brother's a lying, bloodthirsty vampire; the other a considerate, protective vampire who doesn't kill but spends his time covering his brother's reckless and bloody tracks.

With human blood in his system, Stefan's personality changes — he's ostentatious, flirty, fun, cavalier, and mocks his usual broody self. Paul Wesley again puts in a great performance as Stefan unhinged. Like a drug or alcohol addict, Stefan is now a "closet blood junkie," and his primary concern is his next fix — not Elena or the town's safety. Though Stefan denies that there's a problem at all, Damon sees that his brother has become a different person. After revealing to Elena that Stefan is still consuming human blood, Damon explains that Stefan's early decision to starve himself of what his body really wanted prevented him from learning how to control his bloodlust. Stefan's choice to be more human and only drink animal blood has once again made him more vulnerable. It is a daring narrative decision to reveal the monster inside of Stefan, and the writers don't just provide a glimpse — they go all the way showing their hero with the blood of a teenage girl dripping out of his mouth, unable to stop his attack even when Elena sees him. Stefan believes the blood has exposed who he really is, the monster he was hiding from himself. Will the "good brother" be able to come back from this?

While Stefan giving in to the monster within is the primary concern in "Miss Mystic Falls," the episode is also quietly about all that Elena's lost in the past year. She's still part of the Founder's Court but the girl who once signed up for it is gone. Participating in the competition brings the distance between who she is now and who she used to be into sharp relief for Elena. She says to Caroline, "I'm not this person anymore" and Caroline doesn't dispute that but, like the good friend she is, she makes Elena see the competition to its end in order to honor her late mother's wish. Elena tells the panel that the legacy her mother left her is the importance of community, family, honor, and loyalty, and in facing the challenges she has in the past year there's no doubt Miranda Gilbert would be proud of her daughter. Though Sheriff Forbes misses her daughter's big moment, Caroline finally gets first place, winning the title that she wants and deserves (judging by that list of extracurricular activities she rhymed off). Being Miss Mystic Falls is her family legacy and Caroline's efforts have finally paid off.

Without competing for it, Caroline's taken another first place position over Elena — that of best friend to Bonnie. Previously explored in "History Repeating," the friendship between Bonnie, Caroline, and Elena has since changed. Elena realizes that it's not that Bonnie needs space, it's that Bonnie needs space *from her*. Elena wanted nothing more than someone to talk to about her secrets, but the world of the Salvatore brothers has pushed Bonnie away — the tomb spell failed and she holds the brothers responsible for her Grams' meaningless death. Friendships between girlfriends often drift apart when a boyfriend comes into the picture and changes one girl's priorities, and this situation is complicated by the vampire-witch dynamic and the tension-fraught history between the Bennetts and Salvatores that Grams educated Bonnie about. Bonnie has been absent since "Fool Me Once," a long time for the viewer; the writers could have given her more of an opportunity to express the grief and anger that caused her to distance herself. Instead her journey is shown from Elena's perspective. Bonnie doesn't want to give Elena a Stefan-or-me ultimatum but she makes her position clear. She keeps the secret of who attacked Amber from Sheriff Forbes but wants nothing to do with the Salvatore brothers, and this puts a huge divide between her and Elena.

David Anders as Uncle John Gilbert

"I play bad guys, that's what I do," says David Anders, an actor best known for his roles as Julian Sark on *Alias*, Adam Monroe on *Heroes*, and as Josef Bazhaev on the final season of *24*. Originally from Oregon, David moved to Los Angeles to pursue an acting career after doing regional theater in his teens. His other credits include *CSI*, *Charmed*, *Grey's Anatomy*, *Lie to Me*, and *Into the Blue 2*. Though David was unfamiliar with *The Vampire Diaries* when the part of Johnathan Gilbert was offered to him, his girlfriend had read the books and was excited he'd be a part of the show. David watched an episode of *TVD* before flying out to Atlanta to shoot so he'd have a feel for the show. A friend of Ian Somerhalder, David was excited to join *The Vampire Diaries*' family. To his fans, David says, "Thank you for liking the bad guy, for loving to hate me."

Jeremy is also distancing himself from Elena, both glad to not remember Vicki's violence and angry at Elena for taking his memory away. With his new understanding gleaned from Elena's journal, he gets closer to Anna. Forgiving each other for their respective betrayals, Anna and Jeremy find a new openness in their relationship and Anna makes the promise that all good vampires make to their humans: she would never hurt him. Despite what he learned about the potential risk of being with the undead, Jeremy chooses Anna over Elena or his Uncle John to talk with about vampirism. When he's not testing his nephew on how much he knows about vampires, Uncle John tests the limits of Damon's patience. In another display of moral relativism, the writers give us an antagonist for Damon whose mission is noble — to save his town from vampires — and they make it easy for the audience to hate him. Uncle John's motives aren't pure: he's a double agent, working with the secret council and with a murderous vampire at the same time, and having him so close to Jeremy, Jenna, and Elena is worrisome.

To keep the Founder's Council from realizing Stefan and Damon are vampires in their midst, Damon and Elena partner again, as they did in "Let the Right One In." *The Vampire Diaries* masterfully satisfies everybody and nobody at once, as Julie Plec described it, giving those waiting for a Damon-and-Elena romance a glorious moment without having Elena betray her relationship with Stefan. The chemistry, the eye flirting, the "intimacy of the near touch" — their dance feels like a culmination of the developments in their relationship since "Bloodlines."

Saving its best twist for last, "Miss Mystic Falls" closes with a surprising act that elevates Elena to another level of heroism. Elena feels responsible for what's happening with Stefan and she has the strength to make it right. Playing on Stefan's expectations for her behavior, she reprises her speech from the end of "Under Control" and he takes comfort in her arms. It's a confusing moment (why isn't Elena angry or disturbed or heartbroken that Stefan has just mauled Amber?) that turns out to be a beautifully executed fake-out for Stefan and the viewer when Elena stabs him in the back with a vervain dart and, with Damon's help, locks him in the basement, exactly where he himself locked Damon at the end of "Family Ties." She doesn't give up on Stefan; she's determined to fix this even if it means imprisoning her boyfriend and making him remember who he is. It was a no good, very bad day for Elena.

COMPELLING MOMENT: Elena dancing with Damon at the Miss Mystic competition.

CIRCLE OF KNOWLEDGE:
- No Tyler or Matt this episode.
- Miss Mystic Falls is not the first small-town pageant on a Kevin Williamson show; in "Beauty Contest," a season 1 episode of *Dawson's Creek*, Joey competes for the title of Miss Windjammer.
- All the symptoms that Stefan warned Vicki about as she dealt with her first days as a vampire in "Haunted" are what Stefan struggles with, unsuccessfully, in this episode.
- Damon finally gets the dance he asked Elena for in "Unpleasantville." The hand-to-hand, or "palming," dance is similar to choreography in Franco Zeffirelli's *Romeo and Juliet*, the bbc's *Pride and Prejudice* miniseries, and Taylor Swift's "Love Story" video.
- Damon tells Pearl and Anna he had a "no good, very bad day," which is a reference to the classic children's book *Alexander and the Terrible, Horrible, No Good, Very Bad Day* by Judith Viorst.

THE DIABOLICAL PLAN: Damon refuses to play the blackmail game with John Gilbert. Pearl makes a peace offering to Damon. What does Uncle Johnathan Gilbert Sr. Sr.'s invention do? What does Isobel want with it? What is the common goal John and Isobel are working toward?

HISTORY LESSON: The Miss Mystic Falls pageant has been around since the 1860s.

BITE MARKS: Riled up by the smell of blood, Stefan grabs at Alaric's throat. Stefan abducts Amber and feeds on her. Stefan throws Damon. Bonnie inflicts brain pain on Stefan, a trick she learned from Grams (who used it on Damon in "Fool Me Once"). Stefan shoves Elena backward. Elena stabs Stefan in the back with a vervain dart.

MEANWHILE IN FELL'S CHURCH: Stefan's arrival in this episode at Mystic Falls High School in his hot sports car, wearing sunglasses and leather jacket, is very much like his first day at school in *The Awakening*. While there is no Miss Mystic Falls competition, in *The Struggle*, students are selected to represent the "Spirits" of the town for Founder's Day (Caroline is the Spirit of Fidelity, Elena the Spirit of Fell's Church). In *The Struggle*, Damon comes to Elena in a dream and they dance, having a moment of close connection.

MUSIC: Stefan arrives at Mystic Falls High to Faber Drive's "Never Coming Down." Elena and Stefan practice their dance to "On the Beautiful Blue Danube," composed by Johann Strauss II in 1866. Damon and Anna discuss the Gilbert invention to Vitamin String Quartet's cover of Coldplay's "Yellow." Their cover of "Clocks" plays as Uncle John and Jeremy talk about the original Johnathan Gilbert. The Miss Mystic contestants are presented to "Minuet Célèbre," the third movement of Luigi Boccherini's String Quintet in E major, Op. 11, No. 5. Damon and Elena dance to Within Temptation's "All I Need."

Elena: Dying now won't change what happened.

1.20 *Blood Brothers*

Original air date: April 29, 2010
Written by: Kevin Williamson and Julie Plec
Directed by: Liz Friedlander
Guest cast: Evan Gamble (Henry), Joe Knezevich (Johnathan Gilbert)

Starving himself, Stefan flashes back to the night he and Damon died.

Saving the important reveal of how Stefan and Damon actually became vampires for the last flashback episode of the season, "Blood Brothers" defies our understanding of the Salvatore brothers. Locked up without his ring and weakened by vervain and hunger, Stefan does penance for his recent actions — and for those of the past, which he believes make him responsible for all the bloodshed Damon has caused in the past 145 years. There are two stunning revelations. Stefan "created" Damon by luring a girl to him, taking the first bite, and letting the bloodlust do its work. And the human Stefan fed on to complete his change was his father. All of a sudden, Stefan's character is complicated in unexpected ways. Damon refers to Stefan as a martyr, but Stefan acts as his own judge and would-be executioner in "Blood Brothers," willing to die for his own sins, for those of his brother, and to prevent any future transgressions on his own part. In 1864, Stefan's mistake was keeping his faith in his father even after Katherine's capture, not realizing Giuseppe was easily capable of killing his own sons for being vampire sympathizers. Stefan meant his father no harm, and enticing Damon to feed was a mistake he made during the first moments of elation of being a new vampire, realizing not only his physical capabilities but his stunning emotional one — the ability to turn off guilt and pain.

Elena is not a vampire or a witch or even in possession of a protective ring. She is a mere human, and yet she has managed to save the Salvatore brothers just as often as they've saved her, and it's always with the power of her words. Telling Stefan why her parents were in the car the night of the accident (that a simple choice she made to go out instead of staying in for family night led to their deaths) Elena makes a powerful argument: part of life is living with the consequences of actions however painful or shameful. She presents him with a choice, the inverse of the one he made the night he turned — live and keep fighting to be good, or die with the sunrise. Throughout the episode, Elena doesn't let Stefan or Damon get away without a piece of her mind, using her words to help them face the truths they each avoid.

Damon may say he doesn't care about his brother and that he has no friends, but it's becoming increasingly difficult to believe him. Elena and Damon *are* friends; their relationship is playful and honest. He cares about her and protects her and she knows it and returns the feelings. While it would be hard to classify his relationship with Alaric as a friendship, the two share a connection (in being ditched by the women they love) and together make the best vampire-human detective team seen on TV. Alaric realizes that no answer will ever satisfy his need to know why Isobel chose vampirism over him but Damon hasn't entirely given up on Katherine — even though the problem in their relationship predates the tomb, it even predates him turning. Damon hates Stefan because Katherine chose to turn him, too, and, judging by the whispered "I love you, Stefan" in the opening moments of the flashback, Katherine loved Stefan. Damon was willing to become a vampire for Katherine, and he would have chosen death rather than an eternity without her if not for Stefan enticing him with drawn blood.

Anna calls Jeremy her weakness but in the end she chooses her bond with her mother over her new, smoking hot romance. The lurky girl and the loner boy make a great couple who share moments of sweetness, passion, and longing. A weakness for the Gilbert charm runs in the family, but the cruelty John Gilbert shows Pearl is alien to Anna and Jeremy's relationship. John Gilbert's a "hater," like Giuseppe Salvatore and the original Johnathan Gilbert, and he mocks Pearl's affection and proves to be a deadly adversary. Pearl knew she, Anna, and Harper were no longer safe in Mystic Falls, and at least died knowing that Anna was choosing to leave with her. We think of vampires as eternal but all it took was a cheap attack by John Gilbert to kill a vampire over 400 years old. Pearl's and Harper's deaths were not the only final-act twists in "Blood Brothers." Now that Alaric has given up on his quest for answers about Isobel, who should walk into the Mystic Grill . . .

COMPELLING MOMENT: Not one to let Uncle John shame her with a low-blow mother comment, Elena has a feisty reply: "Which mother?"

CIRCLE OF KNOWLEDGE:
- No Matt, Tyler, Jenna, Caroline, or Bonnie this episode.
- While Stefan and Damon are of course brothers by blood, they are also blood brothers in that they are tied together by the exchange of blood that Stefan pushed Damon into to complete his change.
- Grove Hill, where Henry the Friendly Tomb Vamp is staying, is where Trudie Peterson lived and where Isobel grew up ("A Few Good Men").
- Stefan, without his ring, waiting for the sunrise to kill him is reminiscent of the season 3 episode of *Buffy the Vampire Slayer* "Amends." Just as Elena comes to help Stefan, Buffy appeals to Angel to continue to fight despite how hard it is, telling him, "You have the power to do good, to make amends" and "Strong is fighting." In *Buffy*, a sudden snowfall

Bianca Lawson as Emily Bennett

The Vampire Diaries is not the first vampire TV show Bianca Lawson's appeared on: she played Kendra da Vampire Slayer in season 2 of *Buffy the Vampire Slayer.* She has also previously acted in a Kevin Williamson show, as Nikki Green in season 3 of *Dawson's Creek.* Bianca's other credits include *Saved by the Bell: The New Class, Sister, Sister, The Steve Harvey Show, Bones, Save the Last Dance,* and *The Secret Life of the American Teenager.* Bianca plays Maya in the ABC Family adaptation of *Pretty Little Liars,* a series of YA novels by Sara Shepard. She loves her character on *The Vampire Diaries* and adores the show, which she describes as "insanely amazing."

blocks out the sun, whereas in *TVD* Elena has to convince Stefan to keep fighting with her words alone.

- Knowing how Damon completed his transition to become a vampire, the scene with Vicki on the rooftop in "The Night of the Comet" holds another level of meaning. The same dance happened but with Stefan and Damon in reversed roles. With 145 years under his belt, Stefan was able to resist feeding on Vicki on the rooftop, something that Damon, in the confusion of transitioning, couldn't do.

- In the flashback, Damon utters his famous promise to make Stefan's life an "eternity of misery," an oath we heard in their first scene together in the pilot.

- In "Lost Girls," Damon tells Stefan that the deaths of the stoners are "on you, buddy" because Stefan is the one who locked him up and starved him. Here Damon owns his actions, his choices, and their consequences, telling Stefan that the guilt is Damon's alone.

- Damon calls Stefan "little boy lost," possibly referring to William Blake's two poems by that title, one in *Songs of Innocence* (1789), the other in *Songs of Experience* (1794). In the first, a little boy cries out for his father but is in fact alone in the night. In the second, a priest takes the little boy, accusing him of blasphemy, and puts him in an iron chair where he's burned while his parents watch and weep.

THE RULES: Damon clarifies the threshold rule: a vampire must be invited in by an owner, permanent resident, or person of entitlement; hotel rooms and short-term rentals are a grey area (which could explain Stefan and Damon's easy access to the Salvatore boardinghouse).

THE DIABOLICAL PLAN: John Gilbert is still after the device; his motivations and its purpose are unclear. Some of the tomb vampires are still hungry for their revenge on the descendents of the founding families of Mystic Falls.

HISTORY LESSON: For the flashback episode, the blackboard in Alaric's classroom has notes on a Civil War battle, the Siege of Petersburg, Virginia (1864–1865). Seeing Johnathan Gilbert and Giuseppe Salvatore deciding what to record in the founder's archives was a nice commentary on the nature of historical documents: they are written with a particular perspective and purpose, which may or may not align with the truth.

BITE MARKS: In the flashback, Damon attacks a guard in order to free Katherine; both he and Stefan are shot and killed — by their own father. Henry the Friendly Tomb Vamp and Alaric fight. Later, Alaric stakes him. Defending himself in 1864, Stefan impales his father. Damon feeds on and presumably kills the girl Stefan brings him. In the present day, John murders Pearl and Harper.

MEANWHILE IN FELL'S CHURCH: In *The Fury*, Stefan pushes Matt away, feeling guilt and shame about attacking humans. Stefan says, "I am what I am," meaning he is nothing more than the monster he was in his moment of rage. In *The Struggle*, Elena writes in her diary about her faith in Stefan, something that Elena of the show shares: "He can be violent and I know there are some things in his past that he's ashamed of. But he could never be violent toward me, and the past is over." Also in *The Fury*, Stefan is consumed with guilt and refuses to feed in order to punish himself, saying, "I should never have tried to change my nature." In *The Awakening*, Stefan tells his story to Elena, and, though some important details are different, he feels responsible for Damon: "I damned him. . . . I condemned him to live in the night." In *The Fury*, Stefan considers taking off his ring and waiting for the sunrise to finish him off.

OFF CAMERA: Primarily a theater actor and instructor, Joe Knezevich, who plays the original Johnathan Gilbert, has appeared in *The Librarian: Curse of the Judas Chalice* and *Drop Dead Diva*. Also, fans love the Alaric-Damon scenes in this episode and took up "beer and blood" as a moniker for this pairing.

FOGGY MOMENTS: In "Unpleasantville," Stefan says that the founding families burned Emily and took her things. But in this flashback, Emily is still alive after Stefan has attacked his father. Did Giuseppe die that night? If he did, it wouldn't have been possible for Johnathan Gilbert and Giuseppe to discuss him taking Emily's grimoire to his grave (which was the conversation recorded in the Gilbert journal that lead Stefan and Damon to their father's grave in "Children of the Damned").

Sitting on the shore in the flashback, Damon tells Stefan that he watched the church burn with Katherine inside it, but in "History Repeating," *Stefan* saw her enter the church with his own eyes (and thus is surprised Katherine's still alive).

In "Blood Brothers," Emily tells Stefan that Katherine did not use compulsion on Damon, but in both "Lost Girls" and "History Repeating," Stefan believes that Katherine compelled Damon just like she compelled him.

Why does Emily tell Stefan that his pure heart will be his curse? Did she have similar words for Damon that were just not shown or is Stefan somehow "special"?

MUSIC: When Anna surprises Jeremy at the school, he's listening to Timbaland with OneRepublic's "Marchin On (Timbo Version)." Uncle John and Pearl meet at the Grill to Little Boots' "Click." Jeremy and Anna's love scene soundtrack is "In Line" by Robert Skoro. John tries bargaining with Pearl to get the invention while Jamie McDonald's "Thinking of You" plays in the background. The sweet goodbye scene between Anna and Jeremy is to Aron Wright's "Song for the Waiting." Alaric is joined by a surprise guest at the bar while We the Kings' "We'll Be a Dream" plays.

> *Stefan: So, at the risk of sounding like a jealous boyfriend . . .*
> *Damon: Oh, there's no risk. You do.*
> *Stefan: History will not be repeating itself where Elena is concerned.*

1.21 *Isobel*

Original air date: May 6, 2010

Written by: Caroline Dries and Brian Young
Directed by: J. Miller Tobin
Guest cast: Jena Sims (Cherie), Michael Roark (Frank the Cowboy)

As the town prepares for Founder's Day, Elena meets her birth mother.

This episode picks up right where "Blood Brothers" left off with Isobel saying hello to the husband she left behind. Relatively new to being a vamp, Isobel has turned off her humanity as much as she can — roughing up Alaric to get her way, using people as her playthings and minions, crushing Matt's arm to show Elena she means business — but she still loves Alaric and in her own way tries to make amends for leaving him. She's not the only one in Mystic Falls trying to right her wrongs. Unsure about how to come back from "I made out with your mom then beat you up," Tyler makes a first attempt at rebuilding his friendship with Matt, with no success. Elena is similarly rebuffed by Jeremy after learning that he's read her journal and knows what she did to him. Elena has better luck with Bonnie who comes to apologize for turning away from her when she saw Elena in tears at the Grill. Telling Elena that she'll be there for her reconnects these two friends just when Elena needs Bonnie the most.

Though Elena doesn't know it yet, that bond is again being tested as Bonnie decides not to remove the power of the Gilbert weapon. Instead, she fakes it using the "parlor tricks" she's shown before — levitation, playing with fire — in a controversial plot twist. Looking at the situation from Bonnie's perspective, a weapon that works against vampires is a useful tool. She hasn't seen the good in Damon; to her, he's the vampire who fed on and compelled Caroline, killed Tanner, turned Vicki, and tried to kill her. Bonnie has seen Stefan at his best and worst. He saved her life after Damon attacked her. But more recently she witnessed Stefan attack Amber, blood dripping from his chin, and she knows he stopped only when she overpowered him with her witchy-mojo. Bonnie's sense of right and wrong in the supernatural world comes from Grams, and pretending to disarm the weapon could finish what Grams started and it could protect Mystic Falls from the tomb vampires. She's also the latest in a line of Bennett witches whose relationship with the Salvatore brothers and Katherine is tense and complex; it was Emily who armed the Gilbert inventions in the first place. Bonnie's legacy is to honor that choice and help protect the innocent as Emily did. But did Bonnie fully understand the potential ramifications of her decision? She's handing down a

The Shirtless Frequency Index

As it turns out, handsome vampires like to take their shirts off, especially Stefan. Tallied here is the frequency of shirtlessness by character. THE RULES: if a character was never seen with his or her shirt on — like a Sexy Suds Car Wash extra or a Tri Delt — they're not listed. No point for a bare shoulder to suggest shirtlessness, but lifting a shirt to see if a wound has healed or partially hiding under the covers gets half a point. Extra point awarded for multiple instances of shirtlessness in the same episode.

Stefan (Pilot, The Night of the Comet, Friday Night Bites, Family Ties, Lost Girls, 162 Candles, History Repeating, The Turning Point, Children of the Damned, Let the Right One In, Blood Brothers) — 13 points

Damon (Friday Night Bites, Family Ties, Lost Girls, The Turning Point, Children of the Damned, A Few Good Men, Blood Brothers, Isobel) — 9.5

Caroline (The Night of the Comet, Family Ties, You're Undead to Me, A Few Good Men) — 4

Elena (Friday Night Bites, The Turning Point) — 2

Jeremy (You're Undead to Me, Blood Brothers) — 1.5

With one point each: **Bonnie** (You're Undead to Me), **Tyler** (Haunted), **Ben** (Children of the Damned), **Matt** (A Few Good Men), **Anna** (Blood Brothers), **Frank the Cowboy** (Isobel), **Cherie** (Isobel). Special points go to **Vicki** for being the only main character to dance pantless.

death sentence for the Salvatores, deciding that her best friend's boyfriend is expendable. Bonnie may be right: Elena may never forgive her for this.

Bonnie is not the only one making decisions without the consent of the affected people. Back in "Haunted" Elena decided to take away Jeremy's memory and she's suffering the fallout from that now: he says it wasn't her call to make. Isobel and Uncle John (or rather Papa John) believe they are doing what's best for their daughter by plotting to kill the Salvatore brothers; they don't want Elena to have a life full of vampires or to become one herself. Isobel also decides to make it "easier" for Alaric, using her compulsion to free his heart of her. Perhaps least effectively, Stefan attempts to keep the love triangle that Isobel outed from developing any further with an appeal to his brother.

For a vampire who claims to have turned off his emotions, Damon has a whole lot of feeling for Elena. With Bonnie withdrawing from their friendship, Elena turned to Damon to deal with Stefan. And in dealing with the Stefan Blood Crisis, Damon and Elena grew closer. Elena has shown empathy for Damon in his darkest hours, she's saved his life twice, and she never hides her feelings — good or bad — from him. When Damon confronts Isobel at her hideout, it's clear to her, and to the audience, that Damon's alliance is no longer to Katherine; it's to Elena. Isobel uses that to her advantage and has no qualms about creating

Mia Kirshner as Isobel Flemming

Toronto-born Mia Kirshner has been a professional actress since she was 14, and one of her first recurring parts was on the Canadian TV show *Dracula: The Series*. In the early '90s, Mia received praise for two of her roles, Benita in Denys Arcand's *Love and Human Remains* (1993) and Christina in Atom Egoyan's *Exotica* (1994). Perhaps best known to TV audiences as Jenny Schecter on *The L Word*, Mia Kirshner also appeared in *Wolf Lake* with Paul Wesley, in *24* as Mandy, and in the films *Not Another Teen Movie*, *The Black Dahlia*, and in another vampire project, *30 Days of Night: Dark Days*. In 2008, with the aid of Amnesty International and others, Mia saw a project eight years in the making published: *I Live Here* is a collection of life stories of refugees and displaced people from Malawi, Burma, Mexico, and Chechnya. Mia dedicates a great deal of her time to the ongoing project of I Live Here, which aims to transform the lives of those in extreme poverty. It was while in Malawi on a dairy farm that she was offered the role of Isobel. "I got this call . . . about the show . . . and it sounded pretty cool," related Mia to TVChick.com. "[I spoke to Kevin and Julie] through Skype and it was a really crackly connection, but there were words: mysterious and unpredictable and stuff like that, I believe, we used in the conversation that made me excited about the character. And I knew that they were talented, so I said yes — not knowing a lot about it. It was kind of a leap of faith." Mia would love to see Isobel go "head-to-head with Katherine one day" and loves the chemistry she and Matt Davis have onscreen. "I think what's most impressive about the cast is something that perhaps people take for granted [which] is that they're professionals," said Mia. "They know their lines, they do their job, and they take their work very seriously. As a result of that, it's a welcoming atmosphere."

a deliciously awkward moment by telling Elena in front of both Damon and Stefan that she knew her plan would work because Damon is in love with Elena. Stefan has been the model of patience and understanding about the growing friendship between his brother and Elena, never saying a word when she hugged Damon, when she did up his shirt buttons, when he left the tomb just because she asked, or even when he handed over the Gilbert weapon at her request, putting his own life in danger to save someone she cares about. But Stefan will no longer stand idly by; Isobel's blunt words about Damon's feelings for Elena force Stefan to follow suit and warn his brother to back off.

Is Elena doomed, as Isobel tells her, as long as she has a Salvatore brother on each arm? Though she's a far cry from the picture of motherhood, Isobel raises questions (and veiled fears) about Elena's future — if she stays with Stefan, is she going to allow herself to age while Stefan stays eternally 17? Will she become a vampire? Will she be torn between the brothers? Family legacy is hugely important to these characters and Elena's heritage is split between the Gilberts who are traditionally vampire haters and the Pierces who take to the darkest sides of vampirism with relish. Will Elena favor one side or the other, or find a balance that's eluded Isobel and John? While these questions are likely to take the duration of the series to answer, at the very least Elena will soon have the question of her parentage resolved as Damon figures out what some fans guessed when Uncle John showed up in "Under Control." Too bad Elena hates that guy.

COMPELLING MOMENT: Alaric in the hallway with Isobel, taking off his ring and vervain, telling her to kill him or compel him because he doesn't believe the Isobel he loves is gone.

CIRCLE OF KNOWLEDGE:
- Isobel tells Elena that Katherine sought her out because of "genetic curiosity," confirming that the Pierce bloodline somehow runs from Katherine to Isobel and from Isobel to Elena.
- Damon picks Jack London's *Call of the Wild* as the book for Bonnie's witchcraft demonstration. London's 1903 novel follows an extraordinarily powerful dog, Buck, as he is passed from owner to owner, some more cruel than others, in the North. The wilderness has a set of rules very different from the domesticated world Buck came from and he eventually answers the call of the wild and breaks his ties to mankind,

joining a wolf pack as its alpha male. But Buck returns every year to the place where his one good master was murdered. Hmm, a wild and powerful creature who is incredibly loyal — wonder why Damon likes the book.

- John Gilbert tells Isobel she wouldn't hurt a kid, and she threatens to kill Jeremy to prove him wrong. In "Friday Night Bites," Damon kills Tanner to prove to Stefan that he has no humanity left. But both Isobel and Damon are lying: they do retain at least some of their humanity.
- Back in "Family Ties," when Zach was still with us, Damon sensed Zach had something on his mind and said, "Go ahead. Purge," nearly the same thing he says to Stefan at the end of this episode.

THE DIABOLICAL PLAN: Isobel relieves Uncle John of his mission (since he's failed) and gets the Gilbert device, a weapon against vampires. A minion just like John, Isobel's following Katherine's orders. Elena's plan to rescue Jeremy without giving Isobel what she wants is solid, but Bonnie has her own plan and it's in line with Uncle John's and Katherine's: destroy the tomb vampires.

BITE MARKS: Isobel roughs up Alaric and Uncle John, makes Frank crush Matt's arm with the trailer, and has Cherie and Frank beat up Uncle John. She and Damon tussle.

MEANWHILE IN FELL'S CHURCH: In *The Struggle*, Stefan is very respectful of Elena's privacy and, while that space is considerate, it also leaves room for Damon and Elena to bond. In the books, their bond tends to be dangerous and destructive rather than a force that helps Damon rediscover his humanity.

OFF CAMERA: Though Alaric was briefly shown at home among unpacked boxes in the beginning of "Bloodlines," Julie Plec explained that there's so much "late-night school action" and scenes set at the bar for him not only because Alaric is a "sexy lush" but because . . . no house set has been built for him yet.

FOGGY MOMENTS: While Gregor Mendel's theory of genetic inheritance may not be entirely reliable, it's seems unlikely that two blue-eyed people like Isobel and Uncle John would produce a child with dark brown eyes like Elena. (Yes, just holding out hope that somehow, someway Uncle John is not Elena's father.)

MUSIC: Vampire Weekend's "Giving Up the Gun" plays as the students prepare the floats for the Founder's Day parade. Uncle John arrives at Isobel's to see her "side show" dancing to Anya Marina's "All the Same to Me." Neon Trees' "Our War" is on at the Grill while Elena waits and thanks Stefan for being there with her. Isobel reveals her reason for wanting to meet Elena with Sounds Under Radio's "Sing" in the background. Damon and Cherie play strip poker to Cage the Elephant's "Ain't No Rest for the Wicked." The Cribs' "We Share the Same Skies" plays as Tyler tries to repair his friendship with Matt. To Band of Horses' "Laredo" the Mystic Falls students work on the floats and Isobel attacks.

Damon: . . . somewhere along the way you decided that I was worth saving. And I wanted to thank you.

1.22 Founder's Day

Original air date: May 13, 2010
Written by: Bryan Oh and Andrew Chambliss
Directed by: Marcos Siega
Guest cast: Mike Erwin (Tomb Vampire), Kevin Nichols (Deputy #1), Jason Giuliano (Deputy #2), Dave Pileggi (EMT #1)

It's the sesquicentennial of Mystic Falls and history looks like it will be repeating itself as Uncle John prepares to round up the vampires. Let the fireworks begin.

The promo for the season finale of *The Vampire Diaries* said it would leave fans breathless and "Founder's Day" keeps that promise. It's an outstanding end to a first season that barely missed a beat in 22 episodes. The only problem with the finale is that you can only fall for the final twist once (so cherish that memory, Damon-Elena shippers). There were clues for the attentive viewer: the opening scene with Elena dressed as Katherine foreshadows the

ending, Katherine's "Elena" outfit is different than Elena's, and the way she kisses Damon (let alone the fact that she is *kissing Damon*) is more minxy Katherine than soulful Elena.

Uncle John only realizes it is Katherine he's pouring his heart out to when his fingers go flying across the cutting board. His survival in question as the season ends, John is a difficult character, one who makes it easy to hate him but it's not entirely fair to, as Jeremy tries to explain to Anna in the finale's opening scenes. His methods are ruthless — since Sheriff Forbes doesn't agree with him, he knocks her out and locks her up — but he saves countless lives by detonating the Gilbert weapon at Founder's Day. His motivation for wanting Stefan and Damon dead is to protect his daughter from the danger of vampires and from the heartache he's suffered loving Isobel; presumably that's also why he stops to kill Anna — to protect Jeremy. His motives don't justify his actions but they do humanize him in the same way that Giuseppe Salvatore's actions were guided by his similar sense of right and wrong. Where both men go wrong is in their close-mindedness and unwillingness to listen to the younger generation's pleas.

Bonnie shares responsibility with Uncle John for saving the townsfolk of Mystic Falls by not deactivating the device. Her decision to honor her family legacy was justified but, unlike John Gilbert, Bonnie rights her wrong against the Salvatore brothers and Elena, taming the fire so Stefan could rescue Damon. Compare Bonnie from the pilot to the character she's become in the finale: she's fierce and powerful and resolved — if Damon spills innocent blood, she's taking him out. Will Bonnie become a sort of slayer in season 2? With great power comes great responsibility, Bonnie.

Stefan lives up to his name in the finale, playing the savior once again as he pulls his brother from the fire. However, his fear that history will repeat itself and he will find himself in another "ménage à threesome" clouds his perception of his brother. After the encounter with Jeremy, Stefan tells Damon that because his intentions aren't honorable, no good deed he does "counts." Being a do-gooder *is* a foreign concept to Damon, but this is the change that Stefan's hoped would come to pass for the past 145 years. It's proven difficult for Stefan to see past the "sense of Damon humor," and not react when his brother relishes in needling him about his insecurities. At the Grill with Elena, Stefan realizes it's pointless to try and hate his brother — he can't stop caring about him. Perhaps with Elena's reassurance that Stefan is the Salvatore she loves, he will be able to see the good that's grown in Damon.

Believing he's talking to Elena, Damon reflects on the immense change that's come over him since he arrived in Mystic Falls. In "Founder's Day,"

Teen Wolf

The writers of *The Vampire Diaries* held onto a major story arc for season 2, only dropping a few hints about the Lockwood curse in season 1 to prepare fans for a new kind of supernatural creature when the show returns for its next season.

In "Family Ties," during a scene with Tyler at the Grill, the song "You're a Wolf" (by Sea Wolf) plays.

The name of the Mystic Falls High School team is the Timberwolves.

When Tyler freaks out and hits Jeremy in "The Turning Point," it's the night of a full moon.

There is also a full moon the night of the kick-off party in "Under Control," when Tyler beats up Matt.

In "Founder's Day," both Tyler and his father react to the Gilbert weapon despite the fact that they are not vampires. When the EMT opens Tyler's eye after the accident, it's not a human eye that looks back....

that growth culminates in a series of kind acts: he thanks Bonnie for deactivating the weapon (which arguably encourages her to come to his rescue in the end); he warns Stefan and Elena about the tomb vampires' impending attack; he lies paralyzed and suffering because he can't save Anna; he tries to do right by Jeremy by telling him the truth, knowing that lies have hurt Jeremy most; and he apologizes for his part in Vicki's death. In "A Few Good Men," Damon drunkenly joked that his newfound purpose was "how can I help people," but by the finale it is the driving motivator in his life — no more diabolical plan to be had. As Damon said to Elena in "Family Ties," it "always comes down to the love of a woman," and after 145 years that woman is no longer Katherine, it's Elena. But when Damon figures out it was Katherine, not Elena, that he spoke to so openly and kissed, will his change be a lasting one? Or will Damon revert to his old ways as quickly as Stefan was able to come out of his dark turn?

When season 2 begins, Damon may also have to face the unintentional role he played in Jeremy's decision to become a vampire. Damon telling Jeremy that life is easier with a vampire's ability to turn off emotion pushes Jeremy to end his human life. By choosing Elena's leftover pain medication from the car accident to kill himself, he ties himself to what he's lost — his parents, Vicki (who he fought with over those drugs), and to Elena (his estranged sister). In drinking Anna's blood, Jeremy lets go of the pain of losing her and takes on the vampiric existence he once hoped to share with her. Jeremy's journey has been a tragic one, losing everyone who matters most to him. Even the attempt Elena made to protect him, by wiping his memory of Vicki's last moments, just made him feel emptier and more isolated. He is without a guide in the ways of vampirism — does he even know he has to feed on human blood to complete the change? Will he make that choice?

Jeremy won't be alone in dealing with a new supernatural identity. After a season of only hints here and there about the Lockwood curse, Tyler's reaction to the Gilbert weapon, thought to only affect vampires, and the reveal of Tyler's eye paves the road for a season 2 with another supernatural element in Mystic Falls. With Mayor Lockwood dead, Tyler will have to deal with the loss of the strongest influence in his life, however destructive his father's example was. It promises to be a meatier season for Michael Trevino.

The Vampire Diaries finishes its first season with cliffhangers galore, ending with its heroine mid-stride down the hallway toward what may be her first encounter with her evil doppelgänger, Katherine.

The Founder's Day parade passes through the streets of Covington. Pictured above is the Miss Mystic Falls float with the actors preparing to film the "Damon waves at Elena" scene.

Marcos Siega, Director and Co-Executive Producer

"I've never had such a good-looking show," said Kevin Williamson. "It's very polished. If you knew what went into it and how we have less money than bigger-budgeted shows, it's even more impressive." The person primarily responsible for establishing the look of *The Vampire Diaries*, from its pilot through its 22 episodes so far, is Marcos Siega. Born in Queens, New York, in 1969, Marcos began his career not in film school but in a hardcore punk band. As a guitar player in Bad Trip, Marcos recorded a handful of EPs and two albums. He began directing music videos for other bands, and his background as a musician helped him relate to the guys in front of the camera. With close to a hundred music video credits to his name, Marcos has worked with artists like System of a Down, Paramore, Weezer, Blink-182, and P.O.D. His video for "Chop Suey" (System of a Down) won a MPVAA award for best video; Blink-182's "All the Small Things" video received three MTV VMA nominations; and Marcos was nominated for a Grammy for Papa Roach's "Broken Home" video. In 1999, Marcos directed his first film, a short called *Stung*. Around this time, he also started shooting commercials and working on TV series like *Rock the House*, *Fastlane*, *Veronica Mars*, and *Oliver Beene*. His feature film directorial debut came with *Pretty Persuasion* (2005), which starred Evan Rachel Wood and received acclaim at film festivals like Sundance. Marcos directed a second feature, *Underclassman* (2005) with Nick Cannon, and continued his work on series with episodes of *The Nine*, *Shark*, *Life*, *Cold Case*, *October Road*, *True Blood*, and *Dexter* (on which he is one of the main directors).

In 2007, his third feature was released; *Chaos Theory* starred Ryan Reynolds and also featured Chris William Martin (Zach Salvatore) and Mike Erwin (the leader of the tomb vampires in TVD's "Founder's Day"). It's not unusual for an actor who works with Marcos and impresses him to get another gig out of him. Marcos had cast Spencer Locke (Amber in "Miss Mystic Falls") in an episode of *Cold Case* and hired her for *The Vampire Diaries*, knowing she could handle the intense scenes opposite Paul Wesley. When Papa Salvatore needed to be cast, Marcos immediately suggested James Remar, who he worked with on *Dexter* — he thought Remar looked like a good halfway point between Ian Somerhalder and Paul Wesley.

Initially, as supervising producer, then as co-executive producer of *The Vampire Diaries*, Marcos worked on the show from its inception. He helped cast it with Kevin and Julie, establish its look, hired the directors who would work on the episodes Marcos wasn't directing, and he was on set in Atlanta overseeing the day-to-day production. In all facets of his job, Marcos had one goal: to make the show as good as possible. That simple goal informed his casting decisions, decided the crew he would work with, affected the attention to detail, and ultimately resulted in a television series that managed a first season without a shaky episode. Marcos directed eight episodes himself ("Pilot," "The Night of the Comet," "Lost Girls," "History Repeating," "Children of the Damned," "Fool Me Once," "Miss Mystic Falls," and "Founder's Day"); for the rest, he hired people he considers better directors than him. In an interview with The VRO, Marcos explained that he chose people who wouldn't normally direct for a CW series, which has a stigma attached to it as neither a cable network (like HBO or

Showtime) or one of the majors (like NBC or Fox). But Marcos managed to bring in people with a strong background who were working on acclaimed shows like *Dexter*, *True Blood*, and *The Shield*, or who were filmmakers with feature credits.

If his job sounds like a lot of work, it's because it is an *incredibly large* amount of work. Add to that hectic schedule a five-hour flight home to Los Angeles on the weekends to spend time with his daughter and wife. As had been his plan with Kevin and Julie from the beginning, Marcos is scaling back his involvement in *The Vampire Diaries* for season 2, having done his job in establishing the look of the series and the caliber of performers and crew. With the roster of directors hired by Marcos for the second season, he is slated to direct four episodes and will spend the rest of his time working out of Los Angeles on shows like *Dexter* as well as being with his growing family. A universally loved guy, who Julie Plec describes as "incredibly talented, passionate, and committed," the TVD family — from actors to crew to writers to fans — will be eager for Marcos' return to the director's chair in Mystic Falls.

COMPELLING MOMENT: The kiss.

CIRCLE OF KNOWLEDGE:

- When the brothers see Elena in her parade costume, looking like Katherine, they have the same in-unison reaction they did in "Lost Girls" when their heads turned to watch Katherine walk by, both smitten.

- John Gilbert refers to the V5 deputies, a term that was introduced in "The Turning Point" when Sheriff Forbes saw Logan, returned as a vampire, at the high school.

- In "History Repeating," Damon says to Stefan of the Battle of Willow Creek, "Don't think it won't happen again," and he's right. The leaders of Mystic Falls gather up the vampires and burn them alive just like they (thought they) did in 1864.

- The Gilbert weapon is armed with Emily's super-strength version of the spell Sheila used on Damon in "Fool Me Once" and Bonnie used on Stefan in "Miss Mystic Falls." John Gilbert's pseudo-scientific explanation of how it works simply carries on the original Johnathan Gilbert's mistaken belief that he was a successful inventor.

- Jeremy asking Damon if it's easier to be a vampire echoes the conversation Stefan and Vicki had outside the Salvatore crypt in "Lost Girls" as she made her choice whether to feed on human blood or die. She asked him, "Is it better?" and Stefan had no reply for her.

- In "Miss Mystic Falls," Damon threatens to sever Uncle John's hand, pull off the ring, and kill him. And here Katherine executes a similar plan.
- The pills Jeremy takes are acetaminophen and hydrocodone, also known by the brand name Vicodin.
- The Gilbert kitchen knives have seen plenty of vampire action this season. In "You're Undead to Me," Elena cuts herself while chopping garlic causing Stefan to vamp out. In "There Goes the Neighborhood," Jeremy slices his hand open to tempt Anna. In "Founder's Day," Katherine takes John's fingers clean off his hand.

THE RULES: When Bonnie dampened the fire with her witchcraft, she appeared to be holding on to Elena's arm not only to stop her from going into the building, but to draw power from her heightened emotion.

THE DIABOLICAL PLAN: John Gilbert succeeds in eradicating the town of the tomb vampires but fails to take out the Salvatore brothers. Did Katherine return to Mystic Falls just to kill John or does she have other targets in mind?

BITE MARKS: John bonks Sheriff Forbes on the head. The Gilbert weapon disables the vampires and the Lockwood men; the deputies control the vampires with vervain; and the captured are burned alive — with the exception of Anna, staked by John; Mayor Lockwood, killed by the leader of the tomb vampires; and Damon. Caroline sustains internal bleeding in the car accident. Jeremy overdoses on pills. Katherine cuts off John's fingers and stabs him.

MEANWHILE IN FELL'S CHURCH: In *The Awakening*, Elena dresses up in an Italian Renaissance era gown for Halloween, making her appear identical to Katherine, just as Elena does to Stefan and Damon in her 1860s gown in "Founder's Day." For Founder's Day in *The Struggle*, Elena and Caroline are both outfitted in dresses from the era of the town's founding. Also in *The Struggle*, Damon helps Elena avert disaster on Founder's Day. His motivation to give aid seems to be his strong affection for her, which she finds undeniable: "Something was building between them, something that frightened Elena with its power." Though Damon is helping solve the problem, it was after all caused by his actions — as were the events of Founder's Day in this episode. In *Dark Reunion*, Stefan admits that Damon "can be a big help if he puts his mind to it." From a storytelling standpoint, the TV series has adopted the same fast pace as L.J. Smith's novels, as well as her tendency to pick up exactly where the last book left off. Hopefully season 2 will open where season 1 left off just as *The Struggle* opens in the same moment that ends *The Awakening*.

OFF CAMERA: Mike Erwin plays the leader of the tomb vampires, adding another name to the list of *Everwood* alumni who've appeared on *The Vampire Diaries*, like Paul Wesley, Steven R. McQueen, and Melinda Clarke.

Nina Dobrev talked to MTV about filming the twist: "What was cool about it was that I had to kind of play both. I didn't want to play it too obvious. I didn't want to give it away for the audience, because you've got to surprise them and keep them thinking that it isn't Katherine that's actually kissing him. So it was a challenge, but it was fun. I think it turned out really, really well."

Playing a more vulnerable Damon was a challenge for Ian Somerhalder, as he explained to Zap2it.com: "It was not easy for me to play. Because Damon's always in control and, as Ian playing Damon, I feel the same way. So we both sort of empower each other in this odd relationship that I have with this alter ego, and having him be even remotely vulnerable took away a bit of that power and sort of leveled me a little bit. Usually when I'm on my way to work, I'm working on my dialogue, just running [my lines] and when I get out of that car, I am so [focused] and I have a little pep in my step, I feel like I've got the world in my hands. I know I'm about to go jab at someone or be funny, always in a position of power. But during the 11 or 12 days that we shot this last episode, I remember getting out of my car and just feeling strange."

After they learned that Anna was due to be killed in the finale, the crew made "Save Anna" T-shirts and wore them on set, showing their love and support for Malese Jow and her terrific performance as the lurky and awesome Anna.

FOGGY MOMENTS: After busting "Elena" and Damon kissing, Jenna says, "You should probably come inside." Is that a solid enough invitation for a vampire to enter a dwelling or has Katherine been in the Gilbert house before?

MUSIC: The preparations for Founder's Day are to Ellie Goulding's "Every Time You Go." Sia's "You've Changed" plays as Bonnie takes a photo of Matt and Caroline. Elena asks Damon to stop flirting with her with Lifehouse's "It Is What It Is" on in the background. At the Grill, the Mayor gets frustrated

with Tyler to Anberlin's cover of the New Order song "True Faith." Damon is on his way out of the Gilbert house and a special mix of "Bloodstream" by Stateless plays as he talks to "Elena."

QUESTIONS FOR SEASON 2

- Will Caroline recover from her injuries?
- Did Uncle John Gilbert die?
- Did Jeremy succeed in killing himself?
- Stefan and Isobel both regret being turned. Assuming Jeremy completes the change, will he regret it too?
- When will Damon realize it was Katherine, not Elena, he just kissed?
- What fallout will Elena experience from Jenna after she busted Damon and "Elena" kissing? How can she talk her way out of that one — "It was my evil twin"?
- In "Under Control," John Gilbert warned Damon that if he, John, dies his secrets — including the real identity of the Salvatore brothers — go to the council. Does that threat still hold? If Katherine killed John, are Damon and Stefan about to be exposed to the town?

- Will Pearl and Anna return in flashbacks? What is their origin story? Could Lexi return in a flashback? Will Noah's connection to Katherine ever be revealed?
- In "Unpleasantville," Elena is exhilarated after the fight at the school where her life is in danger. In "Fool Me Once," Anna says to her, "You must have a taste for it," because Elena keeps returning to darkness and death. Are these two moments hints at a darker turn for Elena in season 2?

Interview with the Vampire Fandom

What good is a great show if no one watches it? Every fandom needs its leaders, and among the multitude of dedicated and loyal TVD fans, two sites in particular take a lead in sharing all the news on *The Vampire Diaries*, feeding fans' insatiable hunger for all things TVD. Meet Ruthie from VampireDiariesOnline.com and Vee and Red from Vampire-Diaries.net.

When did you first hear about The Vampire Diaries book series?

   Ruthie: My sister Allison had read them and then heard they were going to be doing the TV show based on the books, so she talked me into reading them. I really enjoyed them and immediately became very excited about the show!

   Vee: I've been a Vampire Diaries fan since the series' original publication in the early '90s.
   Red: Same for me, though I found them a year later than Vee, when they were published in the U.K.

How did you get involved in running a fan site for TVD?

   Ruthie: Once my sister found out they were doing the TV series, she decided to create the fan site. She immediately started posting casting information for the show, and created a Twitter account for the site. Then later in the year after the show had been picked up for the fall, she had to return to work full time, so she asked me to take over working on the site, and I ran with it and have built this amazing fan base on the site and on Twitter.

Vee: I talked Red into founding the site.
Red: I think it went along the lines of me saying, "It would be really insane to do this," and Vee insidiously whispering, "Doooo iiiiit!"
Vee: I'm very convincing. Or is it tricky?

It's an incredible amount of work to keep a site constantly up to date. How much time a week do you spend on it?
    Ruthie: Too much . . . haha. I am a stay-at-home mom, so I spend a large portion of my day balancing kids, house, and working on the site. I don't set hours for myself; I just work on the site and Twitter when I can, off and on, all day long. Let's just say I'm great at multitasking!

    Vee: I work full time in addition to working on the site and I do not exaggerate when I say I feel like I'm working two full-time jobs.
    Red: It definitely feels like a full-time job. When we're not blogging, Twittering, or watching the forums, we're doing things behind the scenes like adding information to the wiki and the website pages, and also making sure that the site is working from a technical point of view, too. It's not unheard of for me to dream about running this site!

How would you describe the TVD fandom as a whole? Or a typical TVD fan.
    Ruthie: This has been the most amazing experience. I have never been involved with a fan community like this. My sister had in the past; she has created fansites for *American Idol* contestants and ran several other sites for TV shows. But this fandom, I believe, is like no other. We have all become very close via Twitter. Also, having the connection with the cast and crew has added to our experience in ways you can't imagine. They make us feel a part of the show. A typical TVD

fan would be someone who is so dedicated to the show, they don't record it because they know that watching it live will help ratings. Someone who spends a good portion of their day tweeting about the show, in hopes of getting the phrase "Vampire Diaries" trending on Twitter. *That* is a typical TVD fan.

Kat Graham poses with Ruthie from Vampire Diaries Online.

Vee: One of our friends once said that you could spot an L.J. Smith fan by their twisted sense of humor, and I think that's particularly true of Vampire Diaries fans. We're definitely seeing that come to fruition in the TV fandom, too. The fact the Stefan/bunny jokes actually made it into the second episode of the TV series is a testament to that.

Red: I was actually very (pleasantly) surprised at just how much the twisted sense of humor transferred from the book fandom over to the TV series fandom. As for typical TVD fans? I don't think there are any, really. The series seems to draw fans of all ages from all walks of life, making each fan pretty unique. Perhaps that describes the fandom best: diverse with a wicked sense of humor.

Have you ever been involved in other fan communities?

Ruthie: Not really. This is my first time being involved in something like this, at least at this level.

Vee: The LJS fandom is the only one I'd say I've been involved in, and I've always been a participant, not a siterunner or mod or anything like that.

Red: I've been involved with running projects within the LJS fandom for over 10 years, but never been actively involved with other fandoms beyond basic participation. This is the biggest project I've ever been involved with, and I'm amazed at just how big it's grown.

Before TVD, was there something else that you were this passionate about? A book series, TV show, . . .

> **Ruthie:** If I had to say, I would say the Twilight Saga books and movies, but my passion for *The Vampire Diaries* has definitely surpassed it.

> **Vee:** Honestly, I'm a music junkie, so if I had to pick another fandom, I think that's it. There are a lot of books, movies, and TV shows that I'm passionate about, but I can't say I've been active in their fandoms, at least not to the extent I've been with this one.

> **Red:** Like Vee, I'm a fan of a lot of other TV series, books, and films, but haven't been moved enough to dedicate as much of my time and energy to them as I have with *The Vampire Diaries*. Though I may have been moved to do so with the *X-Files* if I'd been on the internet back in the early days of that show.

Describe your relationship with the network — friendly, hands-off, hostile?

> **Ruthie:** They have been awesome and [The CW was] one of our first followers on our Twitter. The CW knows that the fansites that are dedicated to TV shows, like *The Vampire Diaries*, help promote the show and build buzz, and I believe that they know that we are essential to the survival of the series. If it weren't for the fans, there wouldn't be a show, end of story. They have been very supportive, and they retweet our posts on Twitter all the time.

> **Vee:** We've been pleasantly surprised by the network's and Warner Bros.' tolerance of us. Keep in mind that we didn't start the website because we were jumping on the *Vampire Diaries* TV show bandwagon. We've been fans of this series for almost two decades, so we had definite opinions about what we liked and what we didn't when the show was in development. We were critical of quite a few things but we *always* tried to be fair and reasonable. So while I can't imagine they were all that thrilled with some of what we had to say, I give them a huge amount of credit for not sending us nasty emails or strong-arming us in any way. I think The CW recognizes that fandom is a force to be reckoned with and if you have a passionate,

devoted fan base, they're an extension of your marketing department. Of course, that fan base will also be more demanding when it comes to promo, but I can think of worse problems to have.

How about your interactions with the cast, crew, and creators of the show?

Ruthie: The interactions with the cast have been awesome! More than I could have asked for. Early on, the director Marcos Siega and the executive producers and writers of the show, Julie Plec and Kevin Williamson, showed their support for the site by following us on Twitter. We appreciated that so much. I have also personally been very fortunate to meet several of the cast members when I visited the set back in January [2010]. They are genuine and humbled and very appreciative of their fans, and have a hard time believing that the show is so popular and they are so loved.

Red: They're all amazing people, who have been extremely approachable and forthcoming with what amounts to a couple of fans. Though it's not just us they communicate with; we see them chatting with fans all the time on Twitter, taking time out to answer questions. I don't know if it's down to social networking making people more accessible, but it seems to me that the *Vampire Diaries* cast and crew are an exceptionally friendly and down-to-earth bunch of people.

Vee: We've received nothing but respect and kindness from those connected to the show.

Are you into the other vampire franchises — Twilight, *True Blood*?

Ruthie: Actually yes, as I mentioned, I've read the Twilight book series and *True Blood* happens to be my and my husband's guilty pleasure, something we look forward to watching together after the kids go to bed during the summer!

Vee: I thought the first Twilight book was interesting, but obviously not for the same reasons Stephenie Meyer did because *New Moon*'s direction completely lost me and I never bothered with the rest of the series. I've read the first few Sookie Stackhouse novels and I'm a big fan of *True Blood*. I just recently got hooked on *Being Human*. I love Richelle Mead's Vampire Academy series. But I think my favorite piece of vampire media is the BBC series *Ultraviolet*, which starred Jack Davenport. I just recently re-watched it and was blown away — *again* — by how sophisticated and gritty it was. I think it's truly unique within the genre.

Red: Oh, *Ultraviolet*, how I miss thee. I've always been disappointed that we never got to see more of that. But yeah, I'm a huge vampire fan, and have been since I was small. I saw a German/American version of *The Little Vampire* on TV back in the '80s and have been hooked ever since. I enjoyed the first Twilight book when I read it, but have issues in hindsight, and didn't like the way the series went after that. While I've not read the Sookie Stackhouse novels, I do love *True Blood*. Roll on June!

And a few questions to wrap up about this season: favorite episode?

Ruthie: My favorite episode would definitely be "Lost Girls." It's a very pivotal episode. Elena has discovered Stefan's secret and we get our first look at Katherine and it's the first flashback episode.

Vee: "Let the Right One In" was an astonishing episode. It took me completely by surprise. I had similar feelings after "History Repeating," but "Let the Right One In" worked on every single level.

Red: Likewise, I was completely blown over by "Let the Right One In." Damon stepping up to the plate as big brother did it for me, and the interaction between Alaric and Damon was the icing on the cake.

What's the one thing you'd like to see happen in season 2?

Ruthie: For Damon to realize that it was Katherine he kissed and *not* Elena, then rush to Elena's rescue.

Vee: I'm looking forward to the "circle of knowledge" growing. I'm waiting for Caroline, Matt, and Tyler to be in the vampire loop. I also can't wait for Caroline and Matt to discover how much Elena has kept from them in regards to Damon's compulsion of Caroline and Vicki's change and death. That's going to rock the friendship boat quite a bit.

Red: I'd love to see more development in Matt and Stefan's friendship. It was my favorite part of the books, so I'm dying to see it on the screen. I'm also really curious to see exactly where they're going with Tyler and his developing "Time of the Month." Given the TV series' Tyler has a lot more depth to him than his book counterpart, it should make it a very interesting journey to watch.

Who would win in a fight: Katherine or Damon?

Ruthie: Well, according to the poll I ran on my site, everyone thinks Katherine would win, because on the TV show they have developed the idea that the older a vampire you are, the stronger you are. So for Damon to win, he would definitely need to outsmart her, and I think he is perfectly capable of doing that. So I say Damon! Plus I think if he is eventually put in this position, he will probably be fighting not only for his own life, but Elena's and possibly Stefan's life as well.

Vee: Damon — but not before Katherine wiped the floor with him a few times.

Red: Evidence from the show tells me that Katherine should be able to win based on strength alone; Damon got his backside handed to him by Pearl and Lexi, after all. But I think that people underestimate Damon's ingenuity, tenacity, and patience. If you give him a little time to plot someone's demise, Damon will ultimately prevail.

Vee: *Exactly.*

Vee and Red were asked to edit a book of essays on The

Vampire Diaries* for Smart Pop Books. Tell us about *A Visitor's Guide to Mystic Falls: Your Favorite Authors on The Vampire Diaries.

Red: We were both really stunned when we got the email asking if we were interested in contributing with an essay, and very honored. It was initially kind of a scary concept for me to wrap my head around (previously, the only thing I've had published was a couple of poems I entered into a competition when I was 15), but now it's really exciting. And still a touch scary.

Vee: I've been a big fan of the Smart Pop series since *Finding Serenity*, their first volume dedicated to Joss Whedon's *Firefly*. This show has inspired incredible conversations amongst the fan base and I think the book is an extension of those back-and-forths. The hard part was narrowing down the essay topics! And the fact that there is so much to say about this show after only one season is pretty amazing. It's not all Stefan versus Damon.

Spirits Talk: Benjamin Ayres

(Coach Tanner)

How did you land the role of Mystic Falls High's mean teacher?

My agent called me, and I auditioned for the role of Mr. Tanner in Vancouver two days before my scenes were to be filmed in the pilot episode.

When you were first cast, did you know Tanner would come to a grisly end?

Originally, I thought I was only to appear in the pilot episode. Once the show got picked up for season 1, it moved its shooting location to Atlanta. I was living in Toronto at that point gearing up to film my current series, *Dan for Mayor*. The *Vampire Diaries'* production called, wanting me for two more episodes. They quickly pulled some immigration strings, papers were signed, and I traveled back and forth a few times for the episodes. I knew, yes, that I was to meet a grisly end. I did not, however, know exactly how that end was to be met.

How did you prepare for the role — any speed-reading of The Vampire Diaries' books?

I did not get the chance to read the books so I used social networking sites and Google to find as much info as I could. The writing on the show is so good that I just put my trust in that. I discovered that the character I was playing was a slight departure from the books.

What's your take on Tanner — a total jerk or just a misunderstood guy? The scene where Jenna "got Tannered" suggests that even though this guy won't sugarcoat anything, he's looking out for his students.

I believe he completely looks out for his students. He just does it with a bigger ego than most. When I did the first episode, I was unaware that Tanner was also the football coach. Once I discovered that, it made more sense that he had that aggressive, competitive chip. I had this exact teacher in high school. He's the one I remember the most.

Does any particular scene stand out for you? That death scene, perhaps?

The death scene, of course. It was a very technical scene for a half-second death. Ramps, crash-pads, and blood. Having a man suck on your neck while pretending to die is not easy. We laughed our way through that scene.

Were you able to keep up watching the rest of the season, post-Tanner?

Unfortunately not. I have to catch up!

Do you have any favorite on-set or crew memories? Quite a few of the actors on TVD are Canadian: you, Nina Dobrev, Sara Canning, Chris William Martin. . . . Did a little Hollywood North community pop up when production moved to Atlanta?

I pretty much rolled into town, shot my scenes, and then left. There was really no chance for me to hang with the gang while not on set. Which is too bad. Sara, Nina, and I have mutual friends back home, and we made an effort to hang. Unfortunately, time did not allow that to happen. While there I had one weekend off but had to fly to Vancouver to be best man at my best friend's wedding.

Were you surprised by the show's success?

It's always a little surprising to see something blow up to this proportion. I knew it would be popular. But this is another level. I'm very proud of the show.

The *Vampire Diaries'* fandom is really active online, and you're on Twitter. Did you interact much with fans? Any "RIP Tanner" @replies?

I interact any and every chance I can, time permitting. Twitter is a great tool for getting to chat with fans of shows I've been on. *VD* fans are great. So are the *jPod* fans.

Dan for Mayor was picked up for season 2 — will your character, Mike, be back with the moustache?

Mike will be back with the soup strainer, yes. I have begun the growth for the girth needed. Begins with a beard, trims to a beautiful 'stache in two months time. I have another project that I'm not allowed to talk about at this time. So I'm gonna end the interview being all elusive :)

On Set in Mystic Falls

Jennifer Ridings (@InTwilightWoods) lives in Atlanta, but on TV she's a resident of Mystic Falls: Jennifer has been on *The Vampire Diaries* many times as a background performer, or extra.

Tell me about your experience as a TVD extra.

Every time I've worked on *The Vampire Diaries*, it has been a great experience. I have found the cast and crew to be very friendly and kind. It's obvious that they have a close bond with each other. I've enjoyed seeing them joke and laugh with one another, and hearing Ian sing when not filming, and I feel grateful to have been a (small) part of such an awesome show.

My first experience as an extra on TVD was in March 2010. I worked the entire day in heels and an evening gown at the Founder's Hall set, filming the "Miss Mystic Falls" episode. It was all so new to me and seemed magical . . . especially as day turned into evening and a group of us extras were taken back to set. All the little twinkling lights were plugged in inside Founder's Hall. Here I am all dressed up, with Nina and Ian standing just a few feet away . . . and then Ian walked up and spoke right to me. Needless to say, I was thrilled.

Since that first experience, I've been blessed to work on the show a handful of other times — sometimes in the Covington town square, sometimes at the "high school" or inside the Mystic Grill . . . which, of course, isn't actually in Covington but on a closed set. A friend of

Not working as an extra that day, Jennifer visits the set during the filming of "Founder's Day," posing with Ian Somerhalder (above) and with her husband, Tim, and Malese Jow (below).

mine who loves *TVD* and lives out of state was so disappointed to find out there isn't really a Mystic Grill here where you can go inside and have a meal. I live close to Covington and go there once in a while to shop, meet friends, or for a meal. It's silly, but at times I have to remind myself that I am not in Mystic Falls. That was especially true during the filming of the finale when there were Mystic Falls signs everywhere and there was a carnival set up in the square.

The highlight of my time as an extra on *The Vampire Diaries* is definitely meeting the cast and crew and getting to see how things work behind the scenes. I watch the episodes differently now, but it doesn't spoil the magic of the show for me — at all. At first, I'm sure my patient husband got tired of me talking through every episode I'd worked on, telling him what was going on that the viewer couldn't see, and then replaying the episode, pausing it to see myself or other extras I'd become friendly with while working. From my time on *The Vampire Diaries* set, I gained an appreciation for the amount of people, time, and effort that goes into making the show.

Spirits Talk: Malese Jow
(Anna)

How did you land the role of Anna?

It was your typical audition/callback situation. I didn't think I had a shot at the callback since I had booked another show that had conflicting filming dates. Fortunately, *Vampire Diaries* was willing to accommodate my schedule so they called last minute, asking if I could read for producers in half an hour. It was crazy!

How much did you know about Anna's storyline when you were first cast?

All that was written for Anna's character description was that she was a geeky girl that befriends Jeremy. Possible recurring. It was that small — no joke!

Were you familiar with the show or the book series before you were cast?

I had actually watched an episode when it first came out, thinking, "This show is awesome; maybe there will be a part that comes through the pipes in the future!"

A favorite Anna-Jeremy moment of mine is the goodbye scene in "Blood Brothers," where he's still half-asleep. Such a sweet moment. Does any particular scene stand out for you?

A lot of scenes are special to me for various reasons. I love the Anna-Jeremy scene when she surprises him outside of the school. They have such a sense of genuine young love and normality in that scene. For Anna, that is a huge deal, so that is one of my favorites.

What do you think about Jeremy's choice in the finale — to turn himself into a vampire using the blood Anna gave him?

I'm actually dying to see what happens with that next season [along] with everyone else. Jeremy was very troubled before Anna came into the picture. When she did, she definitely made him happy again, then very suddenly the fairy tale had such a tragic end. It's like all of his pain came back ten-fold. Him resorting to that surprised me, yet not. If that makes sense!

While a lot of your scenes were opposite Steven R. McQueen, you also had the opportunity to act opposite some of the other TVDers. Was there a particular actor or character you were most excited to be paired with?

Ian, hands down. Back-and-forth banter is always the best when you're opposite someone who is not afraid to dish it out. We would always bring our A-game, and in turn we made it believable to the audience that we were pretty evenly matched (which I look at as an accomplishment considering Damon is such a strong character). I learned so much from him and always looked forward to our scenes together.

Julie Plec said in an interview that the TVD crew wore "Save Anna" T-shirts on set while filming the finale because you were so well loved. Do you have any favorite on-set or crew memories?

I couldn't pick a specific moment! As soon as I stepped onto that set, everyone welcomed me with open arms and each day bonded us all tighter. By the end, we were all so sad (to say the least). That gesture (them making the T-shirts) was definitely special to me. The last week filming I was absolutely overwhelmed by love.

As you know, there's a Bring Anna Back fan movement. If you were writing the episode where Anna returned, how would you reintroduce the character? (For example, in a flashback, as a ghost, in dream sequences, or as a mysterious reincarnation à la Katherine & Elena ...)

There are so many possibilities! I've seen a lot of the "Bring Back Anna" feedback from fans, and they all have an idea of a creative way to bring her back. Flashbacks would be totally cool. But if she would be brought back to life for real . . . maybe Damon was still foggy from the vervain so all of it was hallucination? John's stake was ineffective because Emily put a spell on Anna so she would never be hurt by a Gilbert? The options are endless.

Do you have any theories about how Anna and Pearl first became vamps?

No idea! That's something I do wish was explored a bit more. Answers to how old Anna and her mother were, who her dad was, . . .

Tell me about your upcoming projects.

I'm up for a lot of projects at the moment, so fingers crossed! *The Social Network* will be out in theaters, my guest-starring role on TNT's *Leverage*, and a movie I filmed last year will be released on DVD, all this fall. Exact dates are pending, so keep checking back on my Facebook fan page or Twitter (@xomalese) for updates.

Finally, do you have any words for the heartbroken Anna fans out there?

> I just want to thank you guys from the bottom of my heart for all of the love and support. You guys welcomed a brand new character mid-season and ended up loving her equally to the already established and beloved cast. That means so much!!! As far as Anna making any future comebacks — never say never! With your voice, anything is possible.

The Vampire Diaries Timeline

"Anyone keeping a true timeline on TVD is gonna be stumped. It's currently the month of xxxx. Half-past Halloween, quarter to summer." So said Julie Plec in a tweet during the broadcast of "Isobel." Below is an attempt to piece together the information provided in the first season of *The Vampire Diaries* into a semblance of a timeline. A question mark indicates that a date is only an estimate.

1464? — Pearl becomes a vampire; she has "400 years on" Damon who is turned in 1864 ("There Goes the Neighborhood"). Presumably, Anna also became a vampire around this time.

1659? — Lexi is born; she is 350 years old ("162 Candles").

1692 — The Bennett family moves from Salem to Mystic Falls ("Haunted").

1755 — The Saltzman family comes to America from Germany ("History Repeating").

1792 — Mystic Falls cemetery is established ("Pilot").

October 9, 1810 — Giuseppe Salvatore is born ("Children of the Damned").

Early November 1847 — Stefan Salvatore is born ("Lost Girls," "162 Candles").

1860 — The town of Mystic Falls is founded ("Under Control").

January 23, 1864 — According to his tombstone, Giuseppe Salvatore dies ("Children of the Damned"). This date conflicts with many other details in the timeline and is likely a production error.

June 1864 — Johnathan Gilbert begins writing the journal that Jeremy finds ("History Repeating").

September 1, 1864 — The beginning of the Atlanta Campaign fires, which Katherine uses as a cover story ("Children of the Damned"). Presumably, Katherine arrives at the Salvatore estate shortly thereafter.

September 24, 1864 — The first Founder's Ball is held ("Family Ties"); shortly thereafter, Katherine reveals to Stefan that she is a vampire ("Lost Girls").

1864 — A comet passes over Mystic Falls ("The Night of the Comet").

The Battle of Willow Creek — Mr. Tanner says that the Battle of Willow Creek took place in 1865 ("Pilot"), but the flashbacks suggest it was actually in late 1864. On the day of the battle, Damon is with Katherine and sees her in possession of Emily's crystal ("History Repeating"). Stefan speaks to his father about the vampire situation and unwittingly drinks vervain, which leads to Katherine's capture ("Children of the Damned"). Damon makes a bargain with Emily for Katherine's safety ("History Repeating"). Stefan and Damon are shot trying to rescue Katherine ("Family Ties," "Blood Brothers"). Either one or both of the brothers watch the church burn ("History Repeating" conflicts with "Blood Brothers" on this detail).

The day after the Battle of Willow Creek — Emily gives the Salvatore brothers their rings; Stefan confronts his father and leaves him either dead or close to it; Damon promises Stefan an eternity of misery ("Blood Brothers").

1865 — Damon "made sure" vervain won't grow in Mystic Falls ("Family Ties").

1900? — The Salvatore boarding house is built ("Lost Girls").

1909? — Lexi and Stefan meet ("162 Candles").

1942 — The start date for Anna's research into vampire attacks in the Mystic Falls area.

June 12, 1953 — "Uncle" Joseph Salvatore is killed at the Salvatore boarding-house, presumably by Damon ("Family Ties," "You're Undead to Me").

1953 — Four people are killed by "animal attacks" in Mystic Falls ("Bloodlines"); that number likely includes Joseph Salvatore.

1962 — Five people are killed by "animal attacks" in Mystic Falls ("Bloodlines").

October 1969 — Stefan meets Sheila at an antiwar demonstration ("Bloodlines").

1974 — Three people are killed by "animal attacks" in Mystic Falls ("Bloodlines").

October 17, 1975 — Isobel Flemming is born ("A Few Good Men").

1980s — Elizabeth Forbes and Kelly Donovan go to high school together ("Lost Girls"); Kelly Donovan and Miranda Sommers are best friends ("There Goes the Neighborhood").

1983 — Anna sees Katherine in Chicago ("Fool Me Once").

Late 1980s? — Elizabeth Forbes and Logan Fell have known each other since he was six ("The Turning Point"). Kelly Donovan babysits Jenna Sommers ("There Goes the Neighborhood").

1989? — Damon meets Bree and asks for her help getting into the tomb ("Bloodlines").

August 20, 1991? — Vicki Donovan is born ("Lost Girls").

1992? — Isobel leaves Grove Hill; Elena is born ("A Few Good Men").

1994 — Jeremy Gilbert is born ("The Night of the Comet"). Stefan and Damon see each other for the last time before fall 2009 ("Pilot").

Late 1990s — Logan babysits Caroline ("The Turning Point").

2008 — Damon turns Isobel ("Blood Brothers").

May 23, 2009 — Grayson and Miranda Gilbert die in a car accident ("Pilot"); Stefan rescues Elena ("Bloodlines").

May–September 2009 — Stefan observes Elena and investigates her family history ("Bloodlines").

September 6, 2009 — Damon kills the couple in the car ("Pilot").

September 7, 2009 — First day back to Mystic Falls High ("Pilot").

September 8, 2009 — Damon attacks Vicki during the party by the falls ("Pilot").

September 9, 2009 — The comet passes over Mystic Falls ("The Night of the Comet").

September 10, 2009 — Caroline wakes up with Damon; Stefan tries out for the school football team; Caroline and Damon crash Elena's dinner party with Bonnie and Stefan ("Friday Night Bites").

September 11, 2009 — Stefan gives Elena the vervain-filled necklace; Damon kills Coach Tanner ("Friday Night Bites"). (This date actually was a Friday.)

September 24?, 2009 — The Founder's Ball is held; the date here is based on the original Founder's Ball, which was held on the 24th. Stefan captures Damon ("Family Ties").

September 27?, 2009 — Three days after leaving Elena a cryptic voicemail message, Stefan tries to fix his relationship with her by making her dinner ("You're Undead to Me").

September 28?, 2009 — The Sexy Suds Car Wash is held at the high school; Damon attacks Vicki and kills her friends; Elena figures out that Stefan is a vampire; Stefan asks her to keep his secret ("You're Undead to Me," "Lost Girls").

September 29?, 2009 — Damon turns Vicki into a vampire; Logan is killed ("Lost Girls").

There's a jump in the timeline here. Between "Lost Girls" and "Haunted" only a few days pass, but "Haunted" takes place at the end of October.

October 31, 2009 — Vicki dies ("Haunted").

Early November 2009 — Bonnie reveals her powers to Elena; Stefan turns 162; Damon kills Lexi ("162 Candles").

Mid-November? 2009 — Emily possesses Bonnie and destroys the crystal; Logan returns, now a vampire. Stefan has been asking Damon why he returned to Mystic Falls for "months"; Alaric mentions to Jeremy that they are halfway through the school semester ("History Repeating").

The following day — With a full moon overhead, it's Career Night at Mystic Falls High School; Elena and Stefan have sex for the first time; she discovers the portrait of Katherine; Noah causes her to crash her car ("The Turning Point"). Damon rescues Elena from the car wreck ("Bloodlines").

The following day — Damon takes Elena to Atlanta to visit Bree; Bonnie falls into the tomb and Stefan rescues her ("Bloodlines").

The following day — Elena arrives back in Mystic Falls and Stefan reveals that he rescued her from the car crash in May and that she is adopted ("Bloodlines").

December? 2009 — The 1950s Decade Dance is held at the high school; Caroline passes a Christmas display in a store window ("Unpleasantville").

Shortly thereafter — Stefan unearths the grimoire that was buried with his father; both Elena and Bonnie are kidnapped ("Children of the Damned").

The following day — The tomb opens; Duke has a party at the old cemetery where people are wearing winter coats and hats; Sheila Bennett dies ("Fool Me Once").

Winter 2010 — The ill-fated hiker tells Harper the year; the Bachelor Auction is held at the Grill ("A Few Good Men").

No indication of time of year for "There Goes the Neighborhood" or "Let the Right One In."

One month until Founder's Day — Johnathan Gilbert returns to Mystic Falls; the kickoff to Founder's Day party is held; Stefan gives in and drinks human blood ("Under Control").

Three weeks? until Founder's Day — Bonnie returns to Mystic Falls; the Miss Mystic Falls competition is held; Elena and Damon lock up Stefan ("Miss Mystic Falls").

A few days later — Stefan refuses to eat; Elena convinces him not to commit suicide; Isobel shows up at the Grill ("Blood Brothers").

The following day — The Mystic Falls High students prepare floats for Founder's Day; Elena meets her birth mother, Isobel ("Isobel").

The following day — Isobel gets the Gilbert invention from Elena and gives it to Uncle John ("Isobel").

Founder's Day — The tomb vampires, Anna, and Mayor Lockwood are killed; Tyler, Matt, and Caroline are in a car accident; Katherine impersonates Elena, kisses Damon, and attacks Uncle John ("Founder's Day").

Summer 2010 — Left with so many cliffhangers at the end of season 1, *TVD* fans wish away their summers, awaiting the return of *The Vampire Diaries* in September.

Sources

"10 Questions With *Degrassi* Actress Nina Dobrev," TheTVAddict.com. August 28, 2007.

Abrams, Natalie. "*Vampire Diaries'* Ian Somerhalder on Elena vs. Katherine," TVGuideMagazine.com. January 27, 2010.

Abrams, Natalie. "*Vampire Diaries* Scoop," TVGuide.com. March 10, 2009.

"Acting Like a Hilton," VFS.com/blog. January 29, 2008.

Adams, Patty. "The Betty Interview: *The Vampire Diaries'* Sara Canning," Betty Confidential.com.

Adams, Patty. "The Betty Interview: *The Vampire Diaries'* Zach Roerig," Betty Confidential.com.

Ahearn, Victoria. "Canadian Teen Part of Musical Boom," *The Record.* August 11, 2008. B5.

"An Interview With L.J. Smith," Bookalicio.us. March 2009.

AnneRice.com

"A Runway Exclusive With Sara Canning," *Runway Magazine.* Spring 2010.

Ausiello, Michael. "Exclusive: The Shocking Story Behind Last Night's Killer *Vampire Diaries*," EW.com. October 29, 2009.

"A Witch's Garden: Vervain," ShanMonster.com.

"Bad Trip — 1988–1992 Anthology," BloggedandQuartered.blogspot.com. April 25, 2010.

Barker, Lynn. "Sara Canning Vamps It Up a Notch!," TeenTelevision.com. March 24, 2010.

Barker, Lynn. "*Vampire Diaries* Cast Spills the Latest," TeenTelevision.com. January 11, 2010.

Batu, Patrick. "Zach Roerig from *The Vampire Diaries* Talks Truck Stops, Filming in Atlanta, and Boat Shoes," Travel.AOL.com. November 4, 2009.

Bellafante, Ginia. "Dear Diary: Bitten and It's No Hickey," *The New York Times.* September 10, 2009.

BeneaththeBlue.net

"Benjamin Ayres," Shows.CTV.ca.

Bentley, Jean. "*Vampire Diaries* Exclusive: Steven R. McQueen on Jeremy's New Girlfriend and Werewolf Future," HollywoodCrush.MTV.com. January 19, 2010.

Bentley, Jean. "*Vampire Diaries* Star Malese Jow and Steven R. McQueen Are Best Friends," HollywoodCrush.MTV.com. May 3, 2010.

Bentley, Jean. "*Vampire Diaries* Star Malese Jow Reveals the Secret Behind Those Veiny, Vampire Eyes," HollywoodCrush.MTV.com. April 20, 2010.

Bentley, Jean. "*Vampire Diaries* Star Steven R. McQueen Dishes on Dude-Bonding Road Trips and Filming in Atlanta," HollywoodCrush.MTV.com. January 28, 2010.

Berlanti, Greg. "Why We Write," WhyWeWriteSeries.wordpress.com. December 12, 2007.

Bernstein, Abbie. "Exclusive Interview: *The Vampire Diaries'* Executive Producer Julie Plec Gets Bloody," iFmagazine.com. May 13, 2010.

Bernstein, Jacob. "Good Grief," *Women's Wear Daily*. December 16, 2005. 4.

Beautiful Disaster, ajshadowcat09.wordpress.com.

BeverlyMartelMusic.com

Bianco, Robert. "*Vampire Diaries* Stakes its Claim in a Populated Genre," *USA Today*. September 10, 2009.

Bibel, Sarah. "The Drama Club: Interview With the Vampire (Diaries) Teen Witch," FanCast.com. February 11, 2010.

Bierly, Mandi. "Ian Somerhalder," *Entertainment Weekly*. November 13, 2009.

Bierly, Mandi. "Ian Somerhalder Politely Declines Your Request that He Bite You," Popwatch.ew.com. November 12, 2009.

Bierly, Mandi. "Ian Somerhalder Talks *Vampire Diaries*," Popwatch.ew.com. September 17, 2009.

Bierly, Mandi. "*Vampire Diaries* Costume Designer Jennifer Bryan Talks Shirtless Scenes and Leather Jackets," ew.com. March 25, 2010.

B., Lynn. "Paul and Matt: Superheroes," AGirlsWorld.com.

Boyar, Jay. "Back to School," OrlandoMagazine.com. March 2010.

Brioux, Bill. "TV Brimming With Canadians," *Toronto Star*. August 13, 2009. E9.

Byrne, Suzy. "Kayla Ewell: Interview With a Vampire," StarMagazine.com. October 2, 2009.

Caddell, Ian. "Field of Dreams," *Reel West*. September/October 2009.

Carroll, Larry. "Kevin Williamson's *The Bedroom Window* Remake Coming Between Fourth and Fifth *Scream* Movies," MoviesBlog.MTV.com. November 12, 2009.

Clay, Zettler. "Katerina Graham: The Rebel Princess," ClutchMagOnline.com. March 30, 2009.

Collinwood.net

"Comic-Con 2009 Panel," Teen.com.

"Congratulations to All the CW Awards Winners!" E! Online. February 9, 2010.

"Craven and Williamson Reteam for *Cursed*," *St. Petersburg Times*. October 19, 2002.

Crook, John. "Checking In With Nina Dobrev," *North Bay Nugget*. Online. October 2009.

cwtv.com

DarkShadows.co.uk

DarkShadowsFestival.com

DarkShadowsOnline.com

Dark Shadows: DVD Collection 1. DVD. Mpi Home Video, 2002.

Dark Shadows: The Beginning, Collection 1. DVD. Mpi Home Video, 2007.

"*Dawson's Creek* Creator Kevin Williamson Talks Pacey-Joey-Dawson," Zap2ItVideo, YouTube.com. November 5, 2009.

Dawson's Creek: The Complete First Season. DVD. Sony Pictures, 2003.

Dawson's Creek: The Complete Second Season. DVD. Sony Pictures, 2003.

Depko, Tina. "Oakville Native Sinks His Teeth into Hit Vampire Show," InsideHalton.com. January 29, 2010.

Doug. "Exclusive: *The Vampire Diaries*' Head Makeup Artist Spills Secrets From the Set," RadarOnline.com. September 17, 2009.

Elliott, Sean. "Exclusive Interview: Marguerite MacIntyre Is *Kyle XY*'s Awesome Mom," IFmagazine.com. January 15, 2008.

Elliot, Sean. "Exclusive Interview: Meet *Kyle XY* Mom Marguerite MacIntyre," IFmagazine.com. January 22, 2008.

Eng, Jeanette M. "Actor's Career Has Stops in NYC, Prague, Now L.A.," *Independent*. Online. February 26, 2003.

"Exclusive Interview: Mia Kirshner (Isobel) From *The Vampire Diaries*," TheTVChick.com. May 13, 2010.

"Exclusive Interview: *Vampire Diaries* Star Sara Canning Reveals Show's New Secrets," RadarOnline.com. January 11, 2010.

Fierman, Daniel. "Have Yourself a Scary Little Christmas," *Entertainment Weekly*. November 20, 1998.

FineArtAmerica.com

"Forbidden Tales," NightWorld.net.

French, Dan. "Confessions of a *Vampire Diaries* Insider," DigitalSpy.co.uk. March 17, 2010.

Fretts, Bruce. "High School Confidential: *Dawson's Creek*," *Entertainment Weekly*. January 9, 1998.

Fries, Laura. "Fallen," *Variety*. July 21, 2006. 5, 16.

French, Dan. "Nina Dobrev on the *Diaries*' Love Triangle," DigitalSpy.com. January 21, 2010.

"*Friday Night Lights* Fan Podcast No. 22," *Friday Night Lights Fan*. March 11, 2010.

"From *Degrassi: The Next Generation* to *The American Mall*," *Dance Spirit*. November 2008. 42.

Fusion Music Supervision, ChrisMollere.com.

Garcia, Jennifer. "Six Revelations From Ian Somerhalder," *People*. December 7, 2009. 164.

Gardner, Chris. "Cast Away," *People*. May 2, 2005. 38.

"Getting to Know: Paul Wesley," Teenmag.com.

Ghosh, Korbi. "*Vampire Diaries*' Ian Somerhalder Returns to *Lost*, Loves the Undead & Lets Go as Damon," Zap2it.com. September 17, 2009.

Ghosh, Korbi. "*Vampire Diaries* Season Finale: Ian Somerhalder Talks Damon's Love for Elena, Cliffhangers," Zap2it.com. May 13, 2010.

Gilmore, Karen. "Interview With Katerina Graham," ReelArtsy.com. August 28, 2009.

GlenridgeHall.com

Godwin, Jennifer. "*The Vampire Diaries* Star Ian Somerhalder Says Damon Weasels His Way Into Stefan's World," Watch With Kristin, E! Online. September 17, 2009.

Goldwasser, Dan. "Simply Scoring Interview: Michael Suby," Soundtrack.net. June 10, 2006.

"Grad Sinks Her Teeth into *The Vampire Diaries*," vfs.com/blog. July 31, 2009.

Halterman, Jim. "More tv Vampires?? Thank Kevin Williamson," JimHalterman.com. November 12, 2009.

Hartinger, Brent. "Interview: Kevin Williamson Almost Didn't Do *The Vampire Diaries*," TheTorchOnline.com. September 7, 2009.

Henderson, Shirley. "Vampires and Psychics in High School! Oh, My!" *Ebony*. April 2010. 45.

Hernandez, Lee. "Exclusive: Michael Trevino 'Moving On' From *90210*," Latina.com. December 23, 2008.

Hernandez, Lee. "Hungry Like a Wolf," Kidult.com. February 5, 2010.

Hernandez, Lee. "Michael Trevino Dishes on *The Vampire Diaries*," Latina.com. September 10, 2009.

Hill, Erin. "Sara Canning: *Vampire Diaries* Will Pave Its Own Way," Parade.com. January 28, 2010.

Hinojosa, Stacy. "Why We Heart Zach Roerig," jsyk.com. November 5, 2009.

Howell, Peter. "When Good Horror Goes Bad," *Toronto Star*. February 26, 2005. A19.

"Ian Is Out for Blood," *TV Guide*. September 7, 2009. 8.

"Ian Somerhalder Interview: *The Vampire Diaries*," SciFind.co.uk. January 26, 2010.

"Ian Somerhalder," *People*. December 2, 2002. 155.

"Ian Somerhalder," *Tyra*. Online video. September 18, 2009.

"*I Love Lucy* Episode Guide," LucyStore.com.

"Interview With L.J. Smith," TheAuthorHour.com. November 19, 2009.

"Interview With Nina Dobrev," Teen.com.

"Interview With Sara Canning," *Relate Magazine* via IHeartVampireDiaries.com. March 2010.

Interview With the Vampire. dvd. Warner Home Video, 2000.

"Interview With *Vampire*'s Candice Accola," On Set With Annie. wwhotv.com. February 10, 2010.

"Interview With *Vampire*'s Matt Davis," On Set With Annie. wwhotv.com. February 11, 2010.

"Interview With *Vampire*'s Sara Canning," On Set With Annie. wwhotv.com. February 10, 2010.

"Interview With *Vampire*'s Zach Roerig," On Set With Annie. wwhotv.com. February 10, 2010.

"Interview With Zach Roerig," *KTLA Morning News*. Online. March 16, 2010.

"Interview With Zach Roerig," *Pix 11 Morning News*. Online. November 10, 2009.

Jensen, David. "Kevin Williamson Unbound," *The Advocate*. August 31, 1999.

Jensen, Jeff. "Ian Somerhalder," *Entertainment Weekly*. April 15, 2005.

Jancelewicz, Chris. "Q&A: *Degrassi:* TNG's Nina Dobrev," Entertainment.AOL.ca. January 7, 2008.

Jancelewicz, Chris. "Q&A: Nina Dobrev on *The American Mall*," Entertainment. AOL.ca. August 6, 2008.

"Julie Plec — May 28, 2010," *The VRO*. BlogTalkRadio.com/VampRadio.

"Katerina Graham," TrueHollywoodTalk.com. Online video.

KatGraham.com

KaylaEwell.com

"Kayla Ewell," Maxim.com.

"Kayla Ewell," *Soap Opera Digest*. September 2009.

Keck, William. "Dexter's Dad Does *Diaries*," *TV Guide* via SpoilersGuide.com. November 26, 2009.

"Kevin Williamson," GLBTQ.com.

"Kevin Williamson on Bringing Vampires to The CW," BuzzSugar.com. September 10, 2009.

Khouli, Gabriel. "*Vampire Diaries*' Crew to Film on Square Thursday, Friday," CovNews.com. July 21, 2009.

King, Randall. "Ex–*Dawson's Creek* Star Shooting Third Film Here," *Winnipeg Free Press*. September 23, 2008. D2.

King, Susan. "*Dawson's Creek* Bows Out Looking Ahead," LAtimes.com. May 11, 2003.

Kit, Borys. "*Cradlewood* Robs Somerhalder," *Hollywood Reporter*. October 16, 2009.

Kit, Zorianna. "Plec Surfaces at Ricochet Production," *Hollywood Reporter*. August 1, 2000.

Krantz, Michael. "The Bard of Gen-Y," *Time*. December 15, 1997.

Krentcil, Faran. "The Insider: Candice Accola," NylonMag.com. September 24, 2009.

Kristen, Rebecca. "Q&A: *Vampire Diaries* Star Candice Accola Gets Candid About Fang Frenzy, Co-Stars & More," StarPulse.com. September 8, 2009.

Kronke, David. "Nina Dobrev," *V Plus*. October 1, 2009.

Lacey, Liam. "You Scream, I Scream . . . ," *Globe and Mail*. December 17, 1996.

La Ferla, Ruth. "A Trend With Teeth," *The Gazette* (Montreal). August 11, 2009.

La Franco, Robert. "Hollywood's Idea Moguls," *Forbes*. September 21, 1998.

"Lapis," Gemstone.org.

"Lapis Lazuli," SobrietyStones.com.

Lee, Luaine. "Ian Somerhalder: *Lost* and Now Found as Marco Polo," *Knight Ridder Tribune*. May 29, 2007.

Let the Right One In. DVD. Magnolia Home Entertainment, 2009.

Lewis, Jessica. "Degrassi Gets Schooled," TheEyeOpener.com. November 4, 2008.

"Life After *Lost*: Ian Somerhalder," *People*. August 28, 2006. 98.

LJaneSmith.blogspot.com

LJaneSmith.net

Long, Gabrielle. "*Pretty Little Liars* Star Bianca Lawson Talks Beauty, Fitness, and Her Character Maya," Examiner.com. June 1, 2010.

Long, Gabrielle. "*The Vampire Diaries* Candice Accola Talks Beauty, *The Vampire Diaries*, and Kissing Ian Somerhalder," TheExaminer.com. January 28, 2010.

Lost Boys, The. DVD. Warner Home Video, 2007.

Lowry, Brian. "*The Vampire Diaries,*" *Variety.* September 7–13, 2009.

MacKenzie, Carina. "Kevin Williamson Talks About the Future of *The Vampire Diaries,*" LAtimesblogs.LAtimes.com/ShowTracker. October 29, 2009.

MacKenzie, Carina. "*The Vampire Diaries* Ian Somerhalder: 'Honestly, My Heart Is Crushed,'" LAtimesblogs.LAtimes.com/ShowTracker. May 12, 2010.

MacKenzie, Carina. "*The Vampire Diaries*: Sara Canning Makes Her Own Luck," LAtimesblogs.LAtimes.com/ShowTracker. March 25, 2010.

MacKenzie, Carina. "*Vampire Diaries* Star Nina Dobrev on Elena's Look-alike Dilemma and More," LAtimesblogs.LAtimes.com/ShowTracker. January 21, 2010.

"Marcos Siega," HungryMan.com.

"Marcos Siega — May 23, 2010," *The VRO.* BlogTalkRadio.com/VampRadio.

Martin, Danielle. "The Official Interview," MattDavisFans.com. June 7, 2010.

Maslin, Janet. "Everyone Gets an A in the Dark," *New York Times.* August 20, 1999.

MattDavisFan.com

McCabe, Joseph. "Exclusive: We Talk *Vampire Diaries* With Steven R. McQueen," Fearnet.com. September 7, 2009.

McIntyre, Gina. "Fresh Blood," *Hamilton Spectator.* October 31, 2009.

McIntyre, Gina. "Vampires Rule," *Guelph Mercury.* September 10, 2009.

McNaught, Caroline. "Love Bites," *Elle Canada.* September 2009. 72.

Miller, Mark. "Revisiting His Youth," *Newsweek.* August 23, 1999.

Morton, Rebecca. "*Vampire Diaries* to Give Marlboro Native Star Turn," *Sentinel.* Online. September 10, 2009.

Mugglenet.com

"My City: Katerina Graham," Zinkmagazine.com. March 2010.

MySpace.com/CandiceMusic

MySpace.com/MaleseMusic

Naoreen, Nuzhat. "*Vampire Diaries* Star Nina Dobrev Reveals Method Behind Finale Kiss With Ian Somerhalder," HollywoodCrush.MTV.com. May 14, 2010.

Nelson, Katharine. "Anne Rice: The Vampire Chronicles," http://wsu.edu/~dela hoyd/rice.novels.html.

Night of the Comet. DVD. MGM Video and DVD, 2007.

"Nina Dobrev of *Vampire Diaries* on Getting Advice From the *True Blood* Cast," EW.com. September 10, 2009.

Ng, Philiana. "2010 Paley Festival Coverage: *The Vampire Diaries,*" Reporter.Blogs.com. March 7, 2010.

Norton, Al. "411mania Interviews: *The Vampire Diaries*' Candice Accola," 411mania.com. September 10, 2009.

O'Connor, Brian. "Anti-Hero," *Men's Fitness*. March 2006.

O'Hare, Kate. "*Lost's* Boone and Locke Become Buddies," Zap2It.com. January 4, 2005.

Oh, Eunice. "Travel Tips From *Marco Polo's* Ian Somerhalder," *People*. June 4, 2007. 41.

"PaleyFest 2010 — *The Vampire Diaries'* Paul Wesley," Fearnet.com.

"Paul M. Sommers — May 26, 2010," *The VRO*. BlogTalkRadio.com/VampRadio.

"Paul Wesley 'Blessed' Over Fans," Mirror.co.uk. March 11, 2010.

"Paul Wesley," *Cosmopolitan*. February 2010. 124.

"Paul Wesley," *Soap Opera Digest*. September 2009.

Pierce, Scott D. "Another Lovable Jerk — Actor/Utah Native Matthew Davis Plays Bad Guys You Love to Hate," DeseretNews.com. April 14, 2006.

Pleasantville. DVD. New Line Home Video, 2004.

"Q&A: CW's Ostroff Talks Pilots, *Vampire Diaries* and More," THRfeed.com. March 4, 2010.

"Q&A With *The Vampire Diaries* Star Candice Accola," Saturday Night Magazine. Online.

Radish, Christina. "Exclusive Interview: Katerina Graham Shares her *Vampire Diaries*," IESB.net. January 3, 2010.

Radish, Christina. "Exclusive Interview: Matthew Davis Talks *Vampire Diaries*," IESB.net. April 26, 2010.

Radish, Christina. "Exclusive Interview: Sara Canning Is Writing *The Vampire Diaries*," IESB.net. March 26, 2010.

Radish, Christina. "Exclusive Interview: *The Vampire Diaries* With Steven R. McQueen Not to Be Confused With His Granddaddy THE Steve McQueen," IESB.net. January 28, 2010.

Radish, Christina. "Interview: Ian Somerhalder and His *Vampire Diaries*," IESB.net. August 8, 2009.

Radish, Christina. "Interview: Ian Somerhalder Talks *The Vampire Diaries* and the Final Season of *Lost*," IESB.net. February 1, 2010.

Radish, Christina. "Interview: Kevin Williamson and his *Vampire Diaries*," IESB.net. January 28, 2010.

Radish, Christina. "Interview: Nina Dobrev Is Caught Between Two Vampire Brothers in *The Vampire Diaries*," IESB.net. January 28, 2010.

Radish, Christina. "Interview: Nina Dobrev Is Writing Her *The Vampire Diaries*," IESB.net. August 28, 2009.

Radish, Christina. "Interview: Paul Wesley Is Stefan Salvatore in *The Vampire Diaries*," IESB.net. January 28, 2010.

Radish, Christina. "Interview: Paul Wesley Writes His *Vampire Diaries*," IESB.net. August 12, 2009.

"Ralph Waldo Emerson." *The Columbia Encyclopedia, Sixth Edition*, 2008. Encyclopedia.com.

Reilly, Gabrielle. "Malese Jow Interview," TheGlobalTownHall.com.

Rice, Anne. *Interview With the Vampire.* New York: Ballantine Books, 1997.

Rice, Lynette. "Hope & Glory," *Entertainment Weekly.* January 18, 2002.

Robbins, Stephanie. "Williamson's Scare Tactics Working for The CW," *Broadcasting and Cable.* October 26, 2009.

Rodriguez, Brenda. "Steven R. McQueen," *People.* November 7, 2005. 43.

Rosenberg, Carissa. "Fresh Face," *Seventeen.* April 2010. 136–141.

Rudolph, Ileane. "Ian Somerhalder Defends His *Vampire* Character," TVGuide Magazine.com. January 15, 2010.

Rudolph, Ileane. "*The Vampire Diaries*: Love at First Bite," *TV Guide.* January 20, 2009.

Ryan, Andrew. "From Degrassi to the Dark Side," *Globe and Mail.* September 23, 2009. R3.

Salem, Rob. "Genre Continues to Vamp It Up," *Toronto Star.* October 31, 2009.

SalemWitchTrials.com

"Salem Witch Trials of 1692," Law.umkc.edu/faculty/projects/ftrials/salem.

Schaefer, Glen. "From Busy Kitchen to *Black Field*," *The Province.* October 18, 2009. D4.

Schneider, Michael. "CW Picks Up *Vampire Diaries* Pilot," Variety.com. February 5, 2009.

Scott, A.O. "A Hairy Tale From the Lives of Some Hairy Angelenos," *New York Times.* February 26, 2005.

Serjeant, Jill. "Kinder, Gentler Undead Emerge," *Times-Colonist.* August 15, 2009.

Setoodeh, Ramin. "Q&A: Ian Somerhalder Is Dead Again! This Time on *The Vampire Diaries*," Newsweek.com. September 24, 2009.

"*Seventeen* Chats With Candice Accola About *The Vampire Diaries*," Seventeen.com. September 28, 2009.

"Seventeen Questions: Steven R. McQueen," Seventeen.com.

Simpson, Melody. "*Vampire Diaries* & Odd Details from Kelly Hu," HollywoodTheWriteWay.com. April 15, 2010.

Sixteen Candles. DVD. Universal Studios, 2003.

Smith, L.J. *The Vampire Diaries: The Awakening.* New York: HarperTeen, 2009.

Smith, L.J. *The Vampire Diaries: The Fury* and *Dark Reunion.* New York: HarperTeen, 2007.

Smith, L.J. *The Vampire Diaries: The Struggle.* New York: HarperTeen, 2009.

Soler, Alina. "Five Things to Know About TV's Hottest New Vampire," People.com. August 10, 2009.

Stanhope, Kate. "*The Vampire Diaries:* Ian Somerhalder Talks About Going Bad, *Twilight*, and His Return to *Lost*," LAtimesblogs.LAtimes.com/ShowTracker. September 17, 2009.

Steinberg, Lisa. "Candice Accola: Love Bites," *Starry Constellation Magazine.* Online. September 2009.

Steinberg, Lisa. "David Anders: On the Hunt," Starry.com. March 2010.

Steinberg, Lisa. "Katerina Graham: At First Bite," Starry.com. October 2009.

Steinberg, Lisa. "Michael Trevino: Biting Down," Starry.com. December 2009.

Steinberg, Lisa. "Zach Roerig: Just a Taste," Starry.com. November 2009.

Strachan, Alex. "Love Triangle With Bite," *The Province* (Vancouver). October 29, 2009.

Strachan, Alex. "Nefarious Influences on *Vampire Diaries*," *Windsor Star*. January 28, 2010.

Strachan, Alex. "There Will Be Blood," *National Post*. January 11, 2010. B15.

Strause, Jackie. "*Vampire Diaries* Star: People Are Gonna Die!," NYpost.com. October 15, 2009.

Sullivan, Jaime. "Hollywood Original: Katerina Graham," TheCollectiveMagazine. com. April 2010.

"Supervisor's Spotlight: Chris Mollere," MusicSupervisor.com.

Talbot, Lindsay. "Exclusive Q&A With *The Vampire Diaries*' Zach Roerig," TeenVogue.com. February 25, 2010.

Talbot, Lindsay. "New Blood: *The Vampire Diaries*' Paul Wesley," TeenVogue.com. October 12, 2009.

"Teacher's Guide: L.J. Smith," http://Authors.SimonandSchuster.biz.

"*The Vampire Diaries*: Special Effects and Makeup," *Seventeen*. Online video. March 15, 2010.

The Vampire Diaries. TV Series. Exec. Prod. Leslie Morgenstein, Bob Levy, Kevin Williamson, Julie Plec. The CW. 2009–.

Thomas, Rachel. "An Interview With Matt Davis," TVdramas.About.com. May 2010.

Thorpe, Carla and Ivana Wynn. "Q&A With the Cast of *The Vampire Diaries*," SaturdayNightMag.com.

"Today's TV Addict Top 5 Questions With *Vampire Diaries* Star Nina Dobrev," TheTVAddict.com. March 11, 2010.

Tucker, Ken. "*The Vampire Diaries*," *Entertainment Weekly*. September 11, 2009.

Twitter.com

YouTube.com/CWTelevision

YouTube.com/TheCWSource

VampireDiariesGuide.com

"*Vampire Diaries* Featuring Monroe Set to Air," WaltonTribune.com. September 23, 2009.

"*Vampire Diaries*: Kevin Williamson," THR Network. Online video. September 10, 2009.

"*Vampire Diaries* Launches on ITV2," ITN.co.uk. Online video. January 28, 2010.

"Vampire Diaries Most-Watched CW Premiere Ever," THRfeed.com. September 11, 2009.

Vampire-Diaries.net

VampireDiariesOnline.com

Van Riper, A. Bowdoin. *Science in Popular Culture: A Reference Guide*. Santa Barbara, CA: Greenwood Publishing Group, 2002. 27–29.

Vee. "Getting Tannered," Vampire-Diaries.net. November 26, 2009.

Vena, Jocelyn. "*Vampire Diaries* Star Candice Accola Wants Caroline to End Up With a Nice Guy," HollywoodCrush.MTV.com. December 4, 2009.

"Vervain," Botanical.com.

"Vervain," MagicSpells.in.

Virtel, Louis. "*The Vampire Diaries*' Jasmine Guy and Katerina Graham Discuss Spoilers, Dance, and Prince Proteges," MovieLine.com. November 19, 2009.

Walker, Dave. "Second Bite," NOLA.com. September 9, 2009.

Walker, Dave. "*The Vampire Diaries* Moves Ian Somerhalder Closer to Home," NOLA.com. September 8, 2009.

"Watch This Face: Katerina Graham," TeenMag.com

Weiss Rojas, Sabrina. "The Vampire Diaries Author L.J. Smith Talks *Twilight*," HollywoodCrush.MTV.com. September 24, 2009.

Weiss Rojas, Sabrina. "Vampire Diaries Author L.J. Smith Weighs in on the Series: 'They've Done an Incredible Job of Interpreting It,'" HollywoodCrush.MTV.com. September 24, 2009.

Weiss, Shari. "Exclusive: Melinda Clarke Reflects on *The O.C.*, Dishes on *The Vampire Diaries* and *Nikita*," TeenDramaWhore.com. May 9, 2010.

"We Love Steven R. McQueen," MyBliss.co.uk.

Wieselman, Jarett. "Ian Somerhalder: 'The Stakes to Get This Show Were Really High,'" NYpost.com. September 17, 2009.

Wieselman, Jarett. "Paul Wesley: 'I'd Never Heard of Edward Cullen,'" NYpost.com. September 10, 2009.

Wieselman, Jarett. "*Vampire Diaries* Star: Elena Will Learn Stefan's a Vampire Soon!," NYpost.com. October 1, 2009.

Wiki.Vampire-Diaries.net

Wikipedia.org

"Writer/Co-Producer Julie Plec Answers Questions About the *Kyle XY* Finale," Olliewo.blogspot.com. March 2009.

"Zach Roerig," *Soap Opera Digest*. September 2009.

Acknowledgments

Thank you to Jack David and David Caron, co-publishers at ECW Press, and to Jennifer Hale for trusting me that *The Vampire Diaries* was episode guide-worthy. Thank you to Sarah Dunn for being my first and expert reader, for proofreading, for being my publicist, and for your willingness to help me choose which photo of Ian Somerhalder is handsomest. To the rest of the ECW crew — Erin, Michael, Jen Knoch, Simon, Troy — always a pleasure, you talented bunch. Gil Adamson, it was an honor and a riot to have you as editor on this book. Thank you for the improvements you made to it and to me as a writer. Thank you to those who designed *Love You to Death*: cover and photo-section designer Rachel Ironstone, page designer Melissa Kaita, and typesetter Gail Nina. Thank you to Sylvia Gelinek and Jennifer Hirte at Schwarzkopf & Schwarzkopf for bringing my books to a German audience.

Thank you to Benjamin Ayres, Malese Jow, Jennifer Ridings, Ruthie Heard, and Vee and Red for agreeing to be interviewed. A special thank you also to Jennifer Ridings and Dan Curtis Productions for providing me with photos for the book. *The Vampire Diaries* fandom is a welcoming and friendly bunch — thank you for being so epically awesome (and often quite hilarious). And thanks to my blog readers and Twitter friends for the support and conversation.

To Charlie, Erin, Sarah, and Amie; to the Bird Preservation Society (I hope to attend one of your meetings soon); to Adam for his fangtastic facts; and to my family and the entire extended Ace Gang — I love you to death.

Crissy Calhoun is an editor and the author of *Spotted: Your One and Only Unofficial Guide to Gossip Girl* (ECW Press, 2009). Visit her online at crissycalhoun.com.

Also by Crissy Calhoun

Spotted:
Your One and Only Unofficial Guide to Gossip Girl

"from complete episode synopses to soundtrack information to goofs found in the series, this collection of delicious trivia functions as a veritable *GG* bible."
— *Torontoist*

Also available from ECW Press

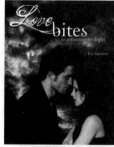

Love Bites:
The Unofficial Saga of Twilight
Liv Spencer

Truly, Madly, Deadly:
The Unofficial True Blood Companion
Becca Wilcott

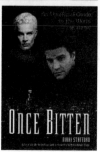

Once Bitten:
An Unofficial Guide to the World of Angel
Nikki Stafford

Bite Me:
The Unofficial Guide to the World of Buffy the Vampire Slayer
Nikki Stafford